D1571180

Original Essays on the Poetry of Anne Sexton

TO VENCIL

“love is the whole and more than all”

Original Essays on the Poetry of Anne Sexton

Edited by Francis Bixler

Associate Editors
Robert Henigan
Katherine Lederer

Editorial Assistant
Dana Bixler

General Editor
Robert E. Lowrey

University of Central Arkansas Press
1988

Jacket Design and Illustrations
Charlotte Story

Library of Congress Cataloging-in-Publication Data

Original essays on the poetry of Anne Sexton.

Includes bibliographies
1. Sexton, Anne—Criticism and interpretation.
I. Bixler, Frances, 1939- II. Henigan, Robert.
PS3537.E915Z83 1988 811'.54 88-4723

ISBN 0-944436-06-4

Manufactured in the United States of America

CONTENTS

III. FORM

IV: QUEST

EPILOGUE

PREFACE

Nearly thirty years have elapsed since Anne Sexton began writing poetry. In those thirty years, Americans have experienced the Vietnam War, economic woes of astounding magnitude, even more astounding leaps in technological sophistication, changing values, and—most gratifyingly—a renewed appreciation for Anne Sexton, whose work we now have begun to respect. As all students of Sexton know, she has not always enjoyed critical acclaim. In fact, the label of a confessional poet seemed to be many critics' strategy for denigrating the quality of her work and denying its seriousness.

Though her writing career was relatively brief (1959-1974), Sexton has left a body of poems worthy of critical reassessment. Until recently, little has been done to challenge the negative confessional label or to see her work as a serious contribution to American letters. Diana Hume George's thoughtful study, *Oedipus Anne: The Poetry of Anne Sexton,* Estella Lauter's article, "Anne Sexton's Radical Discontent," suggesting a striking new method for assessing women's writing, Alicia Ostriker's powerful challenge to critics in *Stealing the Language,* Diane Wood Middlebrook's forthcoming biography, and new collections of reprints of articles edited by Diana Hume George and Steven Colburn suggest that at long last critics have begun to turn a fresh eye on Sexton's poetry.

Time and the maturing of many critics has created the environment for looking anew at the canon of a woman poet who wrote out of her lived experience, having little connection to the feminist movement, yet celebrating and mourning the meaning of being woman, the meaning of life and death, and the fragile hold we all have on sanity and wholeness. Thus it seemed appropriate to send out a call for new critical work. The response has been an outpouring of interest and a truly amazing variety of critical concerns which have, in turn, spawned even further avenues of investigation.

Original Essays on the Poetry of Anne Sexton represents the best of this outpouring. Diane Wood Middlebrook allows us a glimpse into the riches of her forthcoming biography on Anne Sexton in her essay on Sexton and Lowell and their mutually influential friendship. By concentrating on "Her Kind," Kay Capo establishes a unity of voice and character for Sexton's canon which has long been overlooked. A further important context is added by Ann Marie Seward Barry's comparison of Sexton's *Folly* to that of Erasmus. Such a comparison lends insight into possible reasons for Sexton's suicide and increases understanding of the relationship between art and madness.

Taking a step further on the subject of art and madness, Jenny Goodman asserts that Sexton wrote as a stay against her own death wish. That writing poems is the opposite of dying suggests a kind of poetics, one which Sexton appears to endorse in several important selections. Brenda Ameter picks up on John Holmes' famous reprimands to Sexton, asserting that Sexton knew intuitively what kind of poetry she had to write. Ameter treats her work archetypally, citing evidence that Sexton clearly chose to write different poetry in spite of her male mentor's strong disapproval. Employing the metaphor of the mother-daughter relationship, Frances Bixler concentrates on the intimacy between writer and reader in Sexton's poetry, an intimacy resulting in the reader's being nurtured and created by the poet.

Fun house mirrors always make us fatter or taller or misshapen. Caroline King Bernard Hall sees *Transformations* as just this kind of mirror. We move into the book and find ourselves represented, but slightly strange or guilty or ugly or even beastly. These transformations are our nightmares coming true, our favorite tales turning ever so subtly bitter. The form is a part of the meaning. Michael Burns, himself a poet, defends Sexton as a "careful and skilled craftsman," especially in the early work. His close analysis of several important poems reveals strengths hitherto overlooked by many critics. As a kind of counterpoint, Lynette McGrath finds close connections between Sexton's growing use of open forms in her later works and her changing thematic emphases.

One of the major themes of Sexton's canon is the quest. Three essays are devoted to explanations of this quest. Diana Hume George takes the reader on an exploration of Squirrel Island, the place where both sides of Sexton's family spent their summers. It is here that George locates Sexton's god, represented by the father and grandfathers who have made their presence felt in this small part of the world. Borrowing her term "Otherworld" from Mary Daly, Margaret Scarborough suggests that Sexton was moving toward *becoming*—that is, toward a full comprehension of what it is to be a woman. Through her poetry, Sexton makes courageous attempts to create a new order. Finally, Frances Bixler traces Sexton's religious journey from her earliest to her latest work, recognizing the agonizing cost of attempting to achieve a balance between traditional Christian values and newly achieved, hard-won battles for selfhood. Sexton was unable to create a new tradition, nor could she live with the old one. Her struggle, though unsuccessful, deserves recognition.

My special thanks goes to Robert Lowrey for accepting the challenge of publishing a book of original critical works on Anne Sexton and to the University of Central Arkansas for its support of the University of Central Arkansas Press. I also wish to acknowledge the kindness and counsel given to me by Diana Hume George and Diane Wood Middlebrook. Katherine Lederer and Robert Henigan, who read manuscripts and offered valuable advice, cannot be thanked sufficiently. Charlotte Story's wonderfully intuitive drawings and creative insights opened up several new areas of investigation for me. In addition, Dana Bixler deserves recognition for the many hours of typing and editing which made this book a reality. Finally, to all the contributors, some of whom we were unable to include in this collection, I wish to extend appreciation for their enthusiastic and generous response.

Springfield, Missouri FB
January 15, 1988

Abbreviations of Anne Sexton's Works

To Bedlam and Part Way Back	(TB)
All My Pretty Ones	(APO)
Live or Die	(LD)
Love Poems	(LP)
Transformations	(T)
The Book of Folly	(BF)
The Death Notebooks	(DN)
The Awful Rowing Toward God	(AW)
45 Mercy Street	(MS)
Words for Dr. Y	(DY)
The Complete Poems	(CP)

*Although *The Complete Poems* are most often cited bibliographically, we have decided that reader would be more helped by knowing from which particular collection a poem came. Since the collections are listed separately in (CP), the reader should have no trouble finding the poem. A few poems are cited from (CP), having been published for the first time in this collection.

In Memory of Anne Sexton

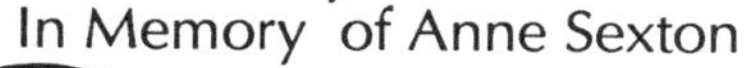

Having, for so very long,
been passionately in love
with not-so-easeful death,
you have at last composed
your final Transformation.

Where is that model's face
ravaged by pure life,
those pain-filled eyes
that saw the words
the wry mouth spoke?

Our Rappaccini's daughter,
you have bitten deeply
into the poisonous fruit
and left us bereft of
your hilarious secret terror.

Robert Henigan

I. Contexts

Sweet weight,
in celebration of the woman I am
and of the soul of the woman I am
and of the central creature and its delight
I sing for you. I dare to live.
Hello, spirit. Hello, cup.
Fasten, cover. Cover that does contain.
Hello to the soil of the fields.
Welcome, roots.

"In Celebration of My Uterus"
Love Poems

ANNE SEXTON AND ROBERT LOWELL

Diane Wood Middlebrook

In the autumn of 1958, Anne Sexton began attending a writing seminar Robert Lowell offered to undergraduates at Boston University. Her productive month at the Antioch Writer's Conference in August that year had opened Sexton's eyes to the usefulness of working with prestigious teachers. Robert Lowell was an obvious choice. Just before the fall term was to begin that September, Sexton wrote to her mentor W. D. Snodgrass, fishing for an introduction to Lowell:

> Where does Robert Lowell live—if I knew I'd write him and ask if he would like me as a student for his graduate course in poetry writing. It says in the catalogue that students may enter without degree with instructor's o.k. . . . There are six Robert Lowells in the book. (*Letters* 35)

With Snodgrass's encouragement, Sexton sent Lowell a sheaf of recent poems. He responded at once:

> Of course your poems qualify. They move with ease and are filled with experience, like good prose. I am not very familiar with them yet, but have been reading them with a good deal of admiration and envy this morning after combing through pages of fragments of my own unfinished stuff. You stick to truth and the simple expression of very difficult feelings, and this is the line in poetry that I am most interested in. (11 September 1958, HRC)

The "unfinished stuff" Lowell refers to was the manuscript of *Life Studies*, undergoing final revision; he mailed it to his publisher only a month later, on October 31 (Hamilton

258). Lowell had been sending the poems around to his friends for the past year, trying out on his most trusted critics a new style of poetry. Phrased in looser, more idiomatic lines than his previous gnarly formalism, the poetry—with prose pieces interspersed—represented a definite stylistic departure form the two previous books for which he had received extravagant praise. Probably more important, where Lowell's earlier work had been learned and thunderously hortatory, the writing in *Life Studies* was contemplative and personal. Based on autobiographical recollection unsparing of his Brahmin family, the new poetry puzzled out the warped invisible connections among the generations, acknowledging madness, fear, and anguish as authentic responses to the dynamics of family life, and by extension, to life in postwar American society.

Lowell had received encouragement in this risky departure into personal themes from Elizabeth Bishop (to whom he dedicated "Skunk Hour" in *Life Studies*) and from Randall Jarrell, both of them old friends who could be counted on for close reading and candor. They liked the work. But an earlier mentor, Allen Tate, was appalled:

> *all* the poems about your family, including the one about you and Elizabeth, are definitely *bad*. . . . the poems are composed of unassimilated details, terribly intimate, and coldly noted, which might well have been transferred from the notes from your autobiography without change. The free verse, arbitrary and without rhythm, reflects this lack of imaginative focus. (qtd. in Hamilton, 237)

These quibbles in letters among Robert Lowell's friends reflected a debate current in American poetry circles between defenders of an ideal of high seriousness (equated with impersonality) and the proponents of a poetry based on self-examination. Many of the latter were undergoing psychotherapies based on psychoanalytic theory, which made family relationships accessible to postwar artists in a new way.

The two world wars of the century had definitively reduced the scale in which human heroism could be credibly recreated in art: it was the age of existential man. Psychoanalysis, however, focuses on the childhood origins of adult behavior, penetrating to that level of consciousness, founded in infancy, where each person has magnified parents and siblings to a gigantic scale. The psychoanalytic point of view permitted the restoration of exorbitant passions and a sense of destiny to individual human history. Though the purpose of psychotherapy is to capture, undress, and demystify one's personal giants and reduce them to manageable proportions, the memory of living among giants lingers in readers, and can be evoked with authority by the poetic image. For Lowell, psychoanalytic reconstruction of his relation to his father and grandfathers helped him explore the theme of depleted masculinity which resonates so powerfully in *Life Studies*. Tate's criticism that the poems on Lowell's family are simply too "intimate" seems like a willful refusal to see their sharply drawn portraits as psychological projections of a man's anxious hostility at his wellborn male forebears for turning out to be so puny, on close inspection.

But in any case, few of Lowell's poet friends shared Tate's skepticism; and Lowell was proud of the new direction he had taken in the poetry he was collecting for publication as *Life Studies* that fall. So Sexton's letter of September 1958, though she could not have known it, was well-timed. Snodgrass's recommendation and the increasingly personal substance of her own writing qualified her for respect as a peer, which is how Lowell addressed her. "You stick to truth and the simple expression of very difficult feelings, and this is the line in poetry that I am most interested in."

Sexton entered the class in September as an auditor, but she did the work too, along with fifteen young B.U. students and others who drifted in and out over the course of the year. Lowell was already a formidable presence on the American poetry scene, and unquestionably the foremost poet of Boston. His poetry courses have been so widely memorialized that it is possible to gain a feeling for what they must have been like when Sexton took her seat there every week, listening, fidgeting, and chain-smoking forbidden cigarettes.

The class met Tuesdays from 2-4 p.m. Students came prepared with typed manuscripts of their poems to circulate in carbon copies. During the first hour Lowell would discuss a poem or two from the anthology students brought to class; he could spend a long time talking about the effects of just one or two lines (Baumel 32). Then he would turn to poems by the students. Poet Alan Williamson recalled Lowell's magisterial procedure in dealing with student poems:

> He would listen to the student read the poem once, then read it aloud himself, his hand hovering like a divining-rod until he reached a particular detail or turn of phrase, then plumping down: "it comes to life here." As often as not he would hand the student back a new poem, constructed on the spot out of the two or three passages that "came to life." . . . he was often uncannily right as to where the emotional center, the possible originality lay. He came as near as I can imagine to teaching the intuitions—about one's real subject; about diction; about structure—which so often distinguish good, let alone great, poets from journeymen. (38)

Lowell's habit of classifying lines, and poets, into minutely differentiated ranks of "greatness" intimidated students, even when it was useful to developing a fine-tuned sense of craft. Sexton had not read much of the poetry Lowell singled out for admiration. After a month in class, she worried to Snodgrass,

> I shall never write a really good poem. I overwrite. I am a reincarnation of Edna St. Vincent . . . I am learning more than you could imagine from Lowell. I am learning what I am not. He didn't say I was like Edna (I do—a secret fear)—also a fear of writing as a

> woman writes. I wish I were a man—I would rather write the way a man writes. (*Letters* 40)

Aside form the work of Emily Dickinson and his friend Elizabeth Bishop, it seemed that *no* poetry by women measured up to Lowell's extreme aesthetic standards. Both in class and in the "office hours" to which Lowell invited a few privileged younger poets every week, Lowell spent a good deal of time mulling over whether this or that poet was "major" or "minor"; women poets were almost inevitably categorized as "Minor, definitely minor."[1] Sexton's boarding school models had been accomplished lyricists in the vein of Edna St. Vincent Millay: Sara Teasdale and Adelaide Crapsey—definitely minor? Suddenly she was confronting the poetry of Robert Browning, Gerard Manley Hopkins, Hart Crane, William Carlos Williams, and assuming they represented what it meant both to be "major" and to "write like a man." "What I am not" was, among other things, male. Was Sexton therefore incapable of artistic "greatness"? The ambiguity was enhanced by Lowell's reputation as a skirtchaser. As one of his friends put it, "Cal had to be 'in love.' Poets were always in love" (qtd. in Hamilton 241); so women themselves came in for another kind of classification. There was always "a girl" somewhere in the background—in the manic phases of Lowell's bipolar mood swings, very much in the foreground—of his professional life (Hamilton, *passim*). Lowell did not cultivate privacy in regard to his erotic adventures; indeed, after he achieved a coveted appointment to the Harvard faculty in 1963, Lowell routinely interviewed the women students—not the men—who signed up for his class, and admitted them on the basis of looks; or so he acknowledged to his friends (Spivack 90).

Sexton wasn't exactly a student, and she didn't engage in a flirtation with Lowell, but she shared the classroom tensions created by what she called Lowell's "soft dangerous voice" (*Letters* 43) as he sorted through the poems in front of him, zeroing in on a phrase or line he might characterize as "almost perfect . . . of its *kind*" (Gilbert 313). Discomfiting his students was a side-effect of one of Lowell's most successful teaching techniques, his focus on small but important achievements in a phrase or line that were worth studying and admiring. A whole poem didn't need to be "great" to manifest qualities almost perfect . . . of their kind. Until she won praise of just this sort, Sexton was convinced Lowell didn't like her, and she was irritated by the attitude of reverence that pervaded the Lowell classroom. "I am very bitchy acting in class," she told Snodgrass.

> The class just sits there like little doggies waggling their heads at his every statement. For instance, he will be dissecting some great poem and will say, "Why is this line so good. What makes it good?" and there is total silence. Everyone afraid to speak. And finally, because I can stand it no longer, I speak up saying, "I don't think it's so good at all. You would never allow us sloppy language like that." . . . and so forth. But I don't do this for effect. But because the line *isn't* good. What do you do—sit there and agree and nod and say nothing . . .? . . . As you say, I do act aggressive. I think the trouble is that my mind, my thinking mind, *is* aggressive. (*Letters* 49)

But something in the writing class catalyzed the best in Sexton: probably Lowell's encouragement to think of writing as a craft, where skill shows in minute particulars; probably also an educational exposure to well wrought lines she would not have found on her own. "Lowell can not have influenced my work with his work as I haven't been reading his stuff . . . just listening to his ideas about other people's work. I do not feel he is influencing me—but teaching me what NOT to write—or mainly," Sexton told Snodgrass in February (*Letters* 53). "I am learning leaps and boundaries" (*Letters* 48). At the end of the term she summed up the experience. "He taught me great. It was as easy as filling an empty vase. After all, I didn't know a damn thing about any poetry really. 2 years ago I had never heard of any poet but Edna St. Vincent . . . and now do know how to walk through lots of people's poetry and pick and pick over" (*Letters* 79-80).

Lowell may not have influenced the style of Sexton's poems that fall and winter, but he certainly validated the direction her work was taking: and this included "writing as a woman." It was in Lowell's class that Sexton began scheming early drafts of "The Double Image," trying to achieve the effect of a spontaneous-sounding first-person voice within the constraints of a complicated, rhyming stanza which slowly and surely built up a dramatic narrative. It was a tall order, and she spent the autumn term on it. When *The Hudson Review* accepted the poem at the end of December—all 240 lines of it—Lowell was suitably impressed.

By early January, most of the poems Sexton was circulating for publication had been accepted. Snodgrass was dazzled: "Jesus God! You're publishing everywhere! Marvelous!" (2 December 1958, HRC). She decided to ask Robert Lowell to help her pull them together for publication as a book.

> I have stuck my poems together as if they could be a book and Lowell is looking it over. Did I make a mistake? I don't know. Still he seems receptive to the idea and said he would tell me frankly if there was enough good stuff for a book. (*Letters* 48)

The manuscript's working title, drawn from lines in "The Double Image," was *To Bedlam and Part Way Back*. It contained 122 pages: all of the poems accepted for publication to date, along with others she still trusted (HRC).[2] Many of these poems did not eventually appear in the published book, which went through repeated, rapid revisions before publication. But the act of selecting and arranging them for Lowell inaugurated a new phase of creativity: during the next five months in Lowell's class Sexton was to write eight new poems, which strengthened the theme of "bedlam" and reduced the number of poems written as formal exercises. (The topic of mental illness, underscored in the title, would eventually attract a wide range of reviewers to the book.) Meanwhile, Lowell reviewed the manuscript, commented on what he saw as strengths and weaknesses to Sexton, and passed it on to other readers for advice about placing it with a publisher. Sexton marveled over Lowell's generosity.

> Lowell is really helping me, De, as kindly as possible and I can't figure it out. I am always so startled by goodness. He likes the looks of my "book," with some critical reservations, and has shown it to Stanley Kunitz and Bill Alfred, who both, he says, agree with his enthusiasm (and his reservations). He is going to show it to somebody Ford at Knopf this week to see if he would be interested. And Houghton Mifflin wants to see it. He thinks that I ought to make my final goal Sept. [. . .] isn't that something, De . . . I mean, I am jeepers creepers about it. He means by Sept. that I might get it accepted now, but should still rewrite and work out the poorer stuff and write some new ones to fill their place.
>
> I am confused and delighted with this—and time and the publishing market will tell the rest. But, I remind my self's self, I've got to stay sane to do it. (*Letters* 51-2)

Houghton Mifflin accepted Sexton's manuscript of *To Bedlam and Part Way Back* on May 19.[3] That same month, Robert Lowell's *Life Studies* was published in the United States (it had been published in England a month earlier). Lowell's book was to receive the National Book Award that year, and in his acceptance speech, Lowell would offer an explanation of his artistic goals in *Life Studies* that was later used to account for Anne Sexton's style too. Borrowing a metaphor from the structuralist anthropologist Claude Levi-Strauss, he distinguished between two "competing" kinds of poetry: "cooked" and "raw."

> The cooked, marvelously expert and remote, seems constructed as

> a sort of mechanical or catnip mouse for graduate seminars; the raw, jerry-built and forensically deadly, seems often like an unscored libretto by some bearded but vegetarian Castro. (noted in Hamilton 279)

"Cooked" was Lowell's way of referring to the poetry of high seriousness and tight, formal effects that he had abandoned in writing *Life Studies;* at the opposite extreme stood poems like Ginsberg's "Howl" (thus the simile of the libretto by a bearded vegetarian). Poetry had taken a turn to the left, and Lowell was throwing in his lot with the new movement—in an aloof, intellectual sort of way.

But at the actual time of the publication of *Life Studies.* Lowell was once again hospitalized at McLean's. He entered the hospital in late April and was there for the whole month of May, 1959. Lowell was manic-depressive, and his life was punctuated with breakdowns followed by rich periods of creativity. In the period of convalescence from one such breakdown in 1956, Lowell had rapidly produced much of *Life Studies;* following another severe breakdown in early 1958, he had finished it (Hamilton, esp. 227-38, 253-68). With the privilege of retrospect, Lowell's biographer Ian Hamilton has speculated that Lowell treasured the "infancy of madness" surrendered in periods of stability. "The diagnosed manic-depressive will surely always have a buried yearning for the 'tropical' terrain of his affliction," Hamilton remarks, "and the pursuit of 'health' will in some measure always be more contractual than voluntary" (257).

In what ways were the psychological tropics of mania affiliated with Lowell's genius? And to what degree were his manic episodes voluntary? Such questions are bound to emerge in discussions of this era of American art, when so many celebrated geniuses were or seemed to be psychologically unstable, manic or depressed. Among Lowell's contemporaries, many had spent weeks or months in mental institutions, and years under psychiatric care. Many were also, like Lowell, abusers of alcohol. To mention only the poets, these included Randall Jarrell and Theodore Roethke, who like Lowell had manic-depressive illnesses; Delmore Schwartz, exiled from friends and profession alike by paranoia; Elizabeth Bishop, hospitalized a number of times for treatment of alcoholism; John Berryman, whose disorders compounded all of the above.

No one who witnessed an episode of actual breakdown was likely to confuse a poet's sometimes freaky or infantile imaginative freedom with the person's pathetic, often frightening insanity. Yet the energy of the poet's obsessional concentration—on language; on the strangeness, the uniqueness of things and being—bore some resemblance to the behavioral disorganization that marked the onset of illness. Lowell himself remarked on the similarities in a letter to Theodore Roethke:

> There's a strange fact about the poets of roughly our age, and one that doesn't exactly seem to have always been true. It's this, that to write we seem to have to go at it with such single-minded intensity that we are always on the point of drowning. . . . I feel it's something almost unavoidable, some flaw in the motor. (qtd. in Hamilton 337)

From Anne Sexton, the spectacle of Lowell's breakdown that April she sat in his class elicited both compassion and voyeuristic fascination. Early that month she reported to Snodgrass that Lowell was squiring a new girl "(shhh secret)"—recognized by gossips as a symptom (letter dated "April in Wednesday," HRC). On May 1 she wrote to Snodgrass, "Lowell has shifted to a manic phase and it seems so disturbing. He is at MacLean's but only for a short while I hear. But I guess he isn't [as] bad as other times" (1 May 1959, HRC). She enclosed, for Snodgrass's eyes only, a poem titled

"Elegy in the Classroom" (and later added it to the manuscript of *Bedlam*):

In the thin classroom, where your face
was noble, and your words were all things,
I find this boily creature in your place;

find you disarranged, squatting on the window sill,
irrefutably placed up there,
like a hunk of some big frog
watching us through the V
of your woolen legs.

Even so, I must admire your skill.
You are so gracefully insane.
We fidget in our plain chairs
and pretend to catalogue
our facts for your burly sorcery

or ignore your fat blind eyes
or the prince you ate yesterday
who was wise, wise, wise.

Lowell almost certainly would have suggested revision of the slack diction ("all things," "some big," "so gracefully," the repeated "place"), had he been invited to comment. It was not Sexton's best poem, but it helped establish *Bedlam's* turf in the poetry world. Lowell, reigning monarch of the kingdom of mad poets, had inadvertently supplied Anne Sexton with an opportunity to appropriate him for *Bedlam* by transforming himself before her eyes from Great Poet into Frog Prince, and she was not going to miss the chance.

Sexton spent more time that summer adding and subtracting poems in the *Bedlam* manuscript, worrying about Lowell's advice to supply fifteen or so new poems. The manuscript had to go to the printer before August 1. In July, riffling through what she called her "bone pile" of discarded work, she picked up a poem that had started life in December

1957 as "Night Voice on a Broomstick," a piece of sentimental verse that might have found a home in the Halloween issue of a woman's magazine. She had sent it to literary journals without success. Still trying to produce work suitable for *Bedlam,* in July 1959 she retitled it "Witch" and reworked it into a 16-line quasi-sonnet form. Then she broke those lines up into very short pieces with irregular but striking rhymes; in that 38-line version, "Witch" ended,

> Who see me here
> this ragged apparition
> in their own air
> see a wicked appetite,
> if they dare.
>
> (Work sheets, folder 2, *TB*, HRC)

This is the sort of poem Sexton had been writing for workshops throughout her apprenticeship. Like "The Farmer's Wife," "Unknown Girl in the Maternity Ward," "For Johnny Pole on the Forgotten Beach," "The Moss of His Skin," Sexton's "Witch" is spoken through a mask, by a dramatic persona, and offers a psychological portrait of a social type. (Later when she was a teacher herself, Sexton referred to the persona in a poem as an identity "applied like a rubber mask that the robber wears," Lecture One, HRC). She polished "Witch" through several revisions. But something about the short lines bothered her; she lengthened the lines again, and this time tried another structuring principle: stanza breaks punctuated with a refrain: "I have been her kind." The poem, titled "Her Kind," begins this way:

> I have gone out, a possessed witch,
> haunting the black air, braver at night;
> dreaming evil, I have done my hitch
> over the plain houses, light by light:
> lonely thing, twelve-fingered, out of mind.

> A woman like that is not a woman, quite.
> I have been her kind. (*TB*)

To the witch as persona, Sexton has added another voice named "I." Now there are two subjectivities, two speakers in the poem: one who registers a state of loneliness, obsession, fear, lust, social outlawry, and punishment; and one who comments on her ("A woman like that. . . .").

Sexton liked this one. The poem had been through nineteen pages of drafting; she noted on the final manuscript, "took one week to complete." From then on she opened each public reading with "Her Kind." She would usually introduce it by saying "I'll read you this poem, and then you'll know just what kind of a poet I am, just what kind of a woman I am. And then if anyone wishes to leave, they may do so" ("Lecture Five," HRC). It was because of such gestures that Sexton was labeled, to her chagrin, one of the "confessional" poets: a label that, like "primitive," conveyed second-class status as an artist. Yet the double subjectivity in the poem insists on a separation between a kind of woman (mad) and a kind of poet (a woman with magic craft): a doubleness that expressed the paradox of Sexton's creativity: transforming the life by making it into a story. "Her Kind" is not a poem spoken through a mask, nor is it a first-person narrative like "The Double Image." It is a poem that calls attention to the distance between pain and the representation of pain, between the poet "on stage" in print—flippant, glamorous, crafty—and the woman whose anguish she knew first hand.

Bedlam went to the printers in mid-July (AS to Frederick Morgan, 20 July 1959, HRC), and was published by Houghton Mifflin the following spring, on April 22. Partly because of Lowell's blurb on the jacket, the book at once created a local stir among literary people; and the book's reception was influenced pronouncedly by the portrait of Sexton by Rollie McKenna printed on the back dust jacket. ("I'm all wrinkles and look like I am about to cry," Sexton commented to Snodgrass. "When I had the picture took I was on a truth and no mask kick." [AS to W. D. Snodgrass, 25 March 1960, HRC].

Immediately, readers' responses established two poles of criticism. One is captured in a note to Sexton from Irving Howe, a distinguished professor of literature at Brandeis: "I don't often write fan notes, but I feel, having just for the second time gone through your book, a strong urge just to let you know that for one reader at least, for me, it has been extremely moving and, in a particular sort of way, pleasing" (20 May 1960, HRC). Howe passed the book on to poet Allen Grossman, who went on to write a review of *Bedlam* for the Brandeis newspaper, enclosing it in a letter to Sexton. The *Bedlam* poems "seem to me incredibly distinguished and compassionate," Grossman wrote to her. "They reach me, and hold me, and give me pleasure" (24 June 1960, HRC). Similar themes appeared in *The New York Times*: the book's "hub has a natural, built-in interest: mental breakdown, pictured with a pitiless eye and clairvoyant sharpness. . . . Mrs. Sexton's craft is quick and deft"(Lask 25).

The other point of view is conveyed in a letter Elizabeth Bishop, residing in Brazil, wrote Robert Lowell after receiving a review copy from Houghton Mifflin:

> I have been seeing some poems around by an Anne Sexton that reminded me quite a bit of you and also were quite good, at least some of them—and the same day your letter came Houghton-Mifflin sent me her book, with your blurb on the jacket and that sad photograph of her on the other side of it. She *is* good, in spots—but there is all the difference in the world, I'm afraid, between her kind of simplicity and that of *Life Studies*, her kind of egocentricity is simply that, and yours that has been—what would be the reverse of *sub*-limated, I wonder—anyway, mad intensely *interesting*, and painfully applicable to every reader. I feel I know too much about her—whereas, although I know much more about you, I'd like to know a good deal more, etc.—oh well it is all fairly obvious isn't it.

> I like some of her really mad ones best; those that sound as thought (sic) she'd written them all at once. I think she really must have been in what Lota called the other day the "Luna bin." (19 May 1960, Houghton Library)

At issue in the praise or criticism of these readers is the question of what *use* Sexton has made of a widely shared, frightening, humiliating, and fascinating human experience: the loss of social functioning labeled "mad." Both sides grant Sexton's work authenticity and skill; but was it interesting, or was it embarrassing? Discussion of the quality of Sexton's work throughout her career tended to question whether the speaker of her poems was the victim or the moral survivor of her illness: that is, to focus on one side or the other of the double consciousness Sexton wrote into "Her Kind." The terms of this debate go back to the oldest work of Western literary criticism, in which Aristotle argues that the highest form of art, tragedy, concerns the fall of persons renowned and prosperous—illustrious men of certain families—through some error or frailty. The function of such art is to illuminate the universal dimension in the tragic fall, bringing the spectator to a higher understanding of human life (*Poetics*, notes on "catharsis" and "character"). But "universality" of meaning could only occur where the protagonist's social status and his tragic flaw were each significant enough to elicit identification from an entire community.

Elizabeth Bishop was perhaps applying just such an Aristotelian standard of significant character, in finding Sexton "egocentric" where Lowell was "painfully applicable to every reader." On first reading the poems of *Life Studies*, Bishop had told Lowell he was "the luckiest poet I know" because, owing to his family lineage, nothing about his personal life was quite without historic interest: "all you have to do is put down the names! And the fact that it seems significant, illustrative, American, etc. gives you, I think, the confidence you display about tackling any idea or theme, *seriously*" (14 December 1957, qtd. in Hamilton 233).

For Grossman, on the other hand, Sexton's personal voice was ennobled by speaking "from the other side of an enormous *dérèglement*, expressing how much one had to give up in order to attain reconstitution, after a dire reduction of the self." Grossman saw this as quite the opposite of egocentrism: "Anne Sexton was the first major writer who was able to be heard as a voice not concerned with itself" as an artistic ego. Rather, she reflected the recuperation of self in the aftermath of madness and then of medical treatment. "Her poetry conveyed an immediacy such as people sometimes experience when first reading Thomas Hardy—but not very many other writers." Having survived, having endured, was also the "psychological collage" of Lowell's work; but Sexton was less digressive, willing to speak of what really happened in the process of reduction: this is what both Howe and Grossman valued in *Bedlam*.[4]

Now, nearly thirty years after its publication, *Bedlam* is readable in a number of contexts impossible for these first critics to have envisioned, from feminist criticism to postmodern psychoanalysis. Today Sexton's work is rarely paired with Lowell's in discussion of contemporary poetry, anyway. But arguably, it was Robert Lowell's influence both on the design of *Bedlam* and on its marketing that gave Sexton's first book an imprimatur of seriousness without which it might have sunk out of sight as rapidly as do most first books of poetry, then and now.

Notes

I am grateful to Linda Gray Sexton, executor of the estate of Anne Sexton, for permission to quote from previously unpublished manuscripts in this article; and to Alice H. Methfessel, executor of the estate of Elizabeth Bishop, for permission to quote from an unpublished letter to Robert Lowell.

[1]Kathleen Spivack recalls the "office hour" in which Lowell transferred Adrienne Rich to that category, after she published a bruising review of Lowell's *The Dolphin* and *For Lizzie and Harriet* ("RL: A Memoir" 190).

[2]Anne Sexton Archive, restricted file, light blue cardboard notebook, with annotations about responses from Lowell, Plath, Snodgrass.

[3]Sexton signed a "General Department Royalty Contract," with a royalty scale, calculated on the list price, as follows: 10% to 5,000 copies; 12.5% from 5,0000-10,000 copies; 15% on all copies over and above. She received an advance of $200. (Anne Sexton Miscellaneous files, HRC).

[4]Allen Grossman, interview with D. M., 13 October 1982, Cambridge, Massachusetts. Grossman's term *dérèglement* refers to Rimbaud's dictum, "le poète se fait voyant par un long, immense et raisonné dérèglement de tous les sens."

Works Cited

Anne Sexton Archive, The Humanities Research Center, The University of Texas, Austin. (Abbreviated HRC in further references.)

Baumel, Judith. "Robert Lowell: The Teacher." *The Harvard Advocate,* Robert Lowell commemorative issue 113.1-2 (1979): 32-33.

Colgate University Lectures, "Lecture One," May 1972, "Lecture Five," May 1972, Anne Sexton Archive, HRC.

Gilbert, Celia. "The Sacred Fire." *Working It Out.* ed. S. Ruddick and P. Daniels, New York: Pantheon Books, 1977.

Hamilton, Ian. *Robert Lowell, A Biography.* New York: Random House, 1982.

Lask, "Books of the Times." *New York Times* 28 July 1960: 25.

Sexton, Linda Gray and Lois Ames, eds. *Anne Sexton: A Self- Portrait in Letters.* Boston: Houghton Mifflin, 1977.

Spivack, Kathleen. "Robert Lowell: A Memoir." *The Antioch Review* 43.2 (1985): 183-93.

Spivack, Kathleen. "Lear in Boston: Robert Lowell As Teacher and Friend." *Ironwood* #25 (1985): 76-92.

Williamson, Alan. "Robert Lowell: A Reminiscence." 36-39.

"I HAVE BEEN HER KIND": ANNE SEXTON'S COMMUNAL VOICE

Kay Ellen Merriman Capo

Critics have argued that Anne Sexton's authoritative style first appears in *Transformations* with the mythic voice of witch and wisewoman.[1] At first, this voice was not universally appreciated, but sensitive reappraisals by Lauter, Juhasz, Middleton, George, and Demetrakopoulos, among others, have reversed the trend. By the same token, Sexton's early verse has been somewhat eclipsed. Her style did change over time, but I feel the perceived split in Sexton's work is unwarranted because the authority so prized by critics appears in her earliest writing. Many poems of *To Bedlam and Part Way Back* prophesy the gnomic voice of *Transformations*, especially "Her Kind," a work this essay will analyze in depth.

Sexton was always sensitive to the collective dimension of poetry, intuiting that just *naming* her feminine experience was worth a life's commitment (Heyen Interview 135). She saw "everyone as writing the same poem, only with many voices. We're all writing the poem of our time, everyone differently" (Fitzgerald Interview 187). Resistance is the base for any paradigm shift, and Sexton invented a tone of resistance to patriarchy which made her voice exemplary. "Self in 1958" (*TB*) critiques a world little changed since Nora slammed the door on her nineteenth-century "doll's house." And "For John, Who Begs Me Not to Enquire Further" (*TB*) was an early effort to "steal the language" (Ostriker), a declaration of independence from male literary censorship.[2] Urging John Holmes to accept "a certain sense of order" that was "Not . . .

beautiful," Sexton's tone of matriarchal wisdom reverses the student-teacher relationship, presenting her mentor with a "lesson." Intimate reassurance—"This is something I would never find / in a lovelier place, my dear"—leads up to a general maxim that confidently blends you and I into we: "although your fear is anyone's fear, / like an invisible veil between us all."

As early as 1962, Sexton wanted to re-envision central myths, such as the story of Jesus (*Letters* 153), and by 1974, she counselled Erica Jong:

> . . . I keep feeling that there isn't one poem being written by any one of us. . . . The whole life of us writers, the whole product . . . is the one long poem—a community effort if you will. . . . It doesn't belong to any one writer—it's God's poem perhaps. Or God's people's poem. . . . It has more rights than the ego that wants approval. (*Letters* 414)

I have noticed that as Sexton transformed life events into exemplary wisdom, she took advantage of *hortatory, admonitory,* and *mystical* anecdotes (Burke 323-338). In her *hortatory* poems (Burke 324; 332-338) a virtuous model—often Sexton herself—becomes the focus of uncritical devotion as she articulates deep hopes and ideals. Embodying motherly wisdom, for example, she writes "herstory" out of her daughter's menarche. Sensing the communal resonance of the day, "the conversation of the old wives / speaking of *womanhood,*" Sexton assures Linda that her new experience has a generic, normative status—"there is nothing in your body that lies. / All that is new is telling the truth"—because "women are born twice" ("Little Girl, My String Bean, My Lovely Woman," *LD*). The mnemonic power of such phrases recurs throughout Sexton's early work, creating maxims to live by. One would be hard-pressed to find better examples of poetry as social praxis, better ways of naming feminine experience and making it holy.[3]

Sexton's grotesque, *admonitory* anecdotes (Burke 330-338), which present her marginal status as a suicide and mental patient, work by a contrary principle, allowing the audience to partake of negative mysteries emblematic of its deepest fears.[4] Repulsive self-images abound: the mad housewife, the witch, the suicide with her "raft and paddle," the drug addict, the adulteress, the exhibitionist. Feces, masturbation, abortion, the taboo realm of impurity, impiety, and social danger became her province as she exploded decorum for the sake of truth. The very subject matter of Sexton's first book—asylum experiences—is admonitory. But the madhouse also offers a mythic sanctuary from guilt and punishment, and Sexton gains moral stature as the book progresses. Salvaging wisdom from her painful way, she warns about the dangers of her passage.[5]

When she presents a *mystical* moment (Burke 305-309) Sexton's authority is transformed by the object of ultimate concern. Exhortation and admonition point to a possible becoming, but mystical moments eat time altogether, allowing contradictory impulses to exist simultaneously, a quality Juhasz (135) has noted in "The Death Baby" (*DN*), where metaphor and simile give way to "literal description of a visionary world," via "mantric language" and "gnomic pronouncements."[6]

Sexton uses the incantatory style to present and control madness in several poems of *TB*, especially "Ringing the Bells" and "Noon Walk on the Asylum Lawn," where refrains from the twenty-third Psalm calm her fears that the sky is falling: *"though I walk through the valley of the shadow . . . I will fear no evil, fear no evil . . . in the presence of mine of enemies, mine enemies."* The worlds of religion and childhood merge in a hallucinatory vision of grass chanting in venomous voices like the "green witches" who taunt Sexton in "The Double Image": "Too late, / too late, to live with your mother . . . / Too late to be forgiven now, the witches said."

I

I have pointed out that while most critics locate Sexton's first use of the transpersonal voice in *Transformations,* I hear edifying and mystical tones in the earliest work. The *nostrum,* which dominates the first three poems of *TB,* recurs throughout that volume, establishing Sexton's "transpersonal" voice at the outset of her career.[7] And the exemplary techniques of exhortation, admonition and mysticism are often woven into the fabric of one poem, as in "Her Kind," a piece which clearly prophesied Sexton's later direction.

Sexton must have intuited the significance of a poetic tone Richard Howard (450) would later call "vatic" because she chose "Her Kind" as the signature poem to open her public readings. According to Middleton, her biographer, "No matter what poetry she had on an evening's agenda, Sexton offered this persona ['Her Kind'] as a point of entry to her art" because the refrain "a woman like that . . . I have been her kind" presented a way to understand her story not as that of a "victim, but witness and witch" (294). And the chamber rock group named "Anne Sexton and Her Kind" provided rhythmic background for one of the most heralded readers of her generation (*Letters* 326).

In "Her Kind" Sexton invented ground rules for the mythic direction currently admired by critics. Hortatory, admonitory, and mystical language reveals the patriarchal pressure against "herstory" as Sexton transforms a culturally-defined saga of feminine passivity and victimage into a heroic tale. Locked into a cultural groove, her gnomic voice records the domestic ritual of women's lives. Each stanza closes with a refrain that declares her generic identity: "A woman like that . . . / I have been her kind." As Spacks has noted (28), feminine autobiography often creates myths which allow women to see themselves "in a great company of their kind, enduring what others have endured and achieving what women have always achieved."

In all three stanzas one is struck by the dual referencing of Sexton's stereotypes. They not only evoke sympathy for the female condition of powerlessness, but warn that women may use this condition to run away from themselves. Initially, Sexton retreats to a posture of feminine "weakness" to gain support. Depicting herself as a "lonely thing, twelve-fingered, out of mind," she adopts helplessness as her panoply against derision. But even amid cries for indulgence and passive imagery, a resistant tone keeps emerging.

The first stanza of "Her Kind" aligns Sexton with a stereotype of instability, irrationality, and also supernatural power—the witch.[8] Being "out of mind" suggests madness, but Sexton's active verb forms—"I have gone out," "haunting" and "dreaming"—signal agency and will. Ulanov (208) has described the witch as a "Medial Woman," an arbiter of the unconscious who may further evil just as her sister, the wise woman, furthers culture. But recent feminist theory has seen the witch more positively, for it is not "wise" to further a culture that demeans women. A resistant, no-saying witch is not just "dreaming evil."

The sorcerer of "Her Kind" is related to the "Sweet witch" whose voice haunts the poet's dreams in "The Division of Parts" (*TB*). It is the voice of a "middle-aged witch" ("The Gold Key," *T*), her dead mother, that "*good dame*" whose verbal authority ("my Lady of my first words") Sexton integrates as "Dame Sexton" in *Transformations*. Accepting the "division of ways" from her mother means finding her own way to express feminine authority and nurturance, the way of a writer who also happens to be a mother during the 1950's. Sexton's "witch" helps her sublimate the "weird abundance" of unconscious life by using "The Black Art" (*APO*) of writing as an exorcism.

That Sexton was ambivalent about witches and the mother-daughter bond they mediate is clear from a quick survey of *TB* and other early books. While their initial message is suicidal, for example, the "green witches" of "The Double Image" (*TB*) do force a necessary separation from Sexton's mother. It is the transfer of death from mother to daughter and back again, "as if death were catching" and a daughter's "dying" could eat "inside of" a mother that invokes the witch, a relative of that "Old Dwarf Heart" (*APO*) who embodies the inherited core of destructive parental energy.[9] As the animus and gnarled crone inside all beautiful women, the witch embodies maternal guilt and anger over the "fact" that "death too is in the egg" ("The Operation," *APO*). A mother's work lacks the permanence of other beautiful objects, a point Sexton explores in "The Fortress" (*APO*), where a mole, an "inherited . . . spot of danger" on her cheek and her daughter's marks the place "where a bewitched worm ate its way through our soul / in search of beauty." The *singular* psychic inheritance ("soul") shared by mother and daughter is worth noting. If the worm inside is "bewitched," does it discover or destroy feminine transcendence in its search for "beauty"?

Ambivalence about key female models—her mother and maiden aunt—figures into Sexton's mixed view of the mother-daughter bond and the witch who represents unsublimated, forbidden aggression. In "The House" (*APO*), her Nana is both a kind mentor and an ancient crone from *The Brothers Grimm* whose knitting needles work "like kitchen shears." The sarcastic voice, irreverent caricatures, and short lines of this poem read like a prelude to *Transformations*. Sexton's fears about psychic inheritance from the aggressive side of her aunt are clearly expressed in later poems—"Anna Who Was Mad" and "The Nana Hex" (*BF*). Sometimes, as in "Live" (*LD*), Sexton's family renders the "witch" and her death-wish harmless by painting her in the "pink" of health.

Returning to stanza one of "Her Kind" we see Sexton described as a neutralized catalyst for the collective unconscious. Being "not a woman, quite," is she more than, less than, or merely different from other women? Does fancy, madness, or the writer's task lure her over the "plain houses" of other women? Sexton presents her night adventures as part of a duty, a social debt analogous to male military service: "I have done my hitch / over the plain houses, light by light. . . ." The unusual rhyme of "hitch" and witch" presents these solo flights as an initiation into a bizarre sorority. A woman "like that" could plot evil against the domestic glow of light below her. If the "hitch" refers to time spent in the watchful role of wife and mother, couldn't "plain" domestic chores drive a woman to insomnia or "dreaming evil?" This domestic role will be explored from inside the house in the next stanza.

Sisterhood and corporate identity are suggested by "hitch." But the first stanza is also self-aggrandizing. Sexton flies "*over* the plain houses," transcending by madness or imagination the domestic lot of housewives whose realm she inhabits. A look at her "insomnia at 3:15 A.M." in "The Ambition Bird" (*BF*) suggests that it is the "business of words," not the business of housewives or madness that "keeps [Sexton] awake" in "Her Kind." I believe the "hitch" refers to her literary apprenticeship: long nights of imagining, writing, and revising poems, dreaming the necessary "evil" of feminine images that embodied a forbidden cultural resistance. Sexton once described the physical conditions of writing when her children were very young: "I just simply wrote when they went to sleep until three in the morning, and then got up at six. I don't know how I did it then, because now I need all my sleep. I had to; I had no choice" (Fitzgerald Interview 197).

While the events of stanza one occur at night, a time when Sexton is "braver" about going outside her realm and role, stanza two shows her trapped in a daytime routine that is harder to escape. The mystery evoked in stanza one spills into the domestic drudgery of stanza two, where Sexton seems less a witch than Snow White herself, that mythic wondergirl who transforms female domestic chores into a magical confinement in "woods" full of "worms" and "elves." Feminine stereotypes of confinement, materiality, and domesticity are evoked by a servitude to men and children (the image of "dwarves" contains both) which requires virginal unsexing.[10]

In a 1960s culture permeated by media images of cleanliness, "Mr. Clean" was the important household god, and Sexton mourns an identity which languished while she nurtured others. Unlike the docile Snow White, whose Disney counterpart whistled while she worked, Sexton questions her tedious lot, "whining" that she is "misunderstood." Stressing the interplay between gender, imagery, and material culture, *The New York Times* recently reported that in the age of working women, the American home is "dirtier" than it has ever been, the sale of most cleaning products has dropped radically, and the image of "housewife" has changed in TV ads, because no one takes pride in that role any longer. As one adman puts it:

> The housewife is no longer evoked as much in advertising because even housewives don't want to be housewives. . . . ads no longer display a pride in cleanliness. Instead, there's an attempt to try to destigmatize the act of cleaning. Advertisers are trying to make cleaning look like an act of power, not wimpish or wifish. (Stark C6)

Perhaps any god, including cleanliness, loses power when identified with women in public discourse.

II

Stanza two of "Her Kind" reflects ambivalence about domesticity by juxtaposing positive and negative images. This enterprising speaker does discover "caves" and tames them into a domestic order capable of supporting life. The "disaligned" chaos of nature ("woods") is sacralized by "goods" she arranges and nurtures. Centering one's life in rearranging (the endless work of women) looks "plain" when surveyed from the high vantage of the "witch" in stanza one. But Sexton has shored up a blend of practical and exotic treasures: carvings, skillets, shelves, closets, "innumerable goods." Like woman's art of quiltmaking, her domestic accomplishment is undervalued, "misunderstood." One feels the pressure of this devaluation in Sexton's voice, as if the home circumscribes a realm of experience so narrow it can produce spiritual lethargy.[11] The tone recalls T. S. Eliot's allusion in "Morning at the Window" to the "damp souls of housemaids / Sprouting despondently at area gates," a passage which assumes that moisture from one's sponge or mop must dampen one's spirits.

The "caves" of stanza two embody the elemental, static aspect of the feminine principle which Ulanov (157) describes as "a receptive, dark, ingoing, moist, enclosing, and containing world of formation that surrounds and holds fast to everything that is created within it." In such a realm, female identity depends less on creating or inventing than on "rearranging" and "fixing." Ellmann has pointed out that while "it is not important that women do things *well*, they must do them neatly" (89), for "*Practicality* is a subdivision of confinement" (91).

It is difficult for Sexton to sculpt identity from the skillets, closets, and shelves which are her props and raw materials. Her "whining" suggests the understated but constant complaint which the passive side of the "Great Mother" archetype evinces. "A masochistic rumination over old hurts, carefully stored and brought out now and again to be reinspected and relived" (Ulanov 200), the term also implies a mother's identification with the nagging demands of her worms and elves.

It is noteworthy that in her later career Sexton's domestic imagery becomes more celebratory while maintaining a spirit of critique. The power and diligence of women's work is invoked as she dares a "man in [his] easy chair" to try and "polish up the stars / with Bab-o and find a new God" ("The Fury of Earth," *DN*). In the "Fury of Sunrises" (*DN*) breakfast is a "sacrament," and though "the dog [is] inside whining for food," she has "the whole day to live through, / steadfast, deep, interior."

Taking delight in the interiority of home life is most obvious in "Clothes" (*DN*) where Sexton ironically explores the relation between Godliness and the cleanliness for which women feel so responsible: "Put on a clean shirt / before you die," she warns herself: "You want me clean, God, / so I'll try to comply." Sexton needs to bring the messy domestic accomplishment of "all my kitchens" along with her to heaven for "They hold the family laughter and the soup." Obeying her "mother's dictum / that nice girls" wear "only white cotton" underpants, she imagines God wants her to be a virginal Snow White who will make no adult, sexual demands and "die like a nice girl / smelling of Clorox and Duz." In "Hurry Up Please It's Time" (*DN*), she is aware that woman's peaceful domestic "routine" is used by patriarchy to keep "shops . . . open" and "sausages . . . still fried" while "wars" and environmental hazards permeate the public sphere where women are silenced.

Whatever the negative self-associations of stanza two of "Her Kind," heroism and self-transcendence are also present. Though compliant, the speaker has "found the warm caves" which shelter her family. Even the Freudian model of feminine identity, which stresses the need for passive receptivity, sees the effort to make a home as an active exertion. Helene Deutsch likens homemaking to the "great achievements of the female animal that tries to find a safe shelter and food for her young and defends them against the dangers of the environment" (20). Describing her dual role as writer and mother, Sexton emphasized the sheer effort of raising children:

> "They would come in and break right into a poem. You get used to that; you adjust to it. 'She hit me. She pinched me.' Or there's always the Band-aid. We've got to get out the Band-aid, *quick*. 'I fell down. Kiss it, and make it well.' Or, 'I want a cookie.' Millions of things go wrong. They might be out lighting matches, burning up leaves. You've got to be *aware*. It's difficult, but not impossible." (Fitzgerald Interview 197)

Sexton presents feminine emotional restraint as a courageous moral achievement. Exercising compassion, she suppresses any natural irritation felt toward those spineless, larval creatures (the worms and elves representing husband and children) who depend utterly on her care. Her only protest takes the nonviolent form of "whining." Dorothy Dinnerstein has proposed that the answer to Freud's famous question, "What do women want?" is that women want men to share the burden of self-repression, the need to curb or sublimate aggressive impulses, which rearing children requires. A woman's psychic strength cannot be understood or appreciated until men share the burden of nurturing.

The psychic resilience and energy of stanza two hinges on Sexton's disalignment in stanza one and the earlier text of *TB*. The heroism of having pulled herself together for the sake of others, having "fixed [all those] suppers," while "rearranging" a home where work is never done, is amplified by the history of mental pain reported throughout *TB*. Because she is "misunderstood" despite efforts to serve others, Sexton gains an aura of heroic martyrdom. Like other female autobiographers discussed by Spacks (29), she "stresses the conscientiousness and good will of her *doing* as evidence of her capacity to surmount and transmute the restrictions of her lot," and extends her range of self-descriptions to protest society's painful undervaluation of the "burden of the trivial" which women assume (Spacks 28).

In a classic essay on feminist theology published the same year as "Her Kind" and *TB* (1960), Goldstein argues that since women's psychic experience is different from that of men, her "sins" must be conceived differently. Theology has encouraged men to root out pride—an excess of selfhood and autonomy—and strive for an other-centered love (101). But since other-centeredness already dominates woman's interpersonal sphere, she faces a moral dilemma opposite to that of men (108). Self, pride, and self-loving behaviors must not be rooted out of women; they should be fostered. A mother learns the depth of "self-transcending love" but also "that it is impossible to sustain a perpetual I-Thou relationship" and that "the attempt to do so can be deadly. Moments, hours, and days of self-giving must be balanced by moments, hours, days of withdrawal into, and enrichment of, her individual selfhood if she is to remain a whole person," since to "give too much of herself, so that nothing remains of her own uniqueness" may make a woman "merely an emptiness, almost a zero, without value to herself, to her fellow men, or, perhaps, even to God" (108).

Goldstein glosses the ethical inquiry of "Her Kind," contending that while "pride" and "will-to-power" are not major problems for women, feminine "sins" are "suggested by such items as triviality, distractability, and diffuseness; lack of an organizing center or focus; dependence on others for one's own self-definition; tolerance at the expense of standards of excellence . . . in short, underdevelopment or negation of the self" (109). Insofar as theology tries to "strangle" woman's impulses to be a separate individual, due to a fear of excess founded in masculine experience, it does women spiritual injustice. A woman who trusts the theologians will presume that the overwhelming needs of a family require utter submission to the feminine domestic role. She will thus relinquish any creative role in the formation of history and culture (110).

I feel that in "Her Kind" Sexton "confesses" the corporate feminine identity of her era. Critics have seen the spiritual problem of being female as a key to Sexton's quest and in this she was somewhat ahead of her time. As Friedan's *The Feminine Mystique* would later catalogue, Sexton's malaise was common among women of her era. "Her Kind's" rhythm of resistance is prophetic of the re-mythologizing of post-War America and of a direction Sexton took in her later work. In this it is akin to "Aunt Jennifer's Tiger's" (1951) which unconsciously contained and predicted the direction of Adrienne Rich's work: "The massive weight of Uncle's wedding band / Sits heavily upon Aunt Jennifer's hand." Only through her art—embroidery filled with fierce tiger images—can one fathom this woman's pride and courage. Like Aunt Jennifer's tigers, the speaker of "Her Kind" leaps out of feminine confinement to protest, defy, and boldly articulate a collective experience of pain.

III

In light of my previous discussion, the last stanza of "Her Kind" is especially revealing. Here Sexton plays her most complicated feminine role as an unnamed "driver" enters the foreground. If he, like Snow White's Prince, was sent to rescue her from the domestic woods of stanza two, it is a mock chivalry, for she leaps from her "skillets" into his "flames." Does she submit herself to this executioner, an agent of sado-erotic death? Or does she resist him?

This stanza embodies a dynamic which George sees at

the center of Sexton's suicide poems, an identity between the wish for death and the fear of death (168). It is also an early example of Sexton's "connection of the death wish with a specifically feminine desire for power and control; and deeper still . . . of the death wish to a protest against human mortality" (George 148). To George's perspective I would add that death is required for reincarnation, the birth of a new self and new "kind" of post-modern woman. In this respect, Sexton's persona is a kindred spirit to the brazen, equally "unashamed" phoenix of Plath's "Lady Lazarus" (*Ariel*).

Eroticized "flames" which "still bite" Sexton's "thigh" associate sex with death through the rhyme of "thigh" with "die." The "driver" is both executioner and spectral suitor, reminiscent of the gentleman caller who "kindly" chauffeured Emily Dickinson in "Because I Could Not Stop for Death." Instruments of public torture conjure up other female martyrs: medieval witches subjected to the "wheels" of the rack and screw which "wind" under their cracked "ribs"; Joan of Arc at the stake with flames biting her thighs; Marie Antoinette refusing to wave her arms at the crowds who watched her ride to the guillotine in a rustic cart.

"Consorting with Angels" (*LD*) clarifies the radical perspective of this last stanza. There Sexton dreams of "a city made of chains / where Joan was put to death in man's clothes," a place where she lost her "gender" and "wove [her] arms together" with Adam and Eve to ride "under the sun" as initiate of a new race unlimited by feminine or masculine typology and unlimited by mortality: "I lost my common gender and my final aspect [death]." Her new "aspect," like "the nature of the angels," resembles no "kind" at all. Like the angels, "no two [beings] made in the same species," she assumes a nature that is immortal and not replicable.

The biggest challenge of "Her Kind" is how to read the last line: "A woman like that is not *ashamed* to die." Is hers the witch's death? The suicide's? Or that of the suburban housewife? It is tempting to read the poem autobiographically, in light of *TB* as a whole. Seen in that light, Sexton transforms suicide into martyrdom, featuring herself as an initiate, one of that elite rank who has seen the edge, the "last bright routes," and "survived" to tell about it. Like a war hero, she has done her "hitch" with madness and been drafted by death, the "driver." Yet she does not brag about her courage before death; she exults over being "not *ashamed* to die." Why does one intuitively expect the last line to read: "is not *afraid* to die?" And what is the effect of our jarred expectations? Does brutal treatment which should call forth anger or aggression produce submission in Sexton? I think not. Her tone is not resigned. It is resistant.

Helen Lynd has pointed out that while guilt responds to internalized standards, shame responds to the criticism or ridicule of others. Shame requires an awareness of others as separate from the self, that others form an "audience—whether the audience gives approval or disapproval" (21). There is grandness in Sexton's waving of her "nude arms to villages going by," and a trust that the offstage audience of authority figures, those clapping hands we see later in "The Play" (*AW*), will watch her pass by. "Guiltless" denotes innocence, but "shameless" is a devil term that means being "insensible to one's self . . . unblushing, brazen, incorrigible" (Lynd 24). It is precisely the devilish tone of a brazen hussy (we all know about *that* kind of woman) which makes this stanza resistant to orthodox views of woman's role. Sexton sees male standards (the "driver") as outside her, and she chooses to die on her own terms. He may escort her to the block for the "crimes" of femininity, but she will die unrepentant.

Recent psychological work distinguishing shame from guilt may illuminate Sexton's stance. Guilt refers to feelings about a specific transgression and so guilt is usually limited in scope. Reparation or atonement can be made by specific acts, such as resolving to change the offending behavior. Shame, on the other hand, goes to the basic sense of self as unworthy or unlovable. It is often experienced as humiliation, embarrassment, or self-loathing, and is generalized into a "subtext" in all one's relationships. But feelings of shame can be alleviated by talking about them with others (Goleman 23, 26).

It is significant that the last stanza of "Her Kind" is about dying—the loss of the whole self—while only the limits of specific roles had been explored earlier. Because Sexton has to overcome shame to speak to us, shame is still present in her denial ("not ashamed"). Speaking both heals and exposes her shame as she remains poised on her polarities.

What complicates this final stanza is that Sexton's fear of death, her resistance to the power of death and her wish for death as a prelude to regeneration cohere in a complex tone. If the poem's early stanzas show the writer / madwoman and the "misunderstood" wife and mother, the "sin" of stanza three is to try to combine these roles, and for that Sexton is executed. Her wish to die is not merely personal, but a wish for her *kind,* that the tormented soul of Western woman be reborn in a healthy form. If housewives are "not ashamed" to die, a new collective identity can emerge. It is notable that Sexton places a little-mentioned poem called "Venus and the Ark" just before "Her Kind." In "Venus" she imagines a new human species generated from the feminine planet of love. Despite their technical expertise, two "Old and withered . . . Ph. D.'s / from Earth" are helpless to effect a new generation. This time around, moral awareness ("the new fruit") springs from a feminine substance.

Having a secret, inner life that does not conform to patriarchy and domesticity (cf. "The Witch's Life," *AW*) is what women of spirit have always been punished for. Such women interrogate not only social reality but its impress on inner discourse and the masculine animus which is in the psychic "driver's" seat, that internalized "audience" which engenders shame, calls the shots, and usurps the power of *directing* women's lives. Being "not ashamed" is not the same thing as being proud, but Sexton has a clue to the puzzle. As in "For John . . ." she seems to feel that if we have no answers, we do have rhetoric to heal the breach and establish the communality from which wisdom emerges. When the "invisible veil" of separation lifts, it reveals the mirror in which two are seen as one, the relation between "my face" and "your face."

In the "Foreword" to Sexton's *Complete Poems,* Maxine Kumin points out that Sexton repeatedly identified herself "through her relationship with the male Other" (xxxix-xxx). Whether in the guise of lover or God, her quest is always to find "a male authority figure [animus] to love and trust." And George brilliantly explores Sexton's imaginary childhood friend, Christopher, as the male principle within her (74-86), the source of creativity and regeneration. While the driver of "Her Kind" impels awareness of difference and otherness, Christopher fosters Sexton's sense of a collective self, that choral mix of "I," "she," and "we" characteristic of the "Psalms" in "O Ye Tongues" (*DN*): "For I became a *we* and this imaginary *we* became a kind company . . ." ("Fourth Psalm"). He assuaged her childhood loneliness and validated her anger or fear about the limits ("Jail") of her environment. Christopher, her creative muse and inner audience, "delivers" Anne with his symbolic magic. For being part of a "kind" *is* kindness, the warmth, "company," and comfort which comes from feeling accepted.

If Christopher symbolizes a positive male presence and inner company, the masculine side of Sexton's nature is not always so generous. "Her Kind" embodies the repression of suburban domesticity, levels a demand for appreciation of women's plight, and defies the masculine animus which induces "shame" in women. These elements give the last stanza its undeniable force and closure. As father, lover, brother, and God, the "driver" is the masculine principle within Sexton which cannot be embraced, which feels consuming and destroying, like "flames."

As Goldstein notes, to internalize masculine caveats against pride does a woman psychic and moral damage; like the people of Third World countries, women need to adopt a theology of liberation rather than a theology of self-humbling. Juhasz argues that women poets cannot easily link the empirical knowledge of their lives with universals "because the universals presently in existence are based upon masculine experience, masculine norms" (139). In "Her Kind," Sexton explores stereotypes of femininity, resorting in the final stanza to an outcome that Durkheim might call "egoistic suicide," a "disorientation resulting from the disintegration of the collective moral life of one's group" (Wallwork 49). Tied to collective roles but rhythmically resisting their male-imposed limits, Sexton chooses Death as the answer to her identity problem. As Alvarez has pointed out, suicide can be a means to indict and create shame in others, an aggressive act committed "at the expense of the guilt and confusion of one's survivors" (108). It is ironic that Sexton places her destructive urge on the driver's shoulders, for he is akin to the aggressive "survivor" inside herself.

Continuing the ambivalent tension of the poem, Sexton's last stanza presents both her sense of victimage and her hope of triumph. If she is death's whore, a silent, "nameless, cooperative, and uncritical" female (Ellmann 123) molded on the "Hetaira" archetype of the eternal daughter who is dominated by the "Great Father," such a person may be saved from eternal fatherly dedication either by a hero who helps her achieve self-integration or by a villain who represents "unrelated aggression, ravaging her, severing ties both within and outside her in destructive ways" (Ulanov 204). Sexton is a damsel in distress but she is not met by Prince

Charming. Her satanic suitor is a symbolic agent who severs her most powerful bond with the father, his embeddedness in the cultural images (stereotypes) which shape and dominate women's lives. If he is God, then her resistance must speak in the voice of a witch, a she-devil.

Sexton's "ribs crack" where the [slave?] driver's "wheels wind" because she is being born again out of herself. Images of labor and delivery not only allude to woman's role in physical creation but reverse Adamic primacy. It is from her *own* ribs and pain that a new woman *kind* will emerge, one freed from slavish obedience to its destructive masculine animus and to the masculine "naming" of feminine life. The motif is similar to that in "Cripples and Other Stories" (*LD*) where her "father-doctor" psychiatrist is the agent: "I'm getting born again, Adam, / as you prod me with your rib," and in her genderless position between Adam and Eve in "Consorting with Angels" (*LD*). However, "Her Kind" claims that a *generic* rebirth emerges from the poet's painful condition. It is not *me* but *we*—a "kind"—that is spiritually reborn.

Sexton's prophecy of a new woman evolves in the no-saying which ends each stanza on a note of defiance: "A woman like that is *not* a woman, quite," "A woman like that is *mis*understood," "A woman like that is *not* ashamed to die." In stanza one, she escapes the degrading dullness of her life in one of the "plain houses" by flying "over" them in the triple garb of witch, madwoman, and poet; in stanza three, she waves farewell to "villages going by" as she rides to her death chamber. While these desperate solutions imply that a woman may escape the household only through madness or death, there is still "dreaming evil," the work of writing and re-imagining.

The hard work of regenerating one's "kind" and one's calling comes through in Sexton's verb choices, which pit self-assertions against the weight of cultural determination. Sexton announces her acts in a litany of uncompromising declarations: "I have gone out . . . I have done . . . I have been her kind . . . I have found . . . filled . . . fixed . . . I have been her kind . . . I have ridden . . . waved . . . I have been her kind." This catalogue of events has the cumulative effect of avowal. On the other side are progressive verb forms—"haunting," "dreaming," "whining," "rearranging," "learning." These present Sexton's acts as part of an ongoing condition which will be difficult to transcend or reverse while affirming her *continuing* resistance to the gravitational pull of "his story."

In "Her Kind," Sexton combines all three types of exemplary rhetoric. Specific details of her life are mythologized into an admonitory realm of "witches," "elves," and a mysterious "driver." She pre-judges the significance of her fallen state by formulating her life as a moral legend. She also exhorts readers to acknowledge the heroism of women who try to transcend domestic limits by "dreaming evil" and those whose domestic achievements are "misunderstood." Exerting the corrective force of proverbial wisdom, Sexton's story ends with a prophetic image of cultic death. She indexes the failure of domestic life to satisfy her needs and sees "madness" as the reimagining of woman's life.

"Her Kind" prophesies that feminine life must undergo painful death and rebirth to achieve focus, authenticity, and power. By 1974, the same year Rich wrote "To an Old House in America," Sexton would also invoke "The Furies" (*DN*) to settle her account with patriarchy. But in "Her Kind" she had already provided a haunting complement to the chilling line which ends Rich's poem: "Any woman's death diminishes me." When Sexton heard the bell toll in 1960, it said: "My death diminishes any woman."

Notes

[1]An exception is Diane Wood Middlebrook (*Parnassus* 298), who feels that "Flee on Your Donkey" (*LD*) marks an important transition in Sexton's sense of her madness: "No longer merely its victim, she is now its interrogator."

[2]The centrality of this poem in Sexton's career has been widely acknowledged. Middlebrook, Sexton's biographer, sees her confrontation with Holmes as a victory over the maddeningly "rational" objections of the literary establishment (*Coming to Light* 195-213). Diana George (8-11) ties the poem to Sexton's ongoing Oedipal quest. For a detailed exegesis of Sexton's rhetoric of apology in "For John. . . ." see Kay Ellen Merriman Capo ("Redeeming Words," forthcoming).

[3]George notes that Sexton is speaking collectively in "Little Girl . . ." saying "what we all want to be saying to our daughters, what we sometimes have not the courage or the attentiveness to say" (xii).

[4]George feels that as Sexton performed the "ritual function" of speaking "the unspeakable" she inspired in readers a "violently negative transference" which led to the denigration of her poetic achievement (xiii).

[5]"The Double Image" closes with a caution to all mothers: "And this was my worst guilt; you could not cure / nor soothe it. I made you to find me." In "Ringing the Bells," Sexton's *nostrum* ("We are the circle of the crazy ladies") announces danger while implicating readers who have been "crazy" enough to follow someone else's drumbeat: "and although we are no better for it, / they tell you to go. And you do." She also advises her daughter in "The Double Image" to avoid self-hatred ("love your self's self where it lives") and imagines being able to save her maiden aunt by warning her (cf. "Some Foreign Letters") that "wars are coming, / that the Count will die," that she will go deaf "one Friday at Symphony."

[6]While I agree with Juhasz' reading of "The Death Baby," I feel the mantric element is present from the first poem of *TB*: "I speed . . . And I am queen . . . We stand . . . The shibboleth is spoken . . . We chew in rows . . . And we are magic talking to itself, / noisy and alone." There is more raw urgency in "The Death Baby" than in "You, Dr. Martin," but the word magic and mysticism are very similar.

[7]The *nostrum* sometimes allows Sexton to be spokesperson for the mad people of *Bedlam* and sometimes creates a "normative" public self. It is used in "Torn down from Glory Daily," "The Kite," "The Exorcists," "The Expatriates," "Elegy in the Classroom," "The Road Back" and

"What's That."

A more limited use of "we" occurs in poems like "Unknown Girl in the Maternity Ward," "The Moss of His Skin," and "The Double Image," where Sexton establishes identity with *one* significant other. In "The Double Image," the "we" of her mother and herself works in dynamic tension with the "we" of her daughter and herself.

[8]The following discussion of feminine stereotypes is indebted to categories developed by Mary Ellmann (55-145).

[9]The "cost" of this psychic inheritance is delineated in "The Dead Heart" (*AW*), where Sexton connects destruction of the self (heart) with the turning back of harsh parental criticism on to the ego: "How did it die? / I called it *EVIL*."

[10]Ulanov (198) explains that a woman who patterns herself after the Great Mother archetype is induced to cherish "those things which are undeveloped, in the process of becoming, or in need of care, help, or protection." In Sexton's poem the images of "caves" and "worms and elves" connote the subterranean fortress in which the nurturing Earth Mother is queen.

[11]In a review of Simone de Beauvoir's *The Second Sex,* written in 1962, Elizabeth Hardwick (182) portrayed the pre-feminist scene that Sexton was up against: "If women's writing seems somewhat limited, I don't think it is only due to psychological failings. Women have much less experience of life than a man, as everyone knows. . . . If you remove the physical and sexual experiences many men have made literature out of, you have carved away a great hunk of masterpieces." So "in the end, it is in the matter of experience that women's disadvantage is catastrophic." Hardwick ignores, of course, the female *bodily* experience which has inspired so much poetry since the 1950's.

Works Cited

Alvarez, A. *The Savage God: A Study of Suicide.* New York: Random, 1972.

Burke, Kenneth. *A Grammar of Motives.* Berkeley: U of California P, 1969.

Capo, Kay Ellen Merriman. "Redeeming Words." *Anne Sexton: Telling the Tale.* Ed. Steven E. Colburn. Ann Arbor: U of Michigan P, forthcoming.

Clark, Arthur Melville. *Autobiography: Its Genesis and Phases.* 1935. Edinburgh: Oliver and Boyd, 1969.

Colburn, Steven E. ed. *No Evil Star: Selected Essays, Interviews, and Prose.* Ann Arbor: U of Michigan P, 1985.

Demetrakopoulos, Stephanie. *Listening to Our Bodies: The Rebirth of Feminine Wisdom*. Boston: Beacon, 1983.

Deutsch, Helene. *The Psychology of Women: A Psychoanalytic Interpretation*. 1945. New York: Bantam, 1973. Vol. 2.

Dickey, William. "A Place in the Country." Rev. of *LP*. *The Hudson Review* 22 (1969): 347-68.

Dinnerstein, Dorothy. *The Mermaid and the Minotaur: Sexual Arrangements and Human Malaise*. New York: Harper, 1976.

Ellmann, Mary. *Thinking about Women*. New York: Harcourt, 1968.

Fitzgerald, Gregory. Colburn 180-206.

Freidan, Betty. *The Feminine Mystique*. New York: Norton, 1963.

George, Diana Hume. *Oedipus Anne: The Poetry of Anne Sexton*. Urbana: U of Illinois P, 1987.

Goleman, Daniel. "Shame Steps out of Hiding." *New York Times* 15 Sept. 1987: 23, 26.

Goldstein, Valerie Saiving. "The Human Situation: A Feminine View." *The Journal of Religion* 40.2 (1960): 100-12.

Hardwick, Elizabeth. "The Subjection of Women." Rev. of *The Second Sex*, by Simone de Beauvoir. *A View of My Own: Essays in Literature and Society*. New York: Farrar, 1962. 167-82.

Heyen, William and Al Poulin. Colburn 130-57.

Howard, Richard. "Anne Sexton: 'Some Tribal Female Who Is Known but Forbidden.'" *Alone with America: Essays on the Art of Poetry in the United States since 1950*. New York: Atheneum, 1969. 442-50.

Juhasz, Suzanne. "'The Excitable Gift,': The Poetry of Anne Sexton." *Naked and Fiery Forms: Modern American Poetry by Women, A New Tradition*. New York: Octagon, 1978. 126-32.

Kumin, Maxine. Foreword to *The Complete Poems: Anne Sexton*. xix-xxxiv.

Lauter, Estella. "Anne Sexton's Radical Discontent." *Women as Mythmakers: Poetry and Visual Art by Twentieth-Century Women*. Bloomington: Indiana UP, 1984. 23-46.

Lynd, Helen Merrell. *On Shame and the Search for Identity*. New York: Harcourt, 1958.

Middlebrook, Diane Wood. "'I Tapped My Own Head': The Apprenticeship of Anne Sexton." *Coming to Light: American Women Poets in the Twentieth Century*. Eds. Middlebrook and Marilyn Yalom. Ann Arbor: U of Michigan P, 1985. 195-213.

—. "Poet of Weird Abundance." Rev. of *The Complete Poems: Anne Sexton*. *Parnassus: Poetry in Review* 12-13 (1985): 293-315.

Ostriker, Alicia. *Stealing the Language: The Emergence of Women's Poetry in America*. Boston: Beacon, 1986.

Plath, Sylvia. *Ariel*. New York: Harper, 1965.

Rich, Adrienne. *Adrienne Rich's Poetry*. Eds. Barbara and Albert Gelpi. New York: Norton, 1975.

Sexton, Anne. *The Complete Poems*. Ed. Linda Gray Sexton. Boston: Houghton Mifflin, 1981.

Sexton, Linda Gray Sexton and Lois Ames. eds. *Anne Sexton: A Self-Portrait in Letters*. Boston: Houghton Mifflin, 1977.

Spacks, Patricia M. "Reflecting Women." *Yale Review* 63 (1973): 26-42.

Stark, Steven D. "Housekeeping Today: Just a Lick and a Promise." *New York Times* 20 Aug. 1987: C1, C6.

Ulanov, Ann. *The Feminine: In Jungian Psychology and in Christian Theology*. Evanston: Northwestern UP, 1971.

Wallwork, Ernest. *Durkheim: Morality and Milieu*. Cambridge: Harvard UP, 1972.

IN PRAISE OF ANNE SEXTON'S *THE BOOK OF FOLLY*: A STUDY OF THE WOMAN/VICTIM/POET

Ann Marie Seward Barry

If Anne Sexton's *The Book of Folly* at first appears to parallel Alice's stop at the Mad Hatter's tea party, with each poem a different chair, and each chair a different view of the relationship between madness and art, one is quickly undeceived in reading on. Sexton's *Folly* implies quite a different sort of consumption—a twentieth-century supper where no matter how hard one tries to escape into the nonsense world of unbirthdays or spontaneous movement, the reality of a world cannibalized by war inevitably intrudes—there is "blood in the gravy," one drinks "bullets from a cup," and the birthday cake is lit by candles of napalm flashed from Promethean eyes ("The Wifebeater" 13).

If it is true, as Martin Gardner suggests, that "the last level of metaphor in the Alice books is this: that life, viewed rationally and without illusion, appears to be a nonsense tale told by an idiot mathematician (15), then the essential difference between the madness which Alice observes and the madness in which Sexton's narrator participates becomes clearer. What Sexton explores is not a world of nonsense but of modern pain in epic proportion—her madness is not an absurd effervescence of life but a rational defense against the evils of her age. As Sexton's title suggests, *The Book of Folly* draws its central metaphor from Erasmus' *Praise of Folly*, a Renaissance work which ultimately pleads that while it is folly *not* to see things as they really are, in the end, "the saddest thing" may very well be "not to be deceived," because without some degree of protective madness, the intellectual search for an ultimate answer must end in suicide.

What a study of Erasmus' *Praise of Folly* contributes to an understanding of *The Book of Folly* more than anything else, however, is its clear resolution to the problem first raised in Sexton's *To Bedlam and Part Way Back*: whether, as Jocasta urged Oedipus, it is better not to enquire further since only "appalling horror awaits . . . in the answer" (vii), or as the narrator of "For John Who Begs Me Not To Enquire Further" suggests, "Not that it [truth] was beautiful, / but that I found some order there. / There ought to be something special / for someone / in this kind of hope." Erasmus' narrator Folly suggests to us a compromise, an acceptance of the limitations of knowledge rather than the despair of a search which both never reassures and never ends.

The fact of Sexton's own suicide shows us the result of her personal struggle and lends insight into the struggle at the heart of *The Book of Folly* as well. Unlike Erasmus, she could not serenely accept either the brutal reality of her world or an idealism which could not be fully justified by faith. In the end, her fate was the fate of the wise, according to Erasmus: "Recall," his narrator Folly tells us, "what kind of people have committed suicide. . . . Have they not been the wise or near-wise? . . . Now you begin to see, I believe, what would happen if all men became wise: there would be need for new clay and another potter like Prometheus" (736).

Thus a study of Erasmus' *Praise of Folly* helps us to frame the central questions of art and madness which haunt Sexton's poetry. First, it reveals that Sexton was writing at least partly out of a humanist tradition, not simply a personal framework. Second, it helps put into perspective the central themes of the roles of woman, victim, and poet which run throughout her poetry and which provide the central focus of *The Book of Folly*. Finally, by acting as a philosophical foil to

Sexton's work, *Praise of Folly* helps us to understand more clearly not only the direction which her poetic search for truth was taking, but perhaps even the inevitability of its outcome as well.

To begin, both Erasmus and Sexton use a female narrator to explore the world of madness and death they see around them. As Erasmus' Folly comes on stage, she speaks directly to her audience as Sexton does, revealing her past, her family and herself in the process. When Folly tells us that her father, Plutus, fathered her out of wedlock while "hot with youth and still hotter with nectar which by chance he had drunk straight and freely at a party of the gods" (731), we are clearly reminded of Sexton's own revulsion toward her father's drinking and the paternal doubts revealed in *Folly's* "Death of the Fathers." Like Sexton who was also born in "the Fortunate Isles," Erasmus' Folly, too, readily admits her foolishness and her commitment to the truth: "Fools have another not insignificant virtue," she tells us, "they alone are candid and truthful." And "what," she challenges, "is more admirable than the truth?" (740).

Underlying both *Praise of Folly* and *The Book of Folly* is this central philosophical preoccupation with truths which both cause and are caused by madness and death. "Not every kind of madness is calamity," Erasmus' Folly says:

> Madness is really of two kinds. The first is sent up from hell by the vengeful Furies. . . . They assault the hearts of men with hot desire for war, with insatiable greed and shameful lust, with parricide, incest, sacrilege. . . . at other times the Furies pursue the guilty and conscience-stricken soul with terror and the fire of wrath. The second kind of madness is far different from this. . . . It arises whenever a cheerful confusion of the mind frees the spirit from care and at the same time anoints it with many-sided delight. It is the state of mind Cicero desired as a defense against the evils of his age. (741)

Like Erasmus, Sexton employs a woman's perspective to come to grips with the same two types of madness which seemed to possess both her world and her soul. The thirty poems of Part I of *The Book of Folly* touch each of the areas mentioned by Erasmus' Folly: war, greed, lust, parricide, incest, sacrilege; the three stories of Part II attempt to resolve the freedom of creativity which her art affords with the outer forces which threaten it; and the Jesus Papers of Part III attempt to resolve these personal and societal conflicts through faith—a feat at which Erasmus, but not Sexton, succeeds by finding forgiveness for the folly of man through the folly of God:

> What do these things declare except that all men, even the pious, are fools? And that Christ himself, although He possessed the wisdom of the Father, became something like a fool in order to cure the folly of mankind, when He assumed the nature and being of a mortal? . . . Surely we should not overlook this argument, that folly is so pleasing to the heavenly powers that forgiveness of its errors is certain; whereas nothing is forgiven to wisdom. (751)

Adopting the role of the twentieth-century woman/victim/poet and paralleling it to the role of Christ, Sexton's narrator ultimately finds salvation only in art. Approaching her poetry and herself with an unflinching and even brutal objectivity, she found wisdom, but not faith. "Need is not quite belief," she tells us in "Mercy for the Greedy" in *All My Pretty Ones*; and in *The Book of Folly*, she reiterates the conviction and parallels the miracles of faith to the magic of her poet's fingers. Like Erasmus, Sexton used her art both to shake free of facile proscriptive explanations of the meaning of life and death and to express that truth through the eyes of a "foolish" woman. For both, the art of discourse was the discipline which allowed them to cut away the superficial: "All form is a trick in order to get at the truth," Sexton told Pat Marx in an interview in 1965 (360).

The Book of Folly is a jester's trick, and the fool who performs it is a woman, victim, and poet. Its artistic process is the attempt to discipline a small circumference of feeling into an expanding philosophical truth, rather than to simply express emotion: the result is a book which speaks as directly to the reader as Erasmus' Folly does, thereby revealing both the woman and the art. For Sexton, however, this process also meant turning the poet herself into her own victim, for unlike the serene Folly of Erasmus who believes that "true prudence consists in not desiring more wisdom than is proper to mortals" (734), Sexton's *Folly* shows only the search for answers, not the finding of them. Like the figures of Jesus and Icarus which haunt all her poetry, Sexton flew headlong into her own suicide with the full knowledge that the faith which was synonymous with her art was both her salvation and her destruction. Sexton's twentieth-century woman poet, who is victimized by both her world and her art, thus serves as an ironic foil to the complacency of Erasmus' Folly.

Accordingly, the narrator of each poem in *The Book of Folly* represents an acutely painful view of the twentieth century and its victims. If these narrators appear mad, it is with the madness of clear perception, the end product of an objective stripping away of veneers to reveal personal and societal pain. Like Icarus, Sexton's narrators don wax wings and fly dangerously close to the truth, knowing that destruction—psychical and physical—is inherent and imminent in the quest.

Like Erasmus, Sexton structures her work in four areas which expand outward to include "Folly Herself"; the "Powers and Pleasures of Folly" which addresses the roles of sex, motherhood, medicine, government, religion, art and the artist; the "Followers of Folly" which for Sexton includes an examination of various people's response to her art; and finally, the "Christian Fool." As Sexton's collection of insights grows concentrically through Poems to Stories to Papers, the central image of the woman/victim/artist becomes a dynamic metaphor for the creative/destructive madness of twentieth-century science and politics, a world devoid of compassion and incapable of believing in anything beyond its own materialism.

Throughout, Sexton combines the madness of the age and its attendant extensions with a vortical structure and an artistic control which is both experimental in form and reflective of the process of creativity and madness. The work expands through the heaping up of components of thought, which then appear to converge according to their own internal laws, in the manner of Pound's *Cantos*. The movement corresponds roughly to Pound's concept of the vortex, where the force of the central image holds together disjunctive elements and redoubles its energy through the rapid nonsequential movement of the internal parts. Her series of female narrators descend into and flow out of a creative and destructive madness where their femaleness both victimizes them and gives them the sensitivity to perceive truth and to express it through art. From the initial metaphor of poetry as box/coffin in the opening poem "Ambition Bird," Sexton expands the image outward into a prison/fortress room in "Stories" and then into the conflict between physical and spiritual existence as cage/coffin in "The Jesus Papers." The vortex moves outward in ever-expanding concentric rings to ultimately encompass the universal quest for salvation in which human and deistic folly merge.

The concept of woman/victim is first introduced in *The Book of Folly* in terms of the conflict between the feeling, sensitive individual and a sterile and unfeeling modern science. In "Doctor of the Heart," the narrator while "sick unto" explores the inadequacy of medical science in coping with the sickness of the heart. The doctor, a "wallowing seasick grounded man" (in contrast to her Icarus of other poems and therefore to the artist in quest of truth), cannot take away her mother's carcinoma, her father's cerebral hemorrhage, or her sister's broken neck. His attempt at a cure for her sickness is shock treatments: his "zigzag machine" plays "up and down like the stock market," but there is no scientific device for her heart. She has only the "magic fingers" of her art to save her.

Art creates rhythmic order out of chaos, where machinery can only spasmodically disorient. Her opening poem, "Ambition Bird," establishes the basic opposition: the natural drive to create keeps her awake, while a "mechanical clock tolls its engine / like a frog following / a sundial yet having an electric / seizure at the quarter hour." Thus "Doctor of the Heart" continues the conflict through the paradox of its title. Her doctor, here addressed as "Herr Doktor," later reappears as "the Hitler-mouth psychiatrist" of her mad grandmother who climbs past her on the stairs "like an undertaker," and then as a metaphor for all men in "The Ballet of the Buffoon." The problem of death which the artist confronts here is intensely and individually personal, but the cry for help is answered only by an impersonal series of prescribed electric shocks.

Faced with the Doctor's unnatural and unfeeling treatment, Sexton's patient becomes a victim whose madness appears as a rational defense and whose only hope for cure resides in her own "magic fingers." Science has the knowledge and power, but it lacks the ability to create or regenerate. Like the Buffoons of the "Ballet" who fail to raise their wives from the dead, the modern doctor is an ersatz savior, an impotent resurrectionist. He is the antithesis of "Jesus Summons Forth":

> Lazarus was whole.
> Jesus put His mouth to Lazarus's
> and a current shot between them for a moment.
> Then came tenderness.
> Jesus rubbed all the flesh of Lazarus

> and at last the heart, poor old wound,
> started up in spite of itself.

The electric wires of "Doctor of the Heart" cannot cure the dead heart, but the faith of Jesus—that "current shot between them"—does achieve the resurrection. Art is faith, and its opposite is science.

Man creates science to cure his physical ills and to extend his powers of productivity and movement, but without faith, his "saving" technology results only in ingenious devices which ultimately destroy him, physically and psychically, individually and *en masse*. The narrator's sister who appears in "Doctor of the Heart" and "Sweeney" and suffers an "unnatural death by car, her slim neck / snapped like a piece of celery" is only one specific casualty of mechanical science. In "The Firebombers," America itself becomes a "grocer of death" dealing as coolly "in the death market" as the doctor "spreading goo" on the suction cups in "Doctor of the Heart." Napalm of the firebombs and electric conducting jelly merge symbolically through the destructive capabilities of science. While Jesus as a positive pole in the vortex puts Lazarus back together and breathes life into his body, technology as a negative force pulls apart and destroys in order to control. Jesus comes to "save" mankind; America, to destroy in the name of saving Vietnam.

While Jesus meets the test, while he can "put on the wrists," "insert the hip bone," and produce life, the "one-legged man" of Sexton's poem of the same name who has been physically and psychically fragmented by war cannot, in typically American materialistic phraseology, "buy his leg back" after it has been blown off. A male victim of a male war, he has lost the tender woman in him—what Jung termed "the anima," and "now there is nothing." As such, he links the specific and familiar circumstance of war with Sexton's mythic view of male domination in "The Ballet of the Buffoon," when the buffoons—in their "finest hour"—kill their wives: "The buffoons were widowers. All the woman in them was gone. There was no theory. There was only death." The despairing cry of the one-legged man—"Lady, lady, / why have you left me?"—both echoes the dying words of Jesus on the Cross and vividly anticipates the merge of the feminine with art and salvation in "The Letting Down of the Hair." His figure also reflects Sexton's ever-present theme of the disintegration of the self in contrast to the integrated wholeness implied by art and promised by religion.

The antithesis of materialism and war, science and male, sterility and unfeeling, then, is faith and domesticity, art and woman, creativity and sensitivity. And because the latter are victimized by the former, the woman as artist appears to be doubly at risk in a world which values only what is antithetical to her nature. As Alvarez points out in his insightful study of suicide, *The Savage God*,

> the more directly an artist confronts the confusions of experience the greater the demands on his intelligence, control and a certain watchfulness; the greater, too, the imaginative reserves he must tap so as not to weaken or falsify what he knows. . . . What is involved then is an artistic intelligence working at full pitch to produce the tentative, flowing continually improvised balance of life itself. But because such a balance is always precarious, work of this kind entails a good deal of risk. And because the artist is committed to truths of his inner life often to the point of discomfort, it becomes riskier still. (230)

It is this sense of risk, first apparent in *Folly's* "Ambition Bird," which makes the artist see her creative work as both immortality box and coffin. The poet within the person "wants to be dropped / from a high place like Tallahatchie Bridge . . . to light a kitchen match / and immolate himself . . . to die changing clothes and bolt for the sun like a diamond."[1] Certainly Sexton is aware of the risk involved in using her "magic fingers," since by the end of the poem, immortality box and coffin are one. But her "ambition bird" also is a phoenix which rises from its own ashes—a resurrected Icarus, parallel to the Jesus who raises Lazarus: the ambition bird "wants to take bread and wine / and bring forth a man happily floating in the Caribbean," to create life through the ritual of her art. Both artist and son of God reflect the creative/destructive nature of the age in which the poet, continually provoking awareness, becomes the representative voice and the victim as well.

Sexton continues to develop the role of the poet as internalizer of the world's external madness as her narrator moves from tea with her psychiatrist in "Oh" to "The Wifebeater," where everything vulnerable is destroyed by Folly's "hot desire for war": "The wifebeater is out, / the childbeater is out / eating soil and drinking bullets from a cup." Men who legislate, promote, and fight the Vietnam War actively counter the poet's "business of words" with the big business of arms, truly manifesting that madness, sent by vengeful Furies from hell to "assault the hearts of men," of which Erasmus speaks.

For Sexton, these men are the calculating victimizers of women and beauty, and throughout her poetry deliberate murder, whether of loved one or country, is both a male function and a metaphor for the modern world where there "is no place for pity. Every man kills his wife. It's a matter of history" (81). Her "Ballet of the Buffoon" reveals a world where men, in the masks of husband and merchant, in love with their guns and whips as in "a Nazi death camp in reverse," sacrifice their wives in order to recreate them in their own image. The buffoons dance "ring-around-the-rosy" as Mr. Ha-Ha manipulates the puppet strings of the world to control the fate of all women: "Each one did a dance. A death dance" (73).

For Sexton, this manipulation represents the destructive forces working against not only the dignity of women, but also art and spirituality as well. The result is a devastation, a Waste Land: "They had been alive without knowing why. They had been young and old without knowing why. They had been jammed in their bodies without knowing why" (75). To further emphasize the continuing nature of the spiritual degeneration, she contrasts the image of art as a communion food for the soul to the omnivorous figure of Sweeney from T.S. Eliot. Her "Sweeney," an Australian, professes to love art and pursues Sexton as Gawain pursues the Holy Grail: "You are the altar cup and from this / I do fill my mouth. Sexton, I am your priest." But he is also an "ersatz press agent man, buying up . . . books / by the dozen." While they are consuming caviar and Dom Perignon, her sister's neck is "snapped like a piece of celery." Eliot's ape-necked Sweeney gulps down grapes, where Sexton's "Aussie gourmet" "eat[s] up men," but both are recognizably from the same mold.

When Eliot's Sweeney, shaving, remains as unmoved as Sexton's "Doctor of the Heart," while a prostitute lies screaming on the bed next to him in an epileptic seizure, he shows no essential difference between himself and Sexton's doctor who administers electrical seizures—both men are exploitative consumers of women's dignity. When Sweeney reappears in Eliot's "Sweeney Among the Nightingales," he evokes the mythical victimizer Tereus who rapes Philomela and cuts out her tongue so that she cannot tell the truth. It is an image which reappears in Eliot's *The Waste Land* and which subsequently appears in Sexton's "The Silence," where she combines the myth of Prometheus with that of Philomela and depicts death as a white bird pecking at "the vibrating red muscle of [her] mouth." *Folly*'s female narrator—who has been violated by both science and materialistic greed—responds like Philomela through the mute tapestry of her art: "Surely the words will continue," Sexton ends her "Sweeney," "for that's / what's left that's true."

The death dance which results from this combination of art and victimization is both characteristic of Erasmus' second type of madness and a result of his first. In the dance, the closest thing to soaring while grounded, whirling becomes both a retreat from the world and an outer protection against it. Like Eliot's narrator of *The Four Quartets* who stands at the still point at the center of the turning world and Sexton's "Assassin" who exists "at the center of feeling," *Folly's* female narrator stands at the center of a structural and metaphorical vortex, facing herself and using the vortical movement to dissipate fear.

First appearing in *To Bedlam and Part Way Back* in "Music Swims Back to Me," the death dance in *Folly*'s "The Red Shoes" encompasses the narrator's past, sexual legacy, and the freedom/confinement conflict inherent in the irresistible pull of her art. As these forces take possession of her, just as in Hans Christian Andersen's fable, Sexton's narrator is "played with" like one of the puppets in "Ballet of the Buffoon":

> They could not listen.
> They could not stop.
> What they did was the death dance.
> What they did would do them in.
>
> ("The Red Shoes")

It is the same dance her mother danced and her grandmother danced, past the suitors, like a "trout on the hook." It is the same vortical dance which the housewife involuntarily performs at the typical suburban cocktail party in "Dancing the Jig":

> I didn't want to . . . But here I am, cavorting over their silent faces. They are blobs of jelly. I think I have eaten the music. It runs through me as if I had swallowed it whole. The music, the music . . . I am the music fisting around. We are the beat and balance of air. (65)

Possessed, the woman/victim whirls beyond people, back into the past to her childhood where the center of the vortex lies, into the napkin ring on the table. Here "the ring in the dead city" (which again ties the dance to Eliot's *Waste Land*) and the circus rings of "The Bells" can be traced to the tree rings of "Where I Live in This Honorable House of the Laurel Tree" of her first work *To Bedlam and Part Way Back.* In "Angels of Flight and Sleigh Bells" she succinctly repeats the image: "I have become a tree." Sexton seems to consciously create a series of concentric rings which expand outwardly both from her narrator's childhood and from her earlier poetry as well.

"Frozen to the chair," the narrator of "Dancing the Jig" stares into the napkin ring "like a mirror and an object of escape, an object to see twice"—another ring growing from "The Double Image" of *Bedlam*, and repeated in *Folly* as "Mr. Doppelganger. In her mental escape, she dreams of Nana up in her room, safe and removed in her madness. Below, eating and being eaten, she can't swallow the meat she is forced to consume at the dinner table. Associated throughout her poetry with the bestiality of men, this eating of flesh both negatively mirrors the Christian miracle of transubstantiation and parallels her inability to believe in the salvation it promises. Instead of eating the meat on her plate piece by piece, she swallows the music whole—an image connected with her art by "The Red Shoes," and in turn is consumed by it, just as the ballerina of the Andersen tale is fated to be danced to death by her shoes.

Immobile in her chair, she relives the tortures of her childhood and the insensitivity of her mother. Caught like Daphne in the tree of "This Honorable House," she reflects on the paralyzing forces of the past and on the desperate freedom which her art alone affords: "the opposite of chair is dancing the jig" (66). Both the dance and the room above seem refuges from eating and being eaten. Together, the stone shoes of the earlier "Angel Flight" and the "Nana Hex" of guilt and insanity function as a mental escape and an imagistic bridge to the stone room of Part III of the woman/ victim/poet trilogy.

In this third section, Folly's woman devotes herself entirely to her art and discovers through her followers that she has again become a victim of those who profess to love her. Both their persecution and her own creative compulsion force her into the isolation of her stone tower, its single window symbolically overlooking the Prudential Center. Above the prudence counseled by Erasmus, past and present merge, and she becomes both her grandmother of the upstairs room and her own mother through the miracle of her art: "The room is my belly," she tells us, "it carries me." But it is a room pregnant with death: a series of destructions link it with the earlier poems and "The Ballet of the Buffoon"—her parents die en route to a cocktail brunch, as in the cocktail party of "Dancing the Jig," their necks snapped like "two broken dolls," her brother becomes "a man of sorrow, a man in painhood." It is the immortality box/coffin of her artistic ambition and her own womb/tomb.

Set against this death imagery, the Lady's hair serves as a connection to her public and a symbol of her femaleness, her creative growth as an artist, and the pregnant past of the child at the dinner table berated for her "terrible" hair—it is the essence of the woman, poet, and victim. Her friend, Ruth, who sends her a crucifix and commits suicide when she loses her faith, declares the hair is "a parable for the life of a poet." And the poet herself declares her art a substitute for faith: "Ruth has Christ, and I, I have only my hair" (89).

Like Christ, she is fated to be a misunderstood victim of her art, and as the poet continues to "let down her hair" (in an obvious reference to the confessional nature of her poetry), her audience enlarges and so, too, does their ignorance. Information given by tour directors and T.V. commentators is false and misleading, and her people become "very devoted or very disgusted." They often write, of course, but she does not answer because she understands that it is the hair—her "trick" of poetry they write to, not to her real self.

This "trick" creates the bridge between Parts II and III of *The Book of Folly* and suggests with heavy irony its central theme—the relation of folly to faith. In parallel to the last division of Erasmus' *Praise of Folly*, Sexton focuses on the essential humanity of Jesus, which she sees as the fatalistic link between the poet and salvation through the practice of their creative arts. But where Erasmus sees the humanity of Jesus as a source of forgiveness for the folly of mankind, Sexton sees only an immortal gift doomed to be locked in the mortal self. Both Jesus and the poet become martyrs who fast, carve their own deaths, perform with magic fingers, and exist outside the world of men. Like the poet locked in the tower, like the woman of "Angel Flight and Sleigh Bells" who has "become a tree," Jesus is continually beset by human frailty and torn by the spiritual/carnal conflict within him.

Knowing He was born to be crucified, the god/man knows the sense of soaring and salvation promised by immortality as well as the purely mortal feelings associated with a sexual being. As a baby, Jesus closes his eyes and sucks in Mary's milk "like a fire." Yet as a god he denies the sensuality: "All lies / I am a truck. I run everything. / I own you." The suckling child is at the same time suckling god and a man who experiences sexual joy. In "Jesus Asleep," "in His dream / He desired Mary. / His penis sang like a dog, / but he turned sharply away from that play / like a door slamming."

As such, he is the counterpart of Sexton's child/woman who finds her sexuality awakening through her father in "The Death of the Fathers":

> You danced with me never saying a word.
> Instead the serpent spoke as you held me close.
> The serpent, that mocker, woke up
> and pressed against me:
> like a great god and we bent together
> like two lonely swans.

Unlike Jesus, however, Sexton's narrator cannot repress her carnal nature. In "Angels of the Love Affair," she combines images of Icarus, a stone room, and red shoes as she pleads for both transcendence and sexuality:

> Angel of flight, you soarer, you flapper, you floater,
> you gull that grows out of my back in the dreams I prefer,
> stay near. But give me the totem. Give me the shut eye
> where I stand in stone shoes as the world's bicycle goes by.

If unlike the poet he can escape his sexuality, Jesus cannot, however, escape the poet's victimization by his own creativity. Continuing the eating/hunger imagery of Parts I and II, in "Jesus Cooks," Sexton shows us that when "the multitudes were hungry" Jesus asks God for the miracle the crowd expects. If the request is spiritual, though, the answer is simply material: "Work on the sly / opening boxes of sardine cans." Jesus, like the poet, creates sustenance out of an idea, and the result of the transubstantiation is the same as for the poet. The crowd doesn't understand him and "kisses his spoons and forks," but not *him*, just as it does with the Lady of the tower, just as Sweeney kisses the poet and declares himself "her priest."

Thus the fisherman who "makes it look easy" becomes a direct parallel to the poet who creates with the "magic fingers" of her art. Jesus' experience in "The Jesus Papers," in fact, parallels the development of the woman/victim/poet explored throughout the Poems and Stories: first a child fed by its mother; then a man whose sexual being cries out, but of necessity is sublimated to his spiritual role; then a miracle worker; then the god/man dying to achieve salvation; and finally, the god/man unborn in an endless, vortical cycle of death-rebirths. Jesus, like the woman/victim/poet, faces shameful lust, incest, and sacrilege, and ultimately he reconciles himself to an inevitable crucifixion.

As a major image connecting the victimization and transcendence inherent in art with the promise of immortality through faith, this crucifixion, for Jesus as for the poet, is a creative, personal thing, the reverse of the mass "death market" of "The Firebombers." It is "a personal matter, / a private affair and God knows / none of your business." It is "man to man"—between himself and the human side of God. Split between his immortal gift and his humanity the way the poet is caught between her creative urge to soar and human weakness, he "needs" as Sexton's poet needs, but he "will do nothing extraordinary." He "will not divide in two," like the One-Legged Man whose leg is delivered of him by war like Eve from Adam's rib, or the poet's Doppelganger in "The Other."

In his extreme need, Jesus recognizes that there is an art in dying which is an essentially private communication between himself and God. Predestined to die, this is what he has lived for; and this penultimate moment is an exclusive one where everyone and everything is shut out. It, too, is a death dance, private and self-contained in meaning, the opposite of the doctor's business in "Doctor of the Heart." When he dies, Jesus is concerned only with his business of dying, in the same way Sexton's poet is concerned with the business of words—unlike Sweeney, the ersatz press agent man who proclaims to the poet, "Martyr, my religion is love, is you."

Like the suffering of the doctor's patient and the Lady in "The Letting Down of the Hair," the death of Jesus can be watched but not understood—except, perhaps, by the artist who in *Folly* nails her hands to a pine box in "Killing the Spring." With "hands in training for a crucifixion," Sexton's poet/victim feels the Spring within her die: a "young person dying for no reason." Just as Jesus declines to die for humanity, leaving his sacrifice with no meaning for the artist, so also does Sexton's poet: "I was the same." The poet of "The Other" puts on the painted mask to "leer at Jesus in his passion" and to giggle at it—just as her sisters giggled when her mother cut her meat at the dinner table—because it is, after all, her own death, too. As Jesus is the ultimate suicide, controlled by a god's death wish and elaborately constructing his own death, Sexton's poet, too, dies of forces beyond herself, while at the same time carefully determining the method of the inevitable death. In *Live or Die* she succinctly verbalizes this fatalism:

> But suicides have a special language.
> Like carpenters they want to know
> which tools.
> They never ask why build.

In *Folly*'s "Oh," she repeats the idea but now sees both herself and God surprised by the inevitability of death, even as she is passively consumed by Him:

> I close my eyes over the steaming
> tea and see God opening His teeth.
> "Oh," He says.
> I see the child in me writing "Oh."
> Oh, my dear, not why.

By the end of *Folly*, this fate extends into a sacrificial ritual for all women as victims: "When the cow gives blood / and the Christ is born / we must all eat sacrifices. / We must all eat beautiful women" ("The Author of the Jesus Papers Speaks").

Thus in Sexton's *The Book of Folly* we find not only the personal emotion of the author, but also a reflection of the same spiritual hunger and cannibalism which Eliot observed at the beginning of the century. Carefully structured to expand her specific opening themes through a series of related images into a vortex, *The Book of Folly* grows concentrically into wider and more complex observations on art and humanity by the narrator in her roles as woman, victim, and poet. In both form and theme, Sexton's work thus becomes a truly ironic contrast to Erasmus' affirmation of Christian humanism. For Sexton, to believe in anything higher than the individual's own transcendence through art, no matter how great the need, is the true folly.

In the end it is wisdom rather than faith which prevails, and Sexton continues the search begun in *To Bedlam and Part Way Back*. Now, however, she does so with the fatalistic understanding that the poet is doomed to repeat the mystical cycle of physical death and spiritual rebirth implied by Christian faith, but in reverse. In the practice of her art, she concludes that art is faith; that resurrection implies death; that art, not science, is the only help for the madness of the world. In the process of living, she observes that personal madness, as an inner psychical fragmentation caused by outer forces, is the inevitable result of domination of women by men, of countries by other countries, of art by business, of creativity by sterility.

In *The Book of Folly* Sexton reminds us that the Furies which Erasmus described in the sixteenth century have truly come to dominate the modern world, and that the clear-sighted "madness," or "folly," of the poet—who creates order out of chaos and reunifies the physical and spiritual through the language of the heart—may in fact be the only true defense against the evils of our age.

Notes

[1]It is interesting to note here that about the same time *The Book of Folly* was published, John Berryman, another poet of the high-risk "Confessional School" committed suicide by jumping from a high Minneapolis bridge.

Works Cited

Alvarez, A. *The Savage God: A Study of Suicide.* New York: Bantam, 1972.

Erasmus, Desiderius. *Praise of Folly.* Trans. Leonard F. Dean. *Continental Edition of World Masterpieces.* Ed. Maynard Mack et al. New York: Norton, 1962. 730-754.

Gardner, Martin. Introduction. *The Annotated Alice.* By Lewis Carroll. U.S.A.: Clarkson N. Potter, 1960. 7-16.

Marx, Pat. "Interview with Anne Sexton." *Hudson Review.* Winter (1965-1966): 560-570.

Sexton, Anne. *All My Pretty Ones.* Boston: Houghton Mifflin, 1962.

—. *The Book of Folly.* Boston: Houghton Mifflin, 1972.

—. *Live or Die.* Boston: Houghton Mifflin, 1966.

—. *To Bedlam and Part Way Back.* Boston: Houghton Mifflin, 1960.

II. Poetics

No. No. The woman is cheerful, she smiles at her stomach.
She has swallowed a bagful of oranges and she is well pleased.
. . . .

For she is a magnitude, she is many. She is each of patting ourselves dry with a towel.
. . . .

For she is seeing the end of her confinement now and is waiting like a stone for the waters.

For the baby crowns and there is a people-dawn in the world.

For the baby lies in its water and blood and there is a people-cry in the world.

For the baby suckles and there is a people made of milk for her to use.

"Eighth Psalm"
The Death Notebooks

ANNE SEXTON'S *LIVE OR DIE*: THE POEM AS THE OPPOSITE OF SUICIDE

Jenny Goodman

Anne Sexton's Pulitzer Prize-winning collection, *Live or Die,* published in 1966, contains in its title the stark theme that dominates a good part of Sexton's work. The poet in *Live or Die* wrestles with the command of the book's epigraph, quoted from Saul Bellow: "Live or die, but don't poison everything. . . ." Not surprisingly, the poems in *Live or Die* have a firm grounding in the body and a great concern with self. These aspects of the poems are essential for the poet to explore life and death as she sees them.[1]

Though death, particularly self-inflicted death, is constantly present in *Live or Die,* the book has, for me, a life wish. Sexton herself said in a 1966 article about Sylvia Plath, "Suicide is, after all, the opposite of the poem" ("Barfly"). The poet in *Live or Die* delves into her own self-destructiveness as well as her search to free herself from it and ultimately gives us a vision of life involving a wholeness of self gained through the process of writing.

Sexton's premise is "live *or* die," as opposed to "live *and* die." The statement of the two antonyms as a choice, instead of a combination basic to the human condition, suggests the poet's struggle with her death wish which pervades the book. The poet depicts her obsession with death vividly. In "Flee on Your Donkey" (*LD*) madness is associated with night. The poet repeats the word *night* three times in describing her return to the mental hospital: "[I] came back last night at midnight,/arriving in the thick June night. . . ." "Today crows play black-jack / on the stethoscope," suggests death through the association of crows, opposed to "my muse," "a mild white mouse," the only hopeful image in the early stanzas of the poem.

In "For the Year of the Insane" (*LD*), the poet can describe vividly her connection to death because she experiences a separation of mind and body which allows her to observe herself. She states:

> In the mind there is a thin alley called death
> and I move through it as
> through water.
> My body is useless.

In fact, the body has no will; "It has given up." Yet in "Wanting to Die" (*LD*), the body is implicated in the poet's wish to kill herself: "Then the almost unnameable lust returns." The comparison of suicidal desire to sexual desire is powerful because it fuses the psychological urge toward death with a biological urge tied to procreation. One is forced to imagine a body made for life which has a will toward death. The juxtaposition is painful. The suicidal state is not so much characterized by the dominance of a contaminated mind or body as it is by the separation of mind and body.

In her self-destructive state, the poet is alienated from her self. The speaker says in "For the Year of the Insane" (*LD*), after the ritual drinking of the wine, which turns into a sort of possession by madness or death, "I see myself as one would see another. / I have been cut in two." The violence of the image is not accidental. The poet also employs violent imagery in "The Addict" (*LD*), describing her ingestion of pills as "a kind of war / where I plant bombs inside / myself." She explains in "Live" (*LD*): "The chief ingredient [of death] / is mutilation."

Sexton also utilizes religious images in relation to death. For instance, in "Live" (*LD*), the poet explains that

> [death] has a hell of a lot
> to do with hell
> . . . .
> and the religious objects
> and how I mourned them
> when they were made obscene
> by my dwarf-heart's doodle.

The wine ritual is an example of a traditional Christian ritual transformed into an experience of madness. As the wine glass moves toward her mouth by its own accord, the poet has "a fear of the horseman / who comes riding into my mouth" ("Year of the Insane," *LD*). Then she says, "I am on fire." The horseman is suggestive of death and the fire of some sort of hell. It is at this moment that the poet feels "cut in two." Just before the wine ritual comes the bread ritual: "Without words one may touch bread / and be handed bread / and make no sound." These lines end the stanza that begins, "Closer and closer / comes the hour of my death." The ritual does not hold the promise of spiritual rebirth for the poet.

It is important to note that the negative ritual must take place "without words" because words, as we shall see, are necessary for the poet to have spiritual transformation, to create herself. The poet speaks to Mary of the rituals she is experiencing, but she is still pleading with Mary to heal her. She tells Mary, "I am in the domain of silence, / the kingdom of the crazy and the sleeper" ("Year of the Insane," *LD*). The traditional Christian image of bread reappears in "The Addict" (*LD*), again in an obviously negative context. The poet describes her ingesting of pills as "eating my eight loaves in a row" and compares her activity to "the black sacrament." Clearly, the poet does not spiritually benefit from these ceremonies of the bread and the wine.

Despite Sexton's vivid portrayal in many poems of the speaker's attraction to death, one also notices the speaker's awareness that death is not her ally. Referring to her suicide attempts, she says, "Twice I have . . . / possessed the enemy, eaten the enemy, / have taken on his craft, his magic" ("Wanting to Die," *LD*). The poet recognizes in the same poem that "Suicides have already betrayed the body." She also says of her behavior when she felt suicidal, "This became a perjury of the soul. / It became an outright lie" ("Live," *LD*). Thus the desire to kill oneself is a betrayal of body *and* mind, of the whole self. Of course, the poet's recognition of the evil nature of suicide does not translate easily into health. Sexton explains, "But suicides have a special language. / Like carpenters they want to know *which tools.* / They never ask *why build*" ("Wanting to Die," *LD*). And yet somehow the suicidal poet implies "Why build?" in the investigation of her madness.

The poet's desire to escape madness is evident in her repeated use of prison metaphors to describe her condition. In "Flee on Your Donkey" (*LD*) she describes herself in the mental hospital as "fastened to the wall like a bathroom plunger, / held like a prisoner / who [is] so poor / he fell in love with jail." "Wanting to Die" (*LD*) contains the remark that death personified waits "[for me] to empty my breath from its bad prison." In "Live" (*LD*) one finds another indication that the speaker feels trapped; she tells us "the body" (as if it were not her own) "was caught / in the first place at birth, / like a fish." We will see how Sexton uses birth imagery to an opposite effect in positive sections of *Live or Die.*

Sexton describes the mind as well as the body as unfree. The speaker in "For the Year of the Insane" (*LD*) tells Mary she is "submerged in [her] own past / and [her] own madness." Then the speaker tells Mary, at the end of the poem, "I am in my own mind. / I am locked in the wrong house." Here is another instance of division of the self, which characterizes the poet's madness. The poet's identification of her condition as a prison leads her to search for a way out. The desire to free herself is clear as early as the title in "Flee on Your Donkey" (*LD*). The image of flight, late in the poem, is sensual:

> Anne, Anne,
> flee on your donkey,
> . . . .
> ride out on some hairy beast,
> gallop backward pressing
> your buttocks to his withers,
> sit to his clumsy gait somehow.

Here, one sees the poet addressing herself as a friend. Presumably the mind, or the spirit, is addressing the body, and there is the sense that they are working together.

The poet seeks health through the paths of the unconscious and the spiritual. Identification of her analyst as God appears to serve as a definition of their relationship and does not appear to relate to the God she seeks on her spiritual route. Nevertheless, it is important to note why the patient thinks the doctor "better than Christ." She says to him in her imagination, "you promised me another world / to tell me who / I was" ("Flee on Your Donkey," *LD*). Clearly, she is looking to unite her separated selves. She uses analysis and dreams to probe her past and speaks of her "eyes circling into [her] childhood, / eyes newly cut." Thus her new vision, gained from analysis, allows her present self to connect with the past, but the process is painful and does not promise sure results. Dreams are "sweet dark playthings, / and above all, mysterious / until they [grow] mournful and weak," and each one is "a bad bet / who might win / because there was no other." The poet's life is at stake, and her only choices for survival are unknown and unguaranteed.

She ultimately pursues an equally difficult spiritual quest. Religion pervades Sexton's work. The poet comes to Mary as "the unbeliever" ("Year of the Insane," *LD*) and asks of Mary, "permit me this grace, / this crossing over." The suggestion is that the poet is trying to reach the "live" side. She also looks for God and perceives accepting God as a surrender: "Soon I will raise my face for a white flag, / and when God enters the fort, / I won't spit or gag on his finger" ("Flee on Your Donkey," *LD*). God's entry is described as military and sexual, a necessary invasion similar to that of Donne's famous Holy Sonnet XIV beginning, "Batter my heart. . . ." The poet also imagines that she will eat God's finger "like a white flower" ("Flee on Your Donkey," *LD*), an image highlighting the opposition of this spiritual moment to, for example, "the black sacrament" of "The Addict" (*LD*). Her connection with Mary is similarly physical. She says to Mary, "I feel your mouth touch mine" ("Year of the Insane," *LD*). Furthermore, she calls Mary "tender physician," underscoring the healing expected from intimate contact with divinity. The juxtaposition of spiritual and physical elements reinforces the concept of health as an acceptance of all parts of the self.

Finally, in *Live or Die*, Sexton does offer a positive vision of life to counter her vision of death. Her life vision involves an integration of the self. The healthy poet copes with the pain of the past and celebrates womanhood and birth. "Mother and Jack and the Rain" (*LD*) includes this memory: "I lay, a blind lake, feigning sleep while Jack / pulled back the wooly covers to see / my body, / that invisible body that girls keep." After this tender memory of her younger body, the poet tells us, "Mother and Jack fill up heaven; they endorse / my womanhood." Hence, the poet is no longer "submerged" in her past, but rather her past validates her present womanhood, encompassing mind and body, past and present. The spiritual connection in this poem is not with traditional Christian figures but with the dead from the poet's own past. She has, in a sense, created her own divinities.

Important symbols associated with life are the sun, sexuality, and dream, in the sense of hope. Even in a poem devoted mostly to madness, "Flee on Your Donkey" (*LD*), the siren of the ambulance is "a noon whistle that kept insisting on life." Noon is the time of the sun, a time opposed to night and darkness frequently associated with death. In "Little Girl, My String Bean, My Lovely Woman" (*LD*), the poet tells her daughter, "Let high noon enter— / the hour of the ghosts," and explains that the idea of noon as a ghost hour comes from the Romans. She then calls the "men bare to the waist," who will "someday" come to her daughter, "young Romans" and says they will come at noon. The association of noon with sexuality is heightened by the command to let noon "enter," and the rest of the poem is filled with images of fertility. In this poem, we certainly receive radically different bodily images from those in the death poetry.

The poet / mother is able to render these images associated with her daughter's body because the poem is about her identification with her daughter. "How can I say that I've known / just what you know and just where you are?" ("Little Girl," *LD*), asks the poet. Thus the poet's statement to her daughter, "there is nothing in your body that lies," is a reminder to the poet herself. The healthy poet must be true to the body as well as the mind; she must not "betray the body." The body in question is clearly a woman's body; the daughter's coming of age is the occasion for the poem. Interestingly, the poet says, "What I want to say, Linda, / is that women are born twice," a statement which celebrates womanhood.

Looking at the imagery in "Live," one might speculate that the poet has been born a third time. In describing her acceptance of life, the poet says:

> Today life opened inside me like an egg
> and there inside
> . . . .

> I found the answer.
> . . . .
> There was the sun,
> her yolk moving feverishly,
> tumbling her prize—
> and you realize that she does this daily!

Here, the sun is associated with birth through the metaphor of the egg, and birth is associated with the daily cycle of the sun. Thus, in what seems to be the most positive statement of the whole book, "Live" (*LD*) suggests a rebirth at the beginning of each day. For the poet, this is a dazzling revelation. She exclaims, "God! It's a dream." Dream takes on the additional meaning of "hope," particularly in the ending lines, "So I won't hang around in my hospital shift, / repeating The Black Mass and all of it. / I say *Live, Live* because of the sun, / the dream, the excitable gift." Because these lines not only end the poem, but also end the book, one cannot help but think that writing is, for the poet, an act affirming life.

Ultimately, the poet creates herself through writing. She says, "I have a room of my own. / . . . / . . . the room affirms / the words that I will make alone" ("Mother and Jack and the Rain," *LD*). The similarity to the title of Virginia Woolf's famous essay, "A Room of One's Own," is either intentional or fortunate because, in the writing room, the poet takes time just for herself and in fact writes the words to create herself. If we recall the bread ritual Sexton associates with death, we should note that it occurs "without words." In addition, the poet, referring to a time at the mental hospital, says, "Everyone has left me / except my muse, / *that good nurse.* / She stays in my hand, / a mild white mouse" ("Flee on Your Donkey," *LD*). Creativity is opposed to madness; it is on the side of health. The muse is a "good nurse" as Mary is a "tender physician."

Another significant way that writing allows the poet to deal with her past is apparent in these lines to her daughter:

> I hear
> as in a dream
> the conversation of the old wives
> speaking of *womanhood*.
> I remember that I heard nothing myself.
> I was alone.
> I waited like a target.
>
> ("Little Girl" *LD*)

Through writing, the poet is able to deal with the pain of her past by saying to her daughter what was not said to her. The unification of her self, with a full recognition of all its parts (mind and body, past and present), is only possible through a grappling with the past. In "Mother and Jack and the Rain" (*LD*), she defines her purpose most poignantly: "to copy out / their two separate names like sunflowers, to conjure / up my daily bread, to endure, / somehow to endure." Here the dead are associated with a life symbol, the sunflower, because they do live on in memory and in writing. Mother and Jack also give the poet life; they even "endorse [her] womanhood." Furthermore, instead of a wordless bread ritual, we get daily bread conjured up by the poet. In addition, we cannot forget the celebration in "Live" (*LD*) of the daily return of the sun. Finally, the prospect of enduring, difficult as it may be, is the opposite of suicide.

The concept of self-making in Sexton's work appears in other collections besides *Live or Die*. As early as "You, Doctor Martin" (*TB*), the speaker states about progress in her treatment for mental illness, "Once I was beautiful. Now I am myself." Similarly, as late as "The Civil War" (*AW*), the poet speaks of "pry[ing] out the broken / pieces of God in me" and putting them back together. One can easily see those pieces of God as parts of the poet's self. The poet then tells us:

> But I will conquer them all
> and build a whole nation of God

in me—but united,
build a new soul,
dress it with skin
and then put on my shirt
and sing an anthem,
a song of myself.

What could be more appropriate than to end a poem about the unification of the self with the title of the ultimate self-making poem by Whitman, the ultimate self-making poet? Sexton's work makes a solid case that the poem truly is the opposite of suicide.

Notes

[1]It is necessary to note outright that my references to "the poet" recognize Sexton's intentional use of the first person in the poems to be discussed as referring to the poet herself; at the same time, my use of "the poet" takes into account the fact that the speaker in the poems is a literary persona.

Works Cited

Sexton, Anne. "The Barfly Ought to Sing." *No Evil Star: Selected Essays and Prose*. Ed. Steven E. Colburn. Ann Arbor: Michigan, 1985.

—. *The Complete Poems*. Ed. Linda Gray Sexton. Boston: Houghton Mifflin Company, 1981.

"PUT YOUR EAR DOWN TO YOUR SOUL AND LISTEN HARD": ANNE SEXTON'S THEORY AND PRACTICE OF ARCHETYPAL POETRY

Brenda Ameter

The greatness of any literature comes from readers recognizing elemental truths about themselves and the people making up their world. Anne Sexton's work portrays a vivid world which runs the gamut of people and situations from a farm wife in Illinois to a Hindu girl in India, from Christian and Greek myths to fairy tales and the bestiary. Many of her poems touch on events in her own life, her stays in mental institutions, her problems with her parents, her relationships with friends, daughters, lovers; yet as she points out, even the most personal poems distort the events of her life to yield greater poetic power and truth. In telling about changing the details in "The Double Image," she says, "I don't imply that I was ever in a mental institution more than once, but that was the dramatic truth." She also tells how she only mentioned one daughter although she had two (Marx 75). The early critics tend to write as if Sexton were giving facts directly from her life. In a review of *Live or Die,* Thomas McDonnell recounts in detail Sexton's autobiographical journey as if it exactly paralleled her art (132-138). Yet Sexton says "You can even lie (one can confess and lie forever) as I did in the poem of the illegitimate child that the girl had to give up. It hadn't happened to me. It wasn't true, and yet it was indeed the truth" (Marx 75). It was a universal truth, an archetypal image buried in the collective unconscious.

Beyond any events that she experienced in her life, her search for the truth, that is for an order of events, compels her to rely upon the unconscious, to search her own unconscious experience so she may understand the collective unconscious shared by all people. From the beginning of her writing, Anne Sexton faced critics who did not understand that it is in the seemingly small events of life that larger events find their meaning. Established traditional writers and critics (especially male ones) criticized her view of the universe, blaming her feminine outlook for an excess of emotion and detail in her writing. She also drew criticism from women because she did not concern herself with political issues. Some contemporary feminists maintain that a woman cannot understand the male experience or a male the female experience. While approving of her poetry that celebrates experiences that are particularly woman related, such as menstruation and motherhood, they argue that she cannot represent a man's experiences. Anne Sexton's greatness proves all her critics wrong. She understood Jungian archetypal theory, not only from her experience with psychotherapy, but from her own experience with her unconscious. Despite attacks on her work from critics and feminists, she had the courage to follow her own vision.

During the period in which Anne Sexton was studying with John Holmes, he objected to her subject matter and style, only approving of poems written in "traditional" form about accepted subject matter. Seventeen years later, Sexton characterized his attitude in these words:

> John Holmes didn't approve of a thing about me. He hated my poetry. I remember, even after Maxine Kumin had left, and I was still with Holmes, there was a new girl who came into the class. And he kept saying, "Oh, let us see *new* poems, *new* poems. We need them." And here I was giving him things that were later anthologized forever. (Showalter and Smith 162)

Sexton realized that she could not do her best work using the methods Holmes advocated. She had enough self-confidence to work in the form that she knew best; however, his criticisms led to her having two concerns during the early years. She labeled herself a primitive writer because she was not well read in literature and did not have much formal education (a year of junior college emphasizing home economics and a year of finishing school emphasizing the art of entertaining), and she became sensitive to differences, or perhaps as she saw it, the inferiority of being a woman poet. In a letter written after she had been writing poetry for a year, she tells W. D. Snodgrass that she has "a fear of writing as a woman writes. I wish I were a man—I would rather write the way a man writes" (*Letters* 40).

The fears and inadequacies raised by Holmes caused Anne to have an ambivalent attitude toward her femininity and her writing. She believed her poetry had value for many people; she believed in her emotional, earthy imagery; but she distanced herself from the women's movement until near the end of her life because she feared reactions such as Holmes'. Many male critics were uncomfortable with poems discussing the uterus, menstruation, nursing, birth. After mentioning Louis Simpson's criticism that "a poem titled 'Menstruation at Forty' was the straw that broke the camel's back," Barbara Kevles asked Sexton if only male critics disliked Sexton's use of biological facts. Anne's answer was classic in its simplicity; she said she had not noticed the gender of her critics (109). Although Sexton referred to herself as a "primitive" throughout her life because she wrote from her inner feelings rather than having a formal background in literature, she actually had two different but equally important methods of attaining knowledge: (1) Formal instruction from television education courses, college writing courses, writing workshops, and her mother's early guidance. (2) Informal instruction from her continuing psychotherapy, which gave her knowledge of Freud and Jung, but more importantly, knowledge of herself; for in herself, she saw the universality of human themes, the collective unconsciousness of archetypes. In her first book of poetry, these two forms of instruction merged as shown by her choice of epigraph at the beginning of the book and her poem "For John, Who Begs Me Not to Enquire Further" (TB).

The epigraph, a quotation from a letter Schopenhauer sent Goethe, says the philosopher must seek answers even though he realizes as did Oedipus that there will be horror in the answers. A strange epigraph for a "primitive," but not a strange one for Anne Sexton who seeks the answers that John Holmes fears. In the poem to him, which sets forth her theory of poetry, she acknowledges that her work is not "beautiful":

> But that, in the end, there was
> a certain sense of order there;
> something worth learning
> in that narrow diary of my mind. . . .

She continues the poem by saying that at first her knowledge was private, but then it became more than just herself,

> it was you, or your house
> or your kitchen.

When this knowledge becomes "you," it has become an archetype. The language evokes comparisons with the Biblical "But as for me and my house" (Joshua 24:14), but it stops short of ending "we shall serve the Lord" just as Anne Sexton never reconciles her beliefs with traditional piety. She brings us back to her femininity by calling up the image of the kitchen. Sexton makes a powerful statement in this first book of poetry; she is going to ask the hard questions and not flinch at the pain that they bring. The questions, set forth in the common images of everyday life, analyze archetypal relationships. In one poem a mother never caresses her child. In another, a daughter commits the one unforgivable sin against her mother—attempted suicide. These situations allow Sexton to probe the mother-daughter relationship. Other poems in the book deal with father-daughter, mother-son, woman-lover, woman-woman friend relationships. Sexton evokes archetypal images written on the psyche of people across cultures, countries, languages, commonly shared experiences from which myths come. During her early readings Anne introduced "The Double Image" (TB) by saying, "The great theme is not Romeo and Juliet. . . . The great theme we all share is that of becoming ourselves, of overcoming our father and mother, of assuming our identities somehow (Letters 28). A curious duality exists in her attitude towards this poem, for by the time that she read it to audiences, the "our" referred to both men and women, but in a letter to Carolyn Kizer written before the poem was published, her anxiety about being a woman writer surfaced again. She described the poem as "a feminine and directly emotional piece that will make most readers flinch and probably the men! most of all" (Letters 56). However, in spite of her occasional insecurities caused by critical reaction to her work, she continued to follow her creative vision.

Three differing but important points are set forth by this first book of Sexton's poetry; and ultimately all three converge in her last four books. The first is that while Sexton refused to accept the perimeters set by men for correct poetry, she also feared their reactions to her writing, and in her most fearful moments early in her career, she regretted the feminine aspects of her writing. However, dependent on her unconscious, she recognized that she could not write like a man or like any other woman for that matter. As she repeatedly insisted, truth came from her unconscious and controlled her poetry.

The second point is that she does use the trivial details of life to find larger truths. She probes this matter of finding our identities in relationships, in religion, and in death by writing about the most trivial details of life. In a review of *The Awful Rowing Toward God,* Joyce Carol Oates notes that Sexton's unsympathetic critics have charged her with "an overvaluing of her private sorrows to the exclusion of the rest of the world" (170). Later in the review, Oates says it is a "risky claim" to suggest that Sexton, Plath, and Berryman deal in collective pathologies (4). Surely in light of Sexton's Jungian view of the unconscious, it is not at all risky to insist that she is exploring the collective unconscious through the details of her experience.

The third point introduced by this first book of poetry is her concern with the ultimate meaning of life that comes with religiously-oriented truth—a truth culminating in the last four books of poetry in which she details her religious visions. While Suzanne Juhasz asserts that *Transformations* marks a new boldness and increased sense of power in Sexton's work (215), Estella Lauter speaks of an impudent stance in which Sexton refuses to "cover up, gloss over or withdraw from what she saw—a refusal to be shamed into silence" (25). The tone of the later works may appear more militant; however, Anne Sexton, while perhaps wishing that she could have "softened" her words, never retreated in any form from the images or visions that her unconscious put forth. The only difference is that in her first works, she speaks of "images"; in the later books she speaks of the "visions." Presumably there was a difference in the form of the material that she was receiving that accounts for the difference that Juhasz and Lauter perceive. This difference can best be seen by analyzing Anne's view of the unconscious.

Rather than taking an intellectualized view of Jungian theory as many feminists do, Anne interacts with the Jungian unconscious through her therapy and her poetry. She describes this relationship in an interview with Barbara Kevles:

> Sometimes, my doctors tell me that I understand something in a poem that I haven't integrated into my life. In fact, I may be concealing it from myself, while I was revealing it to the readers. The poetry is often more advanced, in terms of my unconscious, than I am. Poetry, after all, milks the unconscious. The unconscious is there to feed it little images, little symbols, the answers, the insights I know not of. (85)

Anne even says that judging whether to let an image remain in a poem is done by her unconscious, "May it do me no ill" (Kevles 103). This explanation illustrates the beneficial qualities of the unconscious insisted upon by Jung and acceptable to both Sexton and feminist scholars. However, as Annis Pratt explains in "Spinning Among Fields: Jung, Frye, Levi-Straus," feminist scholars while retaining the machinery of the collective unconscious and archetypical image reject Jung's theory of the *anima* and *animus.* In fact, Pratt rather indignantly tells of her conversation with a therapist in which she said she wished he could be a woman just one day and experience the prejudice against women in the academic world. He maintained that he understood her situation because he had developed his *anima* (97-98). Pratt was outraged by his assumption just as Jung's position seems to outrage many feminist scholars; however, Sexton certainly felt that she had developed her *animus* although she did not speak of it in those terms. She says she feels that she is many people. "When I am writing a poem, I feel I am the person who should have written it. Many times I assume these guises. . . . Sometimes I become someone else and when I do, I believe, even in moments when I'm not writing the poem, that I am that person" (Kevles 103).

Anne gives many examples. She says when she wrote the poem "The Farmer's Wife" (*TB*), that she became the Illinois woman who differed so much from Bostonian Anne Sexton. "When I had the illegitimate child, I nursed it—in my mind—and gave it back and traded life." Most important of all, Sexton says when she wrote "In the Deep Museum" (*APO*), "I felt like Christ. My arms hurt, [sic] I desperately wanted to pull them in off the Cross" (Kevles 104). When Sexton writes "The Hangman" (*APO),* the father's view of the desolation that his retarded child has wreaked on his life conveys a powerful sense of isolation and despair, the same feeling that Christ must have felt, the same feeling that the small boy surely feels when his mother abuses him in "Red Roses" (*MS*), the same feeling conveyed by the description of the old man's room in "Doors, Doors, Doors" (*APO*). Although Sexton has fewer poems in which the persona is a man, the ones she writes are powerful and universal. Sexton also opposed the view that she should make a political statement about any cause, including the women's movement. She asserted, "People have to find out who they are before they can confront national issues" (Kevles 110). Instead, she wrote about "interior events, not Historical ones" (Kevles 110). The people in her poems are struggling for the rights that all people seek, whatever their color; emotions have no color.

Although she makes no political statements concerning women's rights, Sexton's poetry seeks the right for women to preserve and enjoy their womanhood. In "Celebration of My Uterus" (*LP*), Anne tells of a woman's fight to keep surgeons from removing her uterus. This poem certainly describes a situation common in many societies, the popularization of operations, hysterectomies, mastectomies, clitoridectomies, which remove certain parts of women's bodies without sufficient medical reason. Anne's poem in this case parallels very closely the actual incident; moreover, the poem also illustrates another archetype, the desire for a son, which is universal for most people who have daughters, or the desire for a daughter for people with sons. Sexton says she did not realize she wanted a son until the poem came from her unconscious. For the most part, Sexton supports women through an understanding of their feelings and biological needs.

During the early years, she made no formal statements on the women's movement. Interviews during the late sixties portrayed Anne as having non-feminist views on subjects other than those mentioned above. Jane McCabe asserts that "Anne Sexton was not and never claimed to be a feminist" (216). As late as 1965, in an interview with Patricia Marx, Anne Sexton derided Marx's reference to the dilemma of the modern woman with the sarcastic words, "Oh, I don't know! Poor modern Woman!" (77). Marx then asked Sexton how she felt about the "feminine mystique" and if she considered the problems of modern woman worse now than formerly. Sexton replied, "Maybe modern woman is more conscious now, more thinking. I can't tell. Sometimes I feel like another creature, hardly a woman, although I certainly am, in my life. I can't be a modern woman. I'm a Victorian teenager—at heart" (77-78). Surely sophisticated, glamorous Anne Sexton, the former model, is posturing here. Her friend, Maxine Kumin, described Anne at their first meeting in 1957 as a "little flower child; she was the ex-fashion model. She wore very spiky high heels—" (Showalter and Smith 159). In the interview with Marx, Sexton asserted that she was different from other women. In 1965, women still did not admit to friendships with other women. By April 15, 1974 (four months before Anne's suicide), Maxine Kumin and Anne Sexton openly discussed their friendship which involved critiquing each other's poetry. In response to a question concerning whether the women's movement had made them regard their relationship in a different way, Sexton replied, "You see, when we began, there was no women's movement. We were it." This shows a radical change in nine years' time; however, the truth of the situation comes in Kumin's wry comment, "And we didn't know it" (Showalter and Smith 172). In this interview, the two women told how they could enter into each other's consciousness and guide each other in their work, though they produced totally different kinds of poetry (168).

Anne Sexton's final comments on the importance of Jungian theory appear in two letters written late in her life. Six months before her death, she indicated an interest in teaching a course to undergraduate students which she would call "Creative Writing of Poetry[:] Raising of the Unconscious" (*Letters* 411). One month before her death, she wrote a letter to Rise and Steven Axelrod, who asked about her knowledge of Blake. They had written an article comparing her work with his. She replied that she had not read Blake's work but concluded that the parallels are Jungian. "I do think there is somewhere a 'visionary mode' in my work, but I'm usually unaware of it until it comes to me" (*Letters* 421). As early as 1972, she had described religious visions that came to her, saying:

> I have visions—sometimes ritualized visions—that come to me of God, or of Christ, or of the Saints, and I feel that I can touch them almost. . . that they are part of me. It's the same "Everything that has been shall be again." (Kevles 105)

Throughout her poetry Sexton relied on the Jungian concept of the "collective unconscious," progressing from images to visions, but always allowing her unconscious to dictate her art.

Works Cited

Colburn, Steven E., ed. *No Evil Star: Selected Essays, Interviews, and Prose.* Ann Arbor: U of Michigan P, 1985.

George, Diana Hume. *Oedipus Anne: The Poetry of Anne Sexton.* Urbana: U of Illinois P, 1987.

Juhasz, Suzanne. *Naked and Fiery Forms: Modern American Poetry by Women, a New Tradition.* New York: Harper and Row, 1976.

Kevles, Barbara. Interview. Colburn 83-111.

Lauter, Estella. *Women As Mythmakers*. Bloomington: Indiana U P, 1984.
Marx, Patricia. Interview. Colburn 70-82.
McCabe, Jane. "A Women Who Writes: A Feminist Approach to the Early Poetry of Anne Sexton." McClatchy 216-43.
McDonnell, Thomas P. Review of *Live or Die*. McClatchy 132-38.
McClatchy, J. D., ed. *Anne Sexton: The Artist and Her Critics*. Bloomington: Indiana U P, 1978.
Oates, Joyce Carol. "Singing the Pathologies of Our Time: *The Awful Rowing Toward God*." *New York Times Book Review* 23 Mar. 1975: 3-4.
Pratt, Annis V. "Spinning Among Fields: Jung, Frye, Levi-Straus." *Spring: An Annual of Archetypal Psychology and Jungian Thought* (1979): 77-92.
Sexton, Anne. *The Complete Poems*. Ed. Linda Gray Sexton. Boston: Houghton Mifflin, 1981.
Sexton, Linda Gray and Lois Ames, eds. *Anne Sexton: A Self- Portrait in Letters*. Boston: Houghton Mifflin, 1977.
Showalter, Elaine and Carol Smith. Interview with Anne Sexton and Maxine Kumin. Colburn 158-79.

ANNE SEXTON'S "MOTHERLY" POETICS

Frances Bixler

"I look for uncomplicated hymns, but love has none." This is the last line of Anne Sexton's poem for her daughter, Joy. The relationship of mother and daughter evidenced in "A Little Uncomplicated Hymn" suggests that the mother has shared in her daughter's pain through the years. She describes what was probably a traumatic event at one time:

> You fell on your eye. You fell on your chin.
> What a shiner! What a faint you had
> and then crawled home,
> a knocked-out humpty dumpty
> in my arms.

The mother clearly identifies with the child's pain, but acknowledges the limits of her ability to heal. Humpty Dumpty, after all, was never put together again. Yet, she holds the child in her arms, touching, soothing. Later in the poem, she prophesies for this one who has been so bumped and bruised:

> You will jump to it someday
> as you will jump out of the pitch of this house.
> It will be a holiday, a parade, a fiesta!
> Then you'll fly.
> You'll really fly.
> After that you'll, quite simply, quite calmly
> make your own stones, your own floor plan,
> your own sound.

The words of the mother make reality for the daughter, good

reality—that which generates in her a sense of possibility and joy in being woman.

A second poem, this time for Linda, demonstrates Sexton's loving desire to instill in her daughter a sense of the wonder of being female. "Little Girl, My String Bean, My Lovely Woman" (*LD*) catches the mysterious changes going on in the adolescent's body through a catalog of fecund images portraying this ripening time: "the market stalls of mushrooms / and garlic buds all engorged . . . ," "the berries are done / and the apples . . . beginning to swell." Too soon the mother knows that "they will come to you . . . young Romans." Before they do, however, the mother has made certain that she has written words on her daughter's soul that can never be erased by anyone. These are the words of her maternal blessing:

> *Your bones are lovely. . . .*
> . . . .
> What I want to say, Linda,
> is that there is nothing in your body that lies.
> All that is new is telling the truth.
> . . . .
> Darling,
> stand still at your door,
> sure of yourself, a white stone, a good stone—
> as exceptional as laughter
> you will strike fire,
> that new thing.

The source of this blessing is the mother who now describes herself as "that somebody else, / an old tree in the background," and "this hand that formed."

My purpose in this paper is to suggest that Anne Sexton wrote poetry, drawing heavily on her experience of motherhood, not only to create her own soul, but also to mother into life those who read her work. Not content to intellectualize life as John Holmes so strongly encouraged her to do, Sexton delves into the heart of experience in order to reorder the meaning of being woman—"that new thing."[1] In so doing she narrows the distance between reader and writer and reshapes the reality of our lives, asking us to listen closely as she prophesies, takes responsibility for our welfare, suffers with and for us, and bears a "multitude" of children.

Evidence of Sexton's "motherly" poetics appears frequently in poems where the "I" of the poem sacrifices herself for the reader. Such a sacrifice amounts to a "going before" which prepares the way for the naive or uninitiated. In "Eighth Psalm" the mother gives up her life in order that the baby will live: "For the baby lives. The mother will die" (*DN*). Coming where it does in the sequence of psalms, Sexton is hinting at her own imminent death and at the poetic death a poet suffers each time she produces living words; but she also clearly expects that the poetic death will create life in the reader. The final poem of *Live or Die* titled "Live" suggests that the poet's decision to live instead of die grows out of her motivation "to feed our puppies as they come, / the eight Dalmatians we didn't drown. . . ." Black and white, the Dalmations represent all of us who are both good and evil, "fallen angels" Sexton calls us elsewhere ("The Fallen Angels," *AW*). Dalmatians are traditionally firehouse dogs, living where the constant smell of death and danger is present. Thus, Sexton's choice to live is an active choice to become a provider of food and a protector for all of *humanitas*, even though this choice results in pain.

A later poem further supports the idea of Sexton's strong sense of responsibility toward her readers:

> Dolls,
> by the thousands,
> are falling out of the sky
> and I look up in fear
> and wonder who will catch them?
>
> ("The Falling Dolls," *MS*)

The poet continues wondering who or what will save these dolls who appear to have no parents, no mentors, no redeemers. Finally, she says

> I hold open my arms
> and catch
> one,
> two,
> three . . . ten in all. . . .

The metaphor of "catching dolls" implies the close relationship between the writer and her readers. Her poetry, her words, she hopes will serve as a kind of safety net for others.

Sexton uses other methods of closing the gap between herself and her reader; one such method is her use of the witch persona. Though some critics see the witch persona in Sexton's work as a negative aspect of womanhood, a role the poet is forced to accept because of society's unbending attitude toward women poets, I suggest that the witch so poignantly described in "Her Kind" (*TB*) is a deliberate creation of Sexton's which allows her to mediate suffering and reinterpret life in a mode accessible to her readers.[2] Her initial description of the witch suggests both these aspects:

> I have gone out, a possessed witch,
> haunting the black air, braver at night;
> dreaming evil, I have done my hitch
> over the plain houses, light by light;
> lonely thing, twelve-fingered, out of mind.
> A woman like that is not a woman, quite.
> I have been her kind. (*TB*)

The isolation, the loneliness, the exposure to evil are all a part of the witch's experience, one which she expects the reader to share only vicariously. Thus, she has "gone before," suffered the pain of being such a person and has gained for all unusual knowledge. The evidence of this knowledge appears in the character of the narrator of *Transformations,* that middle-aged witch who takes as her audience "this boy. / He is sixteen and he wants some answers. / He is each of us. / I mean you. / I mean me" ("The Gold Key"). The witch's retelling of the familiar stories which have framed our lives establishes her as one who has faced the dark places in our psyches and has lived to warn us about ourselves. Sexton further affirms herself as suffering woman and witch in touch with extraordinary power in "The Witch's Life" where she describes the old witch of her childhood memory: "She had hair like kelp / and a voice like a boulder." She, too, Sexton admits, is becoming much like the old witch. Her appearance and her actions give her away:

> My shoes turn up like a jester's.
> . . . .
> I am shoveling the children out,
> scoop after scoop.
> Only my books anoint me,
> and a few friends. . . .

Finally, she faces the truth about herself and her life:

> Yes. It is the witch's life,
> climbing the primordial climb,
> a dream within a dream,
> then sitting here
> holding a basket of fire. (*AW*)

She is bravely enduring the journey deep into the center of human experience; and though the "basket of fire" charges and warms her with imaginative power, it is also capable of consuming her. For Sexton the danger is real, yet her "climb" cannot be abandoned. For her own soul's sake and for our souls' sake, she continues.

A second aspect of Sexton's "motherly" poetics is her clear suggestion in several poems that she hopes to become a mother of many through the fecundity of her words. The speaker in "Mary's Song" is ostensibly the Virgin Mary, but Sexton uses the vehicle of the Christian story to suggest her own fertility myth:

> Write these words down.
> Keep them on the tablet of miracles.
> . . . .
> My time has come.
> There are twenty people in my belly,
> there is a magnitude of wings,
> there are forty eyes shooting like arrows,
> and they will all be born. (*DN*)

Unlike the Virgin Mary, Sexton prophesies that she will have many children. A similar birthing image occurs in "The Author of the Jesus Paper Speaks" when the narrator, disappointed in her attempt to milk a cow which will give "moon juice," goes to a well and "[draws] a baby / out of the hollow water" (*BF*). Sexton here seems to be saying that she will give up hungering for the milk of Christianity but will instead begin to produce her own babies. And produce she does.

"Eighth Psalm" (*DN*) establishes "the woman" as one who has experienced enormous creative powers:

> No. No. The woman is cheerful, she smiles at her stomach. She has swallowed a bagful of oranges and she is well pleased.
>
> For she has come through the voyage fit and her room carries the little people.
> . . . .
>
> For she is a magnitude, she is many. She is each of us patting ourselves dry with a towel.

The poet and her Reader/Daughters, her babies, have endured and thus find themselves awaiting spiritual rebirth:

> For she is seeing the end of her confinement now and is waiting like stone for the waters.
>
> For the baby crowns and there is a people-dawn in the world.
>
> For the baby lies in its water and blood and there is a people-cry in the world.
>
> . . . .
>
> For the baby lives. The mother will die. . . .

It is true that Sexton projects in these lines her own death and rebirth, her "soul" remade. However, it is also true that the metaphor applies to the reader who, as so often happens in Sexton's work, is pulled into the imaginative world of the writer, identifying closely with the poet/narrator. The stunning birth images of the psalm suggest the powerful connection Sexton makes between writing poetry and mothering *humanitas* into life, even into a new "soul."

"Tenth Psalm" concludes the sequence with many strong allusions to Anne, the child, and to Anne, the mother—complex images and identities which represent both the child/poet's and the child/reader's experience (*DN*). The ambiguity of these images requires a bit of amplification. Constituted as a sequence of celebration narrated by Anne, the mother, who is also Anne, the child, the entire psalm sequence bursts with birthing metaphors. Throughout the sequence the narrative traces the journey of the child from the event of her physical birth where she was "swaddled in grease wool from [her] father's company and could not move or ask the time" to the imaginative birth of Anne and Christopher in the poet's head ("Fourth Psalm", *DN*) to the penultimate moment of the birth of the new child, resulting in the mother's death. Both the mother and the child reappear in "Tenth Psalm," however, suggesting that the death in the prior psalm is a spiritual one and that the entire sequence is to be understood on a metaphorical level. Sexton's deliberate layering of meaning becomes apparent in the line, "For as her child grows Anne grows and there is salt and cantaloupe and molasses for all" (*DN*). The birth which has occurred in "Eighth Psalm" has resulted in new life for both mother and child. One can infer that the "child" and "Anne" are a unified identity. However, the child is also the Reader / Daughter who has been birthed into new imaginative experience by the poet's exploration of her own death and spiritual rebirth. The child "grows to a woman," and "must build her own city and fill it with her own oranges, her own words." Thus, Anne, the mother, comes to the end of her poetic and spiritual journey, having satisfied her own hunger and feeling sure of her success as a Poet / Mother. Two more lines reinforce the idea of Sexton's "motherly" motivation:

> For Anne walked up and up and finally over the years until she was old as the moon and with its naggy voice.
>
> For Anne had climbed over eight mountains and saw the children washing the tiny statues in the square.

Our last glimpse of her is as a tiny speck on the distant horizon where she looks back to see for one last time that "the children" are still fine.

A final poem shows "the woman" at her most fecund, most dynamic. "Somewhere in Africa" describes John Holmes' death from cancer: "cancer blossomed in your throat, / rooted like bougainvillea into your gray backbone, / ruptured your pores until you wore it like a coat." Sexton deplores this image of death. Instead, she substitutes a powerful woman who will carry her former mentor to his final resting place:

> Let God be some tribal female who is known but forbidden.
>
> Let there be this God who is a woman who will place you
> upon her shallow boat, who is a woman naked to the waist,
> moist with palm oil and sweat, a woman of some virtue
> and wild breasts, her limbs excellent, unbruised and chaste.

This goddess, "known but forbidden," will transform Holmes' death into a journey of delight. She concludes with this instruction:

> John Holmes, cut from a single tree, lie heavy in her hold
> and go down that river with the ivory, the copra and the gold.

The awesome creative power of this woman—beautiful, erotic, unspoiled, virtuous, even wild—suggests hidden fountains of creativity hitherto undiscovered by the human race. Her function in this poem is to carry John Holmes into a realm that is secret, unknown, mysterious, redolent of rich fruits as was the Garden of Eden. She literally "carries" him, as a woman carries a child, into the mysterious universe of the dead. Such is the power Sexton often exercises over her readers as she "carries" us into the richness of her "known but forbidden" life.

Notes

[1]I intend here to mean that Sexton, working several years ahead of the feminist movement, had an intuitive sense of the generative powers of women which she constantly sought to express in her poetry. I'd also like to make a clear distinction between the patriarchal notion of the Great Mother and Sexton's portrayal of woman in these and many other poems in her canon. In the former sense, women are servants of a greater good, subject to the needs of men. Sexton's woman is on fire. She explodes with her creative power, establishing a whole new definition of

the meaning of being female.

[2]Kay Capo suggests that "Her Kind" establishes several of the dominant voices in Sexton's poetry—voices which Sexton used to convey various levels of reality.

Works Cited

Anne Sexton: A Self-Portrait in Letters. Eds. Linda Gray Sexton and Lois Ames. Boston: Houghton Mifflin Co., 1977.

Capo, Kay. "'I Have Been Her Kind': Anne Sexton's Communal Voice." *Original Essays on the Poetry of Anne Sexton.* Conway, AR: U of Central Arkansas P, 1988.

Sexton, Anne. *45 Mercy Street.* Ed. Linda Gray Sexton. Boston: Houghton Mifflin, 1976.

_____. *Live or Die.* Boston: Houghton Mifflin, 1967.

_____. *The Awful Rowing Toward God.* Boston: Houghton Mifflin, 1975.

_____. *The Book of Folly.* Boston: Houghton Mifflin, 1974.

_____. *The Death Notebooks.* Boston: Houghton Mifflin, 1975.

_____. *To Bedlam and Part Way Back.* Boston: Houghton Mifflin, 1960.

_____. *Transformations.* Boston: Houghton Mifflin, 1971.

III. Form

Far off she rolled and rolled
like a woman in labor
and I thought of those who had crossed her,
in antiquity, in nautical trade, in slavery, in war.
I wondered how she had borne those bulwarks.
She should be entered skin to skin,
and put on like one's first or last cloth,
entered like kneeling your way into church,
descending into that ascension . . . .

"The Consecrating Mother"
45 Mercy Street

TRANSFORMATIONS: A MAGIC MIRROR

Caroline King Barnard Hall

Like images reflected in a funhouse mirror, the poems of Anne Sexton's fifth volume revisit familiar tales, transforming them into new shapes which are both strange and true. Sexton's recreation of seventeen fairy tales from the brothers Grimm is at once witty, weird, and terrifying; these poems reinvent their models by manipulating proportion and form to express unique insight. They are mythic materials recalled, recast, and reshaped by the poet. In the magic mirror of Sexton's imagination, appearance is distorted and language reinvented.

Sexton's mythopoesis of themes and subjects from her previous work begins in her very choice of Grimm tales to transform. Her method of selection, she tells us, was spontaneous and instinctive; she chose the stories which she liked because they suggested to her a particular meaning. As she comments in a 1973 interview:

> "Sometimes my daughter would suggest 'read this or that, try this one'. . . and if I got, as I was reading it, some unconscious message that I had something to say, what I had fun with were the prefatory things, . . . that's where . . . I expressed whatever it evoked in me—and it had to evoke something in me or I couldn't do it." (Heyen and Poulin 145)

Indeed, fairy tales, which are part of the childhood experience of most of us, suggest a multiplicity of both subconscious and plain messages to readers of any age. Developed within the Western European oral tradition, recorded and overlaid with nineteenth-century didacticism, these tales give voice to the values of western culture. As the scholar and translator Jack Zipes points out in the Introduction to his 1987 translation of the Grimm tales, the Grimm brothers "made major changes while editing the tales," changes which "underline morals in keeping with the Protestant ethic and a patriarchal notion of sex roles" (xxviii).

From these tales, then, which project a mixture of entertainment, folk wisdom, and western morality, we remember the beautiful and beleaguered heroines, the evil and cackling witches, the leering and threatening wolves and monsters, the gentle and helpful doves and fish and ants, the powerful kings, and the incredibly handsome princes. The stories are vivid and exciting. Beautiful Cinderella (we remember the colorful illustrations), kept in bondage and made to do all the dirty housework by her very selfish and clumsy stepmother and stepsister, finds release through the magical intercession of several white birds, the persistent search of a handsome, love-smitten prince, and the essential coincidence of a small, dainty foot. Snow White, whose very name is purity, is finally discovered by her prince, too, with whom we are certain she will live happily ever after. Her preliminary tribulations are caused by a jealous stepmother whose maddeningly honest mirror continues to proclaim Snow White "a thousand times more fair"; she supports herself, before the prince's advent (and before she eats an apple, which of course causes a great deal of trouble) by keeping a tidy little house for the seven cute little dwarfs. The witch, always a female, appears variously and often in fairy tales; she seems most interested in ruining the innocent by burning them, or by imprisoning them, or by magically creating an unwelcome change in their identity.

Though we probably don't know it at the time, when we are children we are being mentally and imaginatively programmed as we are delighted and terrified. A mature reader can plainly see in these tales the patriarchal bias of a male-oriented social view. Bad women are witches, ugly and scheming, wielding over other women and men alike a magical, evil power of transformation, or at least wielding some kind of power. Good women are quiet, domestic, and submissive; they take care of children and/or home while their men go out and "work." Strangely, housework is drudgery for some heroines, like Cinderella, and her reward is escape. But we do not think that revolutionary thought at the time; it is her discovery by the prince which captures our attention. And surely, there will be no housework in her future. And so, like Cinderella, sometimes in these fairy tales if the heroine has not yet become a wife, if she is very lucky and very beautiful (the first depends on the second), and of course if she is virginally pure, her charming prince may come along, discover that the shoe fits, or free her from the tower, or awaken her with a kiss (she has, of course, been only sleeping in all her previous life without the prince). What happens to her then we are never told, except that the beautiful princess and handsome prince live happily ever after.

Though this fairy tale world may be peopled with demure princesses and adventuresome men, however, it is also a world of nightmare and terror, where heroines and heroes must pass through a period of testing before triumphing over the witch, finding their way out of the forest, or breaking the evil spell. While there is in these tales a tendency, which must be recognized, to advocate the maintenance of a sexist status quo, such a structure alone cannot account for the fairy tales' ageless appeal to children and to adults alike. The child psychologist Bruno Bettelheim argues that fairy tales, by enchanting, terrifying, and delighting children, help them to "cope with the psychological problems of growing up and integrating their personalities" (14). By experiencing the fairy tale world, which "simplifies all situations," and in which "characters are typical rather than unique," children face and solve moral, psychological, ethical, and emotional conflicts and learn to master by themselves "the problem which has made the story meaningful . . . in the first place" (18).

Such anxieties and fears as separation from parents, oedipal conflicts, sibling rivalry, sexual awakening, and parental rejection are given both shape and resolution in these tales; Hansel and Gretel survive in the threatening forest without their deserting parents, Gretel burns the witch and frees her brother, Snow White and Cinderella are saved both by males and by their own efforts from their jealous stepmothers and sisters, Rapunzel provides with her own body the means of escaping from the witch to her prince. It is therefore "uninformed," contends Bettelheim, to see the happily-ever-after fairy tale ending as "unrealistic wish-fulfillment" (11), for such an ending assures the child of the desirability of separating from parents to form new relationships.

These stories, then, evoke a multitude of responses which are likely to vary depending upon the age, experience, and predilections of the reader. The "unconscious messages" which they evoked in Anne Sexton appear consistent with the thematic concerns of her previous poetry: guilt, love, anger and madness; uneasy relationships between parents and children; ambivalence over women's roles; imaginative identification of poet with witch; anxiety and fear over sexual awakening, parental rejection, or oedipal conflicts; and the torment and joy of passion. Remarkably, such themes are precisely those which Bettelheim designates as typical fairy tale subjects.

If Sexton's themes in *Transformations* are congruous with fairy tale concerns, her method in these poems is indigenous to the fairy tale mode as well. Each poem follows a prologue-body form, except for the first poem in the series, "The Gold Key," which serves as a general prologue to the whole volume (and which is itself also a "transformation" of a very short Grimm tale called "The Golden Key"). The remaining sixteen poems begin with a prologue of one or more stanzas, intended to emphasize the prefatory nature of the section and to clarify its boundaries. Here, Sexton introduces the context which she has chosen for the tale, providing a thematic focus for the rest of the poem. Sexton's retelling of the tale follows; in this section of each poem we find a story which resembles the Grimm version but which also has been reshaped to some degree by Sexton: "Oh, yes," she comments in an interview, "I embellished [the Grimm tale], oh, indeed, it wasn't that way" (Heyen and Poulin 145). For example, here is part of the prologue of "Rumpelstiltskin":

> In many of us
> is a small old man
> who wants to get out.
> . . . .
> He is a monster of despair.
> He is all decay.
> He speaks up as tiny as an earphone
> with Truman's asexual voice:
> I am your dwarf.
> I am the enemy within.
> I am the boss of your dreams.
> . . . .
> See . . . .
> It is your Doppelganger
> trying to get out.
> Beware . . . Beware . . .

Then the tale begins:

> There once was a miller
> with a daughter as lovely as a grape . . .

The style is campy and humorous (dark and otherwise) as the speaker retells and reinvents the Grimm stories, offering witty embellishments along the way. Such an approach coincides neatly with the original fairy tale mode, for in order to dramatize their meanings clearly and effectively, fairy tales, as well, offer us cartoon characters involved in complex situations which have been reduced to bare essentials. So Sexton announces such an approach in "The Gold Key"; this is, she writes, a "book of odd tales / which transform the Brothers Grimm . . ."

> As if an enlarged paper clip
> could be a piece of sculpture.
> (And it could.)

This volume is to be a pop-art creation, true to the cartoon nature of fairy-tale character and situation. Anne Sexton's volume will have illustrations, as do all respectable fairy tale books; writes Sexton in a 1970 letter, "I'd like [these poems] to be well-illustrated—a real zap of a production even if they aren't the old Sexton style" (*Letters* 361).

Thus, while illustrations designate and simplify theme and character, language and imagery underscore the poems' quality of caricature. Snow White is introduced in breezy language as a kind of pop-art poster, "a lovely number: / cheeks as fragile as cigarette paper"; when revived by the dwarfs from her first encounter with her wicked stepmother, she is "as full of life as soda pop." When the heroine of "Rumpelstiltskin" is unable to spin straw into gold, she weeps "of course, huge aquamarine tears." The parson in "The Little Peasant," discovered hiding in the miller's closet, stands "rigid for a moment, / as real as a soup can." Rapunzel's song pierces the prince's heart "like a valentine." Huntsmen disappear into Iron Hans's forest "like soap bubbles." One-Eye's eye is "like a great blue aggie." After the witch's supper, Hansel and Gretel sleep, "z's buzzing from their mouths like flies."

Shortly before Sexton submitted the completed *Transformations* for publication, she wrote a letter offering her assessment of her new volume. Her comments show her view of these poems both in themselves and as they relate to her previous work:

> I realize that the "Transformations" are a departure from my usual style. I would say that they lack the intensity and perhaps some of the confessional force of my previous work. I wrote them because I had to . . . because I wanted to . . . because it made me happy. I would like my readers to see this side of me, and it is not in every case the lighter side. Some of the poems are grim. In fact I don't know how to typify them except to agree that I have made them very contemporary. It would further be a lie to say that they weren't about me, because they are just as much about me as my other poetry. (*Letters* 362)

The tales which evoked an "unconscious message" in Sexton are precisely those to which she felt a subliminal connection; these poems are, therefore, "just as much about [her] as [her] other poetry." Sigmund Freud theorizes that some individuals may make "fairy tales into screen memories," so that the fairy tales themselves come to symbolize submerged feelings and conflicts, actually "tak[ing] the place of memories of their own childhood" ("Occurrence" 281). Moreover, the creative writer, suggests Freud, is likely to be, at some instinctive, subconscious level, in especially close touch with the meaning of fairy tales and dreams:

> There can be no doubt that the connections between our typical dreams and fairy tales and the material of other kinds of creative writing are neither few nor accidental. It sometimes happens that the sharp eye of a creative writer has an analytic realization of the process of transformation of which he is habitually no more than the tool. ("Interpretation" 246)

It is perhaps this process to which Sexton refers in "The Gold Key": "Do you remember when you / were read to as a child? / . . . have you forgotten? / Forgotten the ten P. M. dreams / where the wicked king went up in smoke?"

The most striking feature of these humorous, witty, and "grim" (pun intended?) poems, and the characteristic which makes them most dramatically Sexton's own, is the sound of the speaker's voice. When we read a fairy tale, or when we remember hearing fairy tales in our childhood, we hear immediately a disembodied, third-person omniscient speaker. "Once upon a time" does not attempt to make either narrator or tale sound individual or "real"; in fact, the attempt is just the opposite. In terms of reality, intensity, and immediacy, the fairy tale is the most distanced of any kind of narrative, and purposely so. By inviting the reader to listen to a little tale of something which might have happened a long, long time ago in make-believe land, the fairy tale narrator clears the way for offering to the widest possible audience a story which entertains while offering a cautionary or didactic message and manages to accomplish this purpose without offending anyone.

Sexton's transformations, on the other hand, are spoken by a very real first person narrator who reminds us constantly, with prologues and frequent interpolations, that mythic materials are being shaped for specific use. In a voice which demands our attention, this narrator is sarcastic, intense, sympathetic, and funny; she warns, or draws conclusions, or makes connections which are entirely her own. Listen, for example, to the opening of "Little Red Cap" in Grimm:

> Once upon a time there was a sweet little maiden. Whoever laid eyes upon her could not help but love her. But it was her grandmother who loved her most. She could never give the child enough. One time she made her a present, a small red velvet cap, and since it was so becoming and the maiden insisted on always wearing it, she was called Little Red Cap. (101)

Now hear the way in which Sexton begins the story of "Red Riding Hood" in *Transformations*:

> In the beginning
> there was just little Red Riding Hood,
> so called because her grandmother
> made her a red cape and she was never without it.
> It was her Linus blanket, besides
> it was red, as red as the Swiss flag,
> yes it was red, as red as chicken blood.
> But more than she loved her riding hood
> she loved her grandmother who lived
> far from the city in the big wood.

This story, says the speaker to the audience, may be cast in a "once upon a time" mode in your memory and imagination, but I am going to make it new for you, for me, for this specific moment. "In the beginning" there may have been "just little Red Riding Hood," but I am taking that basic, original tale and discovering in it my own personal and contemporary meanings.

And this speaker reminds us continually of her presence; her voice is persistent and ubiquitous. As Sexton admits in a 1970 letter in which she asks Kurt Vonnegut to write an introduction to her new volume:

> I've taken Grimms' Fairy Tales and "Transformed" them into something all of my own. . . . I do something very modern to them. . . . They are small, funny and horrifying. Without quite meaning to I have joined the black humorists. I don't know if you know my other work, but humor was never a very prominent feature . . . terror, deformity, madness and torture were my bag. But this little universe of Grimm is not that far away. (*Letters* 367)

The poet has indeed taken these tales, which perpetuate patriarchal and sexist values, which advocate traditional moral behavior, which facilitate ethical, psychological, and emotional growth, which help us to overcome the anxieties and conflicts of childhood and to achieve an integrated identity, and has done "something very modern to them" in precisely those ways which she mentions. The "universe of Grimm" is certainly not very far from the universe of Sexton, and in combining the two, this poet has indeed created "a different language."

We hear this language, the rhythm and sound of this unique voice, in all of the *Transformations* poems; each of them follows the prologue-tale form as well. "Snow White" can serve as an example. In the Grimm tale (196-204), Snow White's mother dies shortly after giving birth to her beautiful daughter. The new stepmother is "beautiful but proud and haughty, and she [can] not tolerate anyone else who might rival her beauty." Until Snow White is seven, the stepmother-queen's magic mirror assures the queen that she herself is fairest in the realm, but then the mirror begins to proclaim Snow White by far the fairest. The queen cannot bear this situation; "Like weeds, the envy and arrogance grew so dense in her heart that she no longer had any peace, day or night." In an attempt to get rid of Snow White, the queen enlists a huntsman to kill her stepdaughter and bring her lungs and liver to the queen, but the huntsman, amazed at Snow White's beauty, instead warns Snow White of her danger and brings to the queen the organs of a wild boar, which the queen eats. Snow White escapes into the forest ("Wild beasts darted by her at times, but they did not harm her"), finds the seven dwarfs' cottage, and agrees to keep house for the dwarfs (who are also impressed by her beauty) in exchange for their protection. The evil queen, meanwhile, discovers from her mirror that Snow White has survived ("As long as Snow White was the fairest in the realm, the queen's envy would leave her no peace"), and tries three times to eliminate her competition, each time by visiting the dwarfs' cottage in disguise and gaining access to Snow White with "pretty wares."

Twice the dwarfs arrive home in time to save Snow White, first by untying a tight staylace which has suffocated the beautiful girl, second by removing from her hair a poisoned comb. The third time, however, the queen entices Snow White to eat a poisoned apple. The dwarfs, unable to revive her, place her in a glass coffin which a passing prince, much later, sees; he falls in love with the beautiful, motionless girl, takes and then drops the coffin so that the apple flies out of Snow White's throat thus reviving her. The evil queen, invited to the wedding of Snow White and the prince, discovers once again from her mirror that Snow White lives and surpasses her in beauty. Arriving for the wedding she finds that "Iron slippers had already been heated over a fire, and they were brought over to her with tongs. Finally, she had to put on the red-hot slippers and dance until she fell down dead."

The contemporary sound of the language Sexton uses to "transform" this tale is the most conspicuous feature of the poem. Here is the first stanza and prologue of "Snow White and the Seven Dwarfs":

> No matter what life you lead
> the virgin is a lovely number:
> cheeks as fragile as cigarette paper,
> arms and legs made of Limoges,
> lips like Vin Du Rhône,
> rolling her china-blue doll eyes
> open and shut.
> Open to say,
> Good Day Mama,
> and shut for the thrust
> of the unicorn.
> She is unsoiled.
> She is as white as a bonefish.

The cadences are apparently effortless, clear and fluent; the diction is slightly slangy, confidential, and irreverent. Metaphor and adverb contribute to the breezy, "contemporary" sound. There is also, as Christopher Lehmann-Haupt points out in a 1971 review of *Transformations*, "the surprise of odd juxtapositioning: similes that deflate romance, humor as black as ebony" (147). Nearly every line of this first stanza uses a simile or metaphor to develop theme and tone: "the virgin is a lovely number," "cheeks as fragile as cigarette paper, / arms and legs made of Limoges," and so forth. Line lengths also express meaning; the three-word lines sound mechanical, doll-like. By all of these means, Sexton deflates characters' pretensions, undercuts most expectations held by readers of Grimm, and rebuilds in their place her own view of things. Later in the poem, when the wicked queen first visits Snow White and sells her a staylace, she fastens it "as tight as an Ace bandage, / so tight that Snow White swooned. / She lay on the floor, a plucked daisy." When the dwarfs undo the stay, "she revived miraculously. / She was as full of life as soda pop." Words and phrases are carefully crafted; the contrast between the older, appropriately fairy-tale usage of "swooned" and the slangy words surrounding it offers subtle demonstration that Sexton is subverting mythic materials for her own use. With this linguistic technique in mind, listen to the poem's second stanza, which follows the prologue:

> Once there was a lovely virgin
> called Snow White
> Say she was thirteen.
> Her stepmother,
> a beauty in her own right,
> though eaten, of course, by age,
> would hear of no beauty surpassing her own.
> Beauty is a simple passion,
> but, oh my friends, in the end
> you will dance the fire dance in iron shoes.
> The stepmother had a mirror to which she referred—
> something like the weather forecast—
> a mirror that proclaimed
> the one beauty of the land.

She would ask,
Looking glass upon the wall,
who is fairest of us all?
And the mirror would reply,
You are fairest of us all.
Pride pumped in her like poison.

Clearly, then, Sexton's use of language is one of the principal means by which she "transforms" fairy tales into modern poems, rebuilding the original Grimm materials into something all her own. Furthermore, what the poet achieves in these poems through language she also accomplishes with content. The analogy of a funhouse mirror is apt (and recalls the queen's magic mirror in "Snow White"): like a distorting mirror which enlarges and collapses parts of the original image reflected in it, both amusing and frightening the viewer, Sexton's *Transformations* poems distort the original Grimm tales, amplifying and magnifying some details, contracting and eliminating others. These poems are in several ways like an "enlarged paper clip" sculpture, both in language and in the content to which that language gives shape.

To continue with the example of "Snow White," the original Grimm version concerns, as we have seen, an innocent girl beset by the jealousy of her evil stepmother, saved by a hunter, by dwarfs, and by a prince, nearly destroyed by her own vanity and by a poisoned apple, and ultimately delivered from her troubles. Bruno Bettelheim discusses the emotional and psychological structure of this story: this tale, he writes, "deals essentially with the oedipal conflicts between mother and daughter; with childhood; and finally with adolescence, placing major emphasis on what constitutes a good childhood, and what is needed to grow out of it" (202). It is narcissism which undoes the queen and almost undoes Snow White; the queen is a jealous mother whose desire to claim Snow White's attractiveness and sexuality for herself is symbolized by her eating of what she thinks are

Snow White's lungs and liver. Snow White's own narcissism causes her to succumb to the queen's evil blandishments; she is nearly destroyed but is ultimately saved by others.

Among those "rescuing male figures" (205), says Bettelheim, are the hunter (a protective father-figure who sides secretly with the daughter but is too weak to stand up to the mother-queen) and the dwarfs (substitute fathers with whom she lives in peace but who, because they are not true relatives but represent only wish-fulfillment, are ultimately unable to protect her). The dwarfs (miners, who dig into the earth) represent, as well, "males who are stunted in their development and, as such, demonstrate along with Snow White "childhood before puberty," a period during which all forms of sexuality are relatively dormant" (211). Snow white's encounters with the queen dramatize her movement into adolescence, showing conflict and unsuccessful attempts to escape back into "a conflict-free latency period" (211) (represented by the dwarfs' cottage), together with the temptation of vanity as Snow White three times lets the queen into the house. After Snow White eats the poisoned apple, which stands for both love and sex (recollecting the apples of Aphrodite and Eden), the child in her dies and she is eventually reborn a woman from the glass coffin. But "before the 'happy' life can begin, the evil and destructive aspects of our personality must be brought under our control"; thus, the queen must die. "Untrammeled sexual jealousy, which tries to ruin others, destroys itself—as symbolized not only by the fiery red shoes but by death from dancing in them" (214).

All of these materials are present in Anne Sexton's transformations of "Snow White," but Sexton's magic mirror elevates Snow White's vanity to a position which moves beyond Grimm and Bettelheim, developing Snow White into someone who promises to follow in her stepmother's shoes, a sort of junior queen. In Sexton's "Snow White and the Seven Dwarfs," as in Grimm, the queen is narcissistic and envious, and Snow White is pre-pubescent, a "dumb bunny," with "china-blue doll eyes" that "open and shut." Unlike Grimm's, however, Sexton's forest through which Snow White passes on the way to the dwarfs' cottage is full of sexual threat: there is a wolf with "his tongue lolling out like a worm"; there are birds which "[call] out lewdly," and there are "snakes hung down in loops." Sexton also emphasizes the phallic nature of Snow White's environment during her stay with the dwarfs: the dwarfs themselves are "little hot dogs," and the poisoned comb which Snow White buys from the queen is "a curved eight-inch scorpion." Furthermore, if as Bettelheim says the eating of food represents in fairy tales the eater's desire to "acquire the powers or characteristics of what one eats" (207), Sexton demonstrates Snow White's sexual urges by having her eat the dwarfs' "seven chicken livers," as the poem has previously shown the queen's will to claim Snow White's beauty by eating her lungs and liver. In Grimm, Snow White eats only the dwarfs' more innocuous vegetables (variety unspecified) and bread.

Thus, in Sexton's "Snow White," as in many other poems of *Transformations*, sexual themes are magnified, and the fairy-tale promise of finding an emotionally mature, psychologically integrated, happy life remains unfulfilled. The heroine of Sexton's tale fails to work her way successfully through the complex problems of growing up and, becoming her mother, remains caught in a nightmarish world. At the end of the poem, the queen, clearly a figure of evil and destructive sexual jealousy, "danced until she was dead, / a subterranean figure, / her tongue flicking in and out / like a gas jet." But her destruction does not represent the lowering of the final barrier to Snow White's happy maturity, for

> Meanwhile Snow White held court,
> rolling her china-blue doll eyes open and shut
> and sometimes referring to her mirror
> as women do.

Sexton's Snow White remains a child who still has "china-blue doll eyes" that "open and shut"; since she now "refer[s] to her mirror," she has become in all ways the new queen. And this behavior is, says the poem's last line, not isolated but typical; it is something which "women do."

Other poems twist the mirror to focus on mother-daughter atrocities in other ways. The Sexton transformation of "One-Eye, Two-Eyes, Three-Eyes" stresses the psychotic and defensive tendency of mothers to bestow inordinate amounts of love upon freakish and crippled children, and concludes (as in "Snow White") with Two-Eyes repeating the maternal behavior which had caused her so much trouble. One-Eye and Three-Eyes, now "beggars, . . . were magical":

> They were to become her children,
> her charmed cripples, her hybrids—
> oh mother-eye, oh mother-eye, crush me in.
> So they took root in her heart
> with their religious hunger.

In "The Wonderful Musician," the fox is another daughter-figure, "a womanly sort," who tries unsuccessfully to kill the musician for deceiving her; in the end, the musician is "Saved by his gift / like many of us— / little Eichmanns, / little mothers— / I'd say." The sins of the mothers are visited upon the daughters in these and in other *Transformations* poems; this is a major theme in Sexton's earlier poetry as well. A daughter is never free from the destructive mother, even if she goes off to live in a castle. Either the mother becomes internalized in the daughter, or marriage offers no escape, or both. There are no fairy tale endings.

"Rapunzel" also explores the complicated mother-daughter relationship, but with a surprising twist. In the Grimm tale, Rapunzel is abandoned by her real mother, who prefers eating lettuce to keeping her first-born child, is imprisoned by her second mother, the witch called "Mother

Gothel," and ultimately finds happiness with her prince "who escorts her back to his kingdom, where he is received with joy, and they live happily and contentedly for a long time thereafter" (49). Sexton transforms this tale into Mother Gothel's story, introducing a theme which concerns love between women. "A woman who loves a woman is forever young," begins the prologue of "Rapunzel"; "The mentor / and the student / feed off each other." In Sexton's "Rapunzel," Mother Gothel is the woman desperately (and futilely) trying to retain her youth through loving a younger woman, and Rapunzel is very much like the "dumb bunny" Snow White, both needing and accepting indiscriminately the advances first of Mother Gothel and then the prince. This mother-daughter relationship is, however, apparently sexual; in the tower where Mother Gothel keeps and often visits her lovely prisoner, "Mother Gothel cried: / Hold me, my young dear, hold me, / and thus they played mother-me-do." The prince complicates this oedipal relationship; he is described in phallic terms (a "beast" with "muscles in his arms / like a bag of snakes," a "prickly plant" with "moss on his legs") and, blinded "by thorns" in his leap from Mother Gothel in the tower, he wanders "for years," "blind as Oedipus." Rapunzel eventually resolves this dilemma by making the heterosexual choice, leaving her mother and going off with her prince-father, "proving that mother-me-do / can be outgrown, . . . / A rose must have a stem." Yet the poem's closing stanza focuses wistfully and sympathetically on the abandoned Mother Gothel:

> As for Mother Gothel,
> her heart shrank to the size of a pin,
> never again to say: Hold me, my young dear,
> hold me,
> and only as she dreamt of the yellow hair
> did moonlight sift into her mouth.

Many other *Transformations* poems explore overtly oedipal materials. "Iron Hans" draws this conclusion: "He who kills his father / and thrice wins his mother / undoes the spell." In "Briar Rose (Sleeping Beauty)" the princess wakens from her long sleep "crying: / Daddy! Daddy!" Here Sleeping Beauty is transformed into Daddy's girl. "Papa" speaks these words to her in Sexton's poem's prologue: "Come be my snooky / and I will give you a root." And the princess' long sleep represents not the "time of quiet growth and preparation" to which Bettelheim refers, from which she will awaken into sexual maturity (232), but rather a recurring nightmare in which she is joined with her father:

> Daddy?
> That's another kind of prison.
> It's not the prince at all,
> but my father
> drunkenly bent over my bed,
> circling the abyss like a shark,
> my father thick upon me
> like some sleeping jellyfish.

Marriage is less than blissful in most of Sexton's transformations, since most heroines marry their "rescuing male figures"; in "The Maiden Without Hands," the king "marries a cripple / out of admiration." And in "The Twelve Dancing Princesses," the marriage of the oldest princess to the soldier who has reported the princesses' nightly escapades to the king may be a reward for the soldier, but it represents the end of fun and dancing for the princesses:

> He had won. The dancing shoes would dance
> no more. The princesses were torn from
> their night life like a baby from its pacifier.
> Because he was old he picked the eldest.
> At the wedding the princesses averted their eyes
> And sagged like old sweatshirts.

> Now the runaways would run no more and never
> again would their hair be tangled into diamonds,
> never again their shoes worn down to a laugh, . . .

In "The Frog Prince," too, marriage offers no happy ending for the princess. The poem seems to come to us from the borders of sanity; in the prologue the speaker chants:

> I write for you.
> I entertain.
> But frogs come out
> of the sky like rain.
> . . . .
> Frog has no nerves.
> Frog is as old as a cockroach.
> Frog is my father's genitals. . . .

Obviously phallic, this father-male-frog, who frightens and repulses the princess in both the Grimm and Sexton versions of the tale, imprisons her, in the Sexton poem, after becoming her prince-husband:

> He hired a night watchman
> so that no one could enter the chamber
> and he had the well
> boarded over so that
> never again would she lose her ball,
> that moon, that Krishna hair,
> that blind poppy, that innocent globe,
> that madonna womb.

As "The Frog Prince" uses imagery, among other poetic devices, to objectify the terror which the princess feels, many other transformations in this volume employ an imagery of violence to link love with torment, anger, and death. The theme so evident in *Love Poems* of lover as killer is present in *Transformations;* Sexton recapitulates it often here through references to World War II horrors, and the lover-killer may be husband, mother, or oneself. "The Frog Prince" is addressed to "Frau Doktor, / Mama Brundig." That Hansel and Gretel's mother does not love them is clear from the plot line and reinforced by diction; her plot to get rid of them is "the final solution." The evil witch, shoved into the oven by Gretel, "turned as red / as the Jap flag." Even Gretel turns from victim to victimizer; "Ja, Fraulein," she says to the witch, "show me how it can be done."

Anne Sexton appropriately begins "The Gold Key" with these words: "The speaker in this case / is a middle-aged witch, me. . . ." Sexton's identification of herself with witch is clear from such earlier poems as "Her Kind" (*TB*) and "The Black Art" (*APO*); in those poems, and in references in many others, the poet-writer-witch characterizes herself as different, misunderstood, and possessed, as one who transforms the ordinary domestic scene into something weird and nightmarish, who pays for her imaginative powers with her sanity or even with her life, but who bravely affirms her power nonetheless. She is subversive, creative, and shunned. This witch-creator shapes the *Transformations* poems; here Sexton's imagination produces outcast, evil, and powerful witch-characters, daughter-women who both love and hate their mothers and fathers but who come to perpetuate maternal transgressions in any case, and wives who are scheming, miserable, numb, or lifeless.

There should be no surprise, then, in Sexton's remark that these poems are not for children: "None of them are children's stories" (Heyen and Poulin 145). They are quite literally not addressed to children. The speaker's "Peers" who "draw near" as the "middle-aged witch" begins her tale are themselves middle-aged, or near it. "Alice" is "fifty-six," "Samuel" is "twenty-two," and we readers (however old we are) are part of that audience as well. The group meets for this story-telling session not to be lulled to sleep but to "have the answers."

In search of those answers, this speaker examines in her magic mirror both her and her fairy tale characters' experience of the joy and torment of love, parent-child relationships, oedipal confusion, personal anguish and suffering, and emotional breakdown. Sexton's new twist in this volume is that fairy-tale characters are sometimes elevated to a position as important as the speaker's own. Yet, as in a dream, all characters and events are projections of the speaker's psyche, and therefore, as in the confessional poem, all poetic materials point to the author-speaker herself.

In *Transformations*, most characters fail to emerge whole from their period of trial, but remain caught in their nightmares for eternity. The quiet, domestic, submissive fairy tale heroines become, in Sexton's poems, mindless, vapid dolls like Snow White or Cinderella. The happy future of these and other heroines is really a kind of living death; the princess of "The White Snake" and her new husband

> played house, little charmers,
> exceptionally well.
> So, of course,
> they were placed in a box
> and painted identically blue
> and thus passed their days
> living happily ever after—
> a kind of coffin,
> a kind of blue funk.
> Is it not?

Through sarcastic language and allusion, these poems tell us that marriage is, for women, either nightmare, or self denial, or imprisonment, or drudgery, or some kind of consolation prize. "Ever after" is not the successful achievement of a mature, integrated personality but rather unrelieved monotony, dehumanized captivity, or madness. The fairy tale promise of happiness remains unfulfilled and forever out of reach.

Sexton has commented that the *Transformations* "end up being as wholly personal as my most intimate poems, in a different language, a different rhythm, but coming strangely, for all their story sound, from as deep a place" (*Letters* 367). Certainly the painful themes of Sexton's more obviously confessional mode either are openly expressed in her "transformations" or lurk just beneath the surface. Yet that surface compels attention. The "different language, . . . different rhythm" is comic, droll, facetious, and brilliant; it is what Sexton calls "a dark, dark laughter" (*Letters* 365). We are delighted and amused by the cartoon quality of these word-sculptures even while recognizing the deadly seriousness of their subjects. We laugh our way through this book even while we are telling ourselves that we shouldn't be laughing; we chuckle in delight at Sexton's gallows humor, at her asides and quips, in spite of ourselves. These poems are, for all their desperate, bitter, nightmarish content, funny. As we have heard, Sexton admits that she was happy while writing them. She no doubt derived as much pleasure from composing these witty, pop-art poems as we experience in reading them.

Works Cited

Bettelheim, Bruno. *The Uses of Enchantment*. New York: Random House, 1977.

Freud, Sigmund. *The Interpretation of Dreams (1900)*. Ed. and Trans. James Strachey, Anna Freud, et al. *The Standard Edition of the Complete Psychological Works of Sigmund Freud*, Vol. IV. London: Hogarth Press, 1958.

Lehmann-Haupt, Christopher. "Grimm's Fairy Tales Retold." *New York Times* September 27, 1971, 37. Reprinted in J. D. McClatchy, ed. *Anne Sexton: The Artist and Her Critics*. Bloomington: Indiana U P, 1978, 146-49.

Heyen, William and Al Poulin. Interview with Anne Sexton. *No Evil Star:*

Selected Essays, Interviews, and Prose. Ed. Steven Colburn. Ann Arbor: U of Michigan P, 1985, 130-57.

Sexton, Anne. *All My Pretty Ones*. Boston: Houghton Mifflin, 1962.

___. *To Bedlam and Part Way Back*. Boston: Houghton Mifflin, 1960.

___. *Transformations*. Boston: Houghton Mifflin, 1971.

Sexton, Linda Gray and Lois Ames, eds. *Anne Sexton: A Self- Portrait in Letters*. Boston: Houghton Mifflin, 1979.

Zipes, Jack, ed. and trans. *The Complete Fairy Tales of the Brothers Grimm*. New York: Bantam , 1987.

CONFESSION AS SACRAMENT

Michael Burns

I was born in 1953, one month before the birth of Linda Sexton, Anne Sexton's older daughter. By the time I came to read contemporary poetry seriously, I was an undergraduate English major and a neophyte poet myself. Except for minor skirmishes, most of the battles of form and content had been fought. The clear winners were those women and men who had chosen to "make a clean breast of it." Indeed, as Maxine Kumin points out in her Foreward to *The Complete Poems,* the attacks on Sexton's subject matter seem today "almost quaint" (xxxiv).

The problem for many of us who started writing poetry when such confessional poets as Sexton, Snodgrass, Plath, Lowell, and Berryman were popular was not that our poetry was weak because we imitated their subject matter but that lost somewhere in our translations was an attention to form. And what has given much confessional poetry and, for many of us, the last books of Anne Sexton, a bad name is this inattention to the craft of the poem. I believe that Sexton should be forgiven her setting aside her craft in her terrible quest for a language that would save her. The "tricks" she mentions in her interview with William Packard in 1970 no longer kept her calm, no longer functioned to make the poem whole (45). She kept looking for the lost ingredients. Who could fault her? Still, when I look back over her work and guide my students to her poems, I want them to see confessional poetry at its best. For me, Sexton is at the height of her poetic powers in her first four books, especially *All My Pretty Ones.* She shows herself there to be not only gifted with image and metaphor, but also to be a careful and skilled craftsman.

Poems are "the tongue's wrangle, the world's pottage" she says in "With Mercy for the Greedy" (*APO*). Her friend has asked that she make an appointment for the sacrament of confession. Her response is often quoted:

> My friend, my friend, I was born
> doing reference work in sin, and born
> confessing it.

She has, in fact, gone beyond entering the booth to anonymously confess to the priest. In a fundamental sense, she has appropriated the sacrament—its formality, its ritual. The tools of her trade are her rhymes, the stanzas, the ways her colloquial diction stands in tension with the formal elements of her poems; they are what Richard Howard describes as her "lucid obstruction to sentimentality" (200). In *All My Pretty Ones* we find a poetry of sentences, and the pleasures we derive are often the result of her careful play of the sentence across the line break, the building of rhythm and rhyme towards a satisfying closure. The effect is not the one of the later poems, too often gimmicky and built of repetition and catalogue. In poems like "The Room of My Life" or "The Dead Heart" from *The Awful Rowing Toward God*, individual lines and images are startling and impressive, but I finish a poem and turn immediately to the next. The power of the poetry depends to a large extent on the accumulated thrust of the collection. In contrast, such poems as "The Truth the Dead Know," "All My Pretty Ones," "The Operation," and the less formal but lyrical "Young" stand easily alone. They reward us on rereading and through explication, as well as in their relationship to other poems.

As the sacrament makes possible a new beginning, a clean slate, "The Truth the Dead Know" seems to be a formal attempt by Sexton to reach a conclusion about the death of her parents and get beyond it. Discussing her epigraph to *All My Pretty Ones,* that a book should serve as "the ax for the frozen sea within us," Sexton makes an important statement about her poetry prior to 1965. She says that "writing puts things back in place" (qtd. in Marx 32). I cannot conceive of a poem that more carefully puts things back in place than this first poem of her second book. Using a traditional quatrain rhyming *abab* and shifting her tone from elegiac to lyric, she sets about the business of dealing with the dead and the living:

> Gone, I say and walk from church,
> refusing the stiff procession to the grave,
> letting the dead ride alone in the hearse.
>
> (from stanza 1)
>
> My darling, the wind falls in like stones
> from the whitehearted water and when we touch
> we enter touch entirely.
>
> (from stanza 2)

If we can impose Kafka's analogy of the ax and the frozen sea onto our reading of this poem alone, I'd have to say there is no instant cleavage of that sea. At this point in my understanding of Sexton's emotional state, I find not a frozen sea but a tightly contained yet moving body of water. In fact, the lines of the poem are like waves within a large room; they turn back on themselves. Out of the stiff elegiac procession of the first stanza, we move to the lyrical healing power of the physical in stanzas two and three, and finally to the carefully modulated "truth" in stanza four where things are put back in their place. The tone becomes emphatic. There is a rocking motion here, but despite the enjambment, the interlocking rhymes allow no forward motion out of the poem. For them, the dead, the iron gate swings shut, and for Sexton it seems a shutting out. The dead have their own refusals.

In "All My Pretty Ones," Sexton plays both parts—transgressor and absolver. She confesses the sins of the fathers and continues to try to put her guilt and their faults into perspective. She faces one of the most difficult problems a poet can face: how to tackle a whole history and find a way of presenting it that will consistently be more than flat prose broken into lines. How can she shape the narrative so that she can go beyond the specific details, no matter how graphic they are and how much they entertain for their own sakes? She needs to provide some interpretation of events, some intellectual and/or emotional response.

The triumph of the title poem of this collection can be attributed to Sexton's graceful crafting. Five stanzas of ten lines each rhyme *ababcdcdee*. No traditional ten-line stanza in English verse exists, so what Sexton has done is create a hybrid. Borrowing from the ottava rima stanza as it was used by Yeats and from the conventional Elizabethan sonnet, Sexton develops her material through the quatrain and punctuates it with the closing couplet. Take stanza one for example:

> Father, this year's jinx rides us apart
> where you followed our mother to her cold slumber;
> a second shock boiling its tone to your heart,
> leaving me here to shuffle and disencumber
> you from the residence you could not afford:
> a gold key, your half of a woolen mill,
> twenty suits from Dunne's, an English Ford,
> the love and legal verbiage of another will,
> boxes of pictures of people I do not know.
> I touch their cardboard faces. They must go.

Sexton is the contemporary confessor. She uses that part of the ritual necessary to give formality to her colloquial diction, but she adapts the traditions to meet her needs. Working in an accentual line, she is less concerned about syllable count than about her rhymes, which are, for the most part, perfect. Especially interesting is the powerful couplet in the last stanza. Here she uses feminine rhyme to emphasize the heart of the poem and perhaps the essential element of the sacrament of confession—to live and forgive:

> Whether you are pretty or not, I outlive you,
> bend down my strange face to yours and forgive you.

If Christ be not God and need is not belief, some men and women are faced with internalizing their rage and guilt for lack of an outlet. Sexton turns to her poetry as an outlet for the personal trauma of "The Operation." One important American writer, Denise Levertov, has expressed concern that Sexton's readers may confuse the pain of her poems with art itself—that one is necessary for the other (77). Maybe it is that "The Operation" deals less with the madness and self-inflicted pain than do many of the other poems and this fact makes it successful, but it is also clear that Sexton has found a voice to elevate a painful experience to the level of art. The trick is, of course, to make the story seem artless, simple yet honest, to hide the artifice. I'm reminded of Yeats's line:

> I said: a line will take us hours maybe,
> Yet if it does not seem a moment's thought,
> Our stitching and unstitching has been naught.
>
> ("Adam's Curse")

In "The Operation," enjambed lines of varying lengths, carefully placed caesuras, and a diction and rhyming that are most obvious for their commonness create the effect of the speaking voice, one that wants to get it all down in the right order so she can separate the guilty from the innocent:

> No reason to be afraid,
> my almost mighty doctor reasons.
> I nod, thinking that woman's dying
> must come in seasons,
> thinking that living is worth buying.

Kumin tells us that Sexton worked hard in this three part poem to establish through rhyme and shaping a "direct rendition of the actual experience" (Foreword to *The Collected Poems* xxvii). She achieves this effect through her narrative's chronology and her use of the present tense, but it is most important to consider what Kumin means when she says rhyme and shape affect us so. I believe that there is always some element of her form that is pulling away from our traditional expectations, paralleling the narrator's reluctance and skepticism. She creates her own form, and the tricks of her unusual rhyme schemes in part one and two propel the poem. They create the tension between the casual idiom of the speaker and the dramatic situation's demand for form and ritual, and this tension results in a level of language and metaphor that functions as the "lucid obstruction to sentimentality" which Howard describes. I quote from the last lines of stanza four, Part I:

> I walk out, scuffling a raw leaf,
> Kicking the clumps of dead straw
> that were this summer's lawn.
> Automatically I get in my car,
> knowing the historic thief
> is loose in my house
> and must be set upon.

And surely there is some parody of tradition in Sexton's choice of stanzaic pattern for Part II of the poem. Her manipulation of the form reminds me of her attitude towards the true sacrament of confession—that she has her own version which is better suited to her personal truth. Somewhere between Wordworth's "I Wandered Lonely As a Cloud" and Shakespeare's "Venus and Adonis," we find our narrator suspended in mid-air in the operating room, having her own sexuality threatened, altered by the surgeon's knife:

The great green people stand
over me; I roll on the table
under a terrible sun, following their command
to curl, hand touching knee if I am able.
Next, I am hung up like a saddle and they begin.
Pale as an angel, I float out over my own skin.

The technique that controls "Young" is an obvious one. The poem is one long sentence. The strategy is not so special in itself, but the poem seems to be an example of what we learn to look for in good poems—the successful marriage of form and content. Kumin tells us that "The Truth the Dead Know," "All My Pretty Ones," and "The Operation" were "sought after and hard-won poems" while "Young" was "achieved almost without effort" (Foreword to *The Complete Poems* xxvi). I come to it finally here because I do not mean to suggest that every good poem by Sexton was laboriously crafted and that all the bad ones could have been saved by craft. Some of her poems are what might be called "organically" right. Take "Young" for example. How many ways can we see that the shape and flow of the poem are connected with its imagery? I see it in the doors opening back into time and the way the lines are enjambed, giving us this "funnel of yellow heat running out" or in the boards that make up the house like the piling of line on line makes up the poem or, finally, in the narrow shape of the poem like the strange stalk of the young girl's body. This poem, which recalls that innocence of the girl not yet a woman, requires no learned forms, no borrowed ritual. She says "I . . . told the stars my questions / and thought God could really see . . . ."

A popular creative essay in our time has been "Total Eclipse" by Annie Dillard. I think Sexton would have liked it, that she would have understood and approved of its central metaphor. Jungian in her premise, Dillard creates a dark analogy. The human soul is like a mine thousands of feet below the surface, she says, and the brave among us must go down into the mine to discover and salvage the treasure. Sometimes we bring up a frightening, nameless beast; sometimes we find gold. Did Sexton have the same idea in mind when she wrote these lines in "Flee On Your Donkey"?

> You taught me
> to believe in dreams;
> thus I was the dredger.

If she did, then maybe she would not be offended by my perhaps too simple appraisal of her work. Dillard tells us that our only tools to bring back the treasure, our bucket and shovel, are grammar and lexicon. I like to think the poet has, along with the bucket and shovel and grammar and lexicon, another set of tools—the pick and the chisel, the stanza and the line. Unlike the axe for the frozen sea which may break loose a torrent of image and emotion, the pick carefully shapes and defines what is otherwise unmanageable and ugly. It and the chisel, the line, are capable of taking the personal confession of pain and suffering and madness and transforming it into a sacrament. They make it art. The poems Sexton brings to the surface are sometimes beast and sometimes gold. They are her sacrament, what she has to offer to us as readers who have chosen to hear her confession. I am most satisfied as a listener when she invokes her poetic tradition, yet tells her own honest tale.

Works Cited

Howard, Richard. "Anne Sexton: 'Some Tribal Female Who Is Known but Forbidden.'" McClatchy 200.

Kumin, Maxine. Foreword. *The Complete Poems*. By Anne Sexton. Boston: Houghton Mifflin, 1981. xix-xxxiv.

Levertov, Denise. "Light Up the Cave." McClatchy 77.

Marx, Patricia. "Interview with Anne Sexton." McClatchy 32.

McClatchy, J.D., ed. *Anne Sexton: The Artist and Her Critics*. Bloomington: Indiana U P, 1978.

ANNE SEXTON'S POETIC CONNECTIONS: DEATH, GOD, AND FORM

Lynette McGrath

I

In the work of any poet, adjustments in theme and form inevitably occur, sometimes signaling increased control of the poetic craft, sometimes a gradual decline of poetic power. The majority of Anne Sexton's readers, feminist and non-feminist alike, seem agreed that the changes in her poetic practice are signs of progressive decline rather than increased poetic power. In addition, the sensational details of her life and death have fed the accepted judgment that, because she was losing control of herself, at the end of her career Sexton abandoned the formally controlled style of her early work and took to writing loose, episodic poetry concentrated on themes of death and suicide. This view implies that Sexton's death brought to a tidy close the collapse into madness and despair already evident in her poetry. Alicia Ostriker, in her influential and much-needed study of women poets, further suggests that Sexton's failure to edge out of a relationship with an incorrigibly patriarchal God in some sense led to what Ostriker still sees as Sexton's ultimate self-defeat (Stealing 159-163).

All of these critical responses, however, are colored by their partisans' insufficient analysis of two cultural problems affecting women's poetry. In the first place, biographical material is, for a woman writer, especially susceptible to a type of unsympathetic or hasty interpretation which, in Sexton's case, encourages a reading of her life as a psychological failure. Second, such biographical references often determine value judgments about women writers' style and form. The readings of Sexton's life as a personal failure have thus promoted the view that her poetry also was doomed to fail, breaking down into necessarily confused and indeterminate forms of expression. I think that these readings, all emphasizing psychological and poetic failure and conditioned by culturally condoned notions of what a woman might or might not be expected to achieve, need an immediate adjustment. Dominant cultural attitudes toward women and suicide make an understanding of Sexton's biography and especially her view of death very difficult. A patriarchal view that expects in women weakness and loss of control will tend to interpret a woman's suicide not as a heroic act but as a sign of failure, seeing it as "hysterically" interruptive of her more appropriate biological and nurturing functions. On the other hand, even a sympathetically feminist view like Ostriker's may see a suicidal woman like Sexton as victimized by patriarchal pressures and betrayed by a "sex-rejecting misogynist zealot" hiding behind the image of a "gentle Jesus" (Stealing 162). Agreeing with Roland Barthes that a language of "innocence," "freed from responsibility in relation to all possible contexts," is unavailable (75-77), I would nevertheless like, insofar as is possible, to move away from a reading context that assumes that a woman's life and work must be interpreted only in terms of a dominant male hegemony and attempt a more independently feminist assessment of the successes Sexton achieved and the freedoms she grasped, however painfully, within her own self-defined contexts.

This admittedly tricky endeavor is further complicated by the commonly adopted critical point of view that considers poetry wholly successful only when it is organically structured, autonomous, whole, and achieving closure through metaphoric and thematic coherence, for these are not conventions that encourage sufficient appreciation of

Sexton's unique poetic accomplishments. To understand Sexton's poetic performance, we need to allow for the deconstruction of those principles that insist on poetic authority and packed-up "works of art." A critical approach that does not demand thematic and structural closure may better reveal how Sexton's later poetry, especially, functions.

I intend to develop an argument, just as feminist in sympathy as Ostriker's, to celebrate the remarkable degree to which, against all cultural odds, Sexton challenged the contexts that at first conditioned her writing. Negotiating these contextual circumstances required an ongoing and devastatingly honest self-examination, shifts in theme, an adjustment of the image of her Muse as an inspirational divinity whom Sexton struggled to release from the oppressive role of the traditional patriarchal God, and finally the structural experimentation made possible by these other risky and courageous explorations.

In particular, my argument annotates thematic changes in Sexton's poetry that are significant, not casual, and that indicate a growth away from feelings of confinement and infantilism toward a sense of openness, power, and freedom. These thematic changes are accompanied by a changing poetic style which produces a poem that opens itself to include the reader instead of closing itself around the poet. The shift away from metrically, stanzaically, and syntactically ordered pieces to loose, open-ended forms does not, in my view, represent poetic failure but a brave choice to involve the reader with the poem and with the poet's experience.

Reading through the codes of Sexton's poetic and personal context, we find that these thematic and structural changes reflect the increased confidence she achieved in midlife and mid-career. This confidence she based in a Muse-like divinity whose nature she adjusted to fit her poetic and female experience. Under the aegis of this inspiriting image, the once tight, closed statement, centered on self-disclosure, expands toward liberation and draws the reader into the experience the poem describes. As the audience is urged more insistently into the poetic experience, formal polish and subtlety diminish, and the whole poem shifts into a relaxed form, structurally open and latent rather than closed and already realized.

Such a reading of Sexton's work (in the nature of an *apologia*), documents poetic growth instead of failure and perplexity. It implies also a connection between her suicide and the epigraph to the last book of poetry published under her supervision before her death: "There are two ways to victory—to strive bravely, or to yield. How much pain the last will save we have not yet learned" (*AW*). Sexton's last poetry and her death may well represent her brave yielding to a psychological possibility which she had already actualized in overt poetic configuration.

In any case, Sexton wanted, I believe, to develop a poetry based on an interaction among what she called a "story-telling" poet (Kevles passim), an open text, and a responsive reader. The success of this interaction depended heavily on Sexton's decision to take conscious risks with the form of her poems—risks that have led to some critical misjudgments, but which, in the long run, will be acknowledged as having successfully extended her poetic range rather than reducing it.

II

Although major thematic and metaphoric constructs remain constant throughout Sexton's poetry, their range of reference and significance changes. Fundamental in Sexton's poetry is the project of self-exploration. She engages in a prolonged and valiant effort to know herself, while realizing that this kind of self-analytic writing might require of both poet and reader violent and even potentially self-mutilating means: "a book should serve as the ax for the frozen sea within us" (epigraph to *All My Pretty Ones*). Initially, Sexton's poetry sought a means to break up the frozen sea within herself; the later poetry expands its therapeutic goals by attempting to release the reader from the frozen role of passive observer. With regard to the early poetry, there may be some truth in Joyce Carol Oates's observation that "Sexton emphasizes her private sorrows to the exclusion of the rest of the world" (review of *The Awful Rowing Toward God*). The unashamed self-exposure in "The Operation" (*APO*) is typical:

> After the sweet promise,
> the summer's mild retreat
> from mother's cancer, the winter months of her death,
> I come to this white office, its sterile sheet,
> its hard tablet, its stirrups, to hold my breath
> while I, who must, allow the glove its oily rape.

Furthermore, we know that Sexton began to write poetry seriously at the urging of her therapist; she records her absorbed fascination with the self-healing process of poetry in "For John, Who Begs Me Not to Enquire Further," (*TB*) a poem addressed to her teacher John Holmes, who tried to dissuade her from writing what he saw as "selfish" poetry (Middlebrook, "Housewife" 493):

> in the end, there was
>
> a certain sense of order there;
> something worth learning
> in that narrow diary of my mind,
> in the commonplaces of the asylum
> where the cracked mirror
> or my own selfish death
> outstared me.

Although Sexton's honest self-confrontations may strike

a sympathetic response from the reader, the early poems are not really designed to produce this result. There are no invitations to shared experience, only fortuitous connections between Sexton's perceptions and the reader's. To begin with, Sexton seems to have used the self-revealing poem as a medium of self-discovery. For example, in "To a Friend Whose Work Has Come To Triumph" (*APO*), or "With Mercy for the Greedy" (*APO*), Sexton addresses her early poems outward to a particular person rather than to a general audience. The widely communicating, reaching poems, characteristic in the last books, are exceptional in these early works. In typical early poems, Sexton records her confinement within the "wifely" domestic role bounded by the house or kitchen—"Some women marry houses. / It's another kind of skin" ("Housewife")—and within the "womanly" sexual role invaded and possessed by the male body:

> I looked long upon you,
> love-bellied and empty,
> flipping my endless display
> for you, my cold, cold,
> coverall man
> . . . .
> It is virtually guaranteed
> that you will walk into me like a barracks.
>
> ("Moon Song, Woman Song," *APO*)

Seeking to dramatize her sense of restriction and alienation, Sexton frequently writes of herself as a child, speaking in a child-like voice, confined and dominated by the adult world. The plight of the child parallels the woman's. Neither is free or articulate; both remember—and are directed by—"the song my mother / used to sing" ("The Fish That Walked," *AW*). This late poem implies that, through poetry, the child grown to womanhood will eventually become freely eloquent, but Sexton does not explicitly draw connections with poetry as a means to freedom until her last work. More typically, in the early poetry, as in "Those Times" (*LD*), Sexton associates her present woman's frustrations with those of her childhood. The voice of a rejected and confined child is heard in the rhythms and language of much of the poetry, although the alienated, unripe personality does occasionally deride itself. This level of ironic self-appraisal, when it occurs, betokens a degree of mature self-understanding that in the later poetry becomes most vivid and emphatic and begins there to include the reader in the ironic transaction.

"Baby Picture" (*DN*) is exemplary of this later style of self-analysis. As the poet gazes at an old, peeling picture of her seven-year-old self, she sees, without nostalgia or self-pity, what she then was and now is. The view of herself as she is now is telescoped into what she was as a child, and the juxtaposed images are appraised with ironic detachment. By the time of *The Death Notebooks*, in which this poem appears, Sexton has substituted self-appraisal for self-pity. She casts herself now in the saving role she has sought all along: she needs to write "real," as she puts it, "because that is the one thing that will save (and I do mean save) other people" (Sexton and Ames 110). In her last two books, Sexton emphatically insists on connections between herself and her audience and God. These connections facilitated the self-discovery through affiliation—which feminist theorists now understand to be characteristic of women's experience—more effectively than did her initial attempts to achieve a detached, solipsistic sense of the self. The unexpected "wild card" for Sexton in this eventual arrival at self-recognition is the assisting factor of death.

As Sexton's early poems develop the theme of confinement in its varying aspects, the imagery of death as enclosure also insistently recurs. Death is the extinction of love: "The end of the affair is always death" ("The Ballad of the Lonely Masturbator," *LP*). One enters into death as into an enclosed space: "Thief!— / how did you crawl into, / crawl down alone / into the death I wanted so badly and for so long" ("Sylvia's Death," *LD*), and: "In the mind there is a thin alley called death / and I move through it as / through water" ("For the Year of the Insane," *LD*). Death is an "old belonging" ("Sylvia's Death"), into which one grows backwards, regressing to the narrow restricted place where childhood and death converge: "Closer and closer / comes the hour of my death / as I rearrange my face, grow back, / grow undeveloped and straight-haired. All this is death" ("For the Year of the Insane" *LD*).

Yet the symbolic weight of death is much more complicated than this for Sexton. Even attached as it is in the early poetry to a sense of restriction, death is still yearned after as a cessation from pain: "Death's a sad bone; bruised, you'd say, / and yet she waits for me, year after year, / to so delicately undo an old wound, / to empty my breath from its bad prison" ("Wanting to Die," *LD*), and as an escape: "and I know at the news of your death, / a terrible taste for it, like salt" ("Sylvia's Death"). This early taste for death establishes a foundation for a later treatment of death as the means of freedom instead of the way to confinement.

As with the themes of self-exploration and childhood, the early treatment of death contains an undercurrent of feeling which foreshadows a subsequent change of attitude. The central lines of "The Starry Night," (*APO*)—a crucial poem in Sexton's development—read: "This is how / I want to die: / into that rushing beast of the night, / sucked up by that great dragon, to split / from my life with no flag, / no belly, / no cry." The longing for death is at the same time a longing for release and freedom: "Sexton's death wish is envisioned as a slow diffusion of the self into air, elements, separation. . . . There is the suggestion not of diminishment so much as assimilation into a larger whole" (Mizejewski 342). The representation of death as both engulfing and releasing is not usual in the early poetry, but by the time of *The Death Notebooks,* with its ambiguous epigraph—"Look, you con man, make a living out of your death"—death has become a means to life. The last poems see the self as passing through death, whether symbolic or literal, into a more spacious, freer mode of existence within which the personal and poetic self can be defined and affirmed through connections, made at one end of the poetic process with a divine Muse, and at the other with the reader.

III

The Death Notebooks and *The Awful Rowing Toward God* present this wider, freer prospect in the context of a poetic and personal alliance with God, but revise the traditional aspect of a restrictive and disciplinary patriarchal divinity. What amounts to a redefinition begins most clearly in "Somewhere in Africa" (*LD*):

> Let God be some tribal female who is known but forbidden.
> Let there be this God who is a woman who will place you
> upon her shallow boat, who is a woman naked to the waist,
> moist with palm oil and sweat, a woman of some virtue
> and wild breasts, her limbs excellent, unbruised and chaste.

In "For Eleanor Boylan Talking With God" (APO), "God has a brown voice, as soft and full as beer"; "God is as close as the ceiling"; "Now he is large, covering up the sky / like a great resting jellyfish." In "For God While Sleeping" (*APO*), the Christ figure is a "poor old convict"; the relationship between the poet and her God is familiar, equalized, reciprocally intimate. This kind of relationship, which allows for devotion but rejects a hierarchically-based reduction of the worshipping woman, is thoroughly typical in Sexton's late religious verse. God becomes all-inclusive, literally omnipresent, Protean, androgynous, non-authoritarian. Sexton discovers that the divine is utterly pervasive and sanctifying, even to the extent that "the gods of the world were shut in the lavatory" ("Gods," *DN*). The beauty of musical harmonies also includes God: "A flute came too, / joining the five strings, / a God finger over the holes" ("The Fury of Guitars and Sopranos," *DN*). And in "The Rowing Endeth" (*AW*), a liberating union with God accompanies the experience of death, which is a crucial component in a unified and equalized creation. The project to eliminate God's oppressive and judgmental aspects enables Sexton to make spiritual peace with a more expansive divinity. In the context of this new relationship, Sexton thematically welds together her enhanced self knowledge, her willingness to engage with death, her sense of psychological freedom, and her text's connection with the now all-important reader. Unhappy self-absorption and a sense of restriction are replaced by a sense of self-acceptance and of freedom from the harrying demons that pervade the early poetry. Self-critical complaint changes into ironic and even affectionate self-appraisal:

> I am a fortunate lady.
> I've gotten out of my pouch
> and my teeth are glad
> and my heart, that witness,
> beat well at the thought.
> Oh body, be glad. You are good goods.
> Middle class lady,
> you make me smile.
>
> ("Hurry Up, Please, It's Time," *DN*)

Where Sexton now assumes the role of the child, it is to mock kindly and ironically what remains of the child in herself, and also to emphasize the child's need for the connection and support she now finds in divine love. She now sees the domestic role as salvaging and soothing instead of destructively restrictive. Accepted freely, the elements of domestic life may be small means to saving ends, especially to human connections—"Herbs, garlic, / cheese, please let me in! / Souffles, salads, / Parker House rolls, / please let me in! / Give me some tomato aspic, Helen! / I don't want to be alone" ("The Fury of Cooks," *DN*). The creative offices of God may bring to resolution even the contest for power between man and woman: the concluding injunction in "Two Hands" (*AW*), to the two God-created hands, one "man," the other "woman," is: "Unwind hands, / you angel webs, / unwind like the coil of a jumping jack, / cup together and let yourselves fill up with the sun / and applaud, world, applaud." Sex, once seen as invasive, now becomes a divinely blessed connection: "All the cocks of the world are God, blooming, blooming, blooming / into the sweet blood of woman" ("The Fury of Cocks," *DN*).

An analysis that styles itself feminist can hardly pass over in silence this kind of association of masculine sexual virility and divine power, especially in light of Alicia Ostriker's claim that Sexton was engaged in a "grotesque attempt to placate and conciliate a God of our Fathers who is being experienced as atrocious, brutal, a betrayer" (Writing 82)—a reading which I think should be contextualized differently. Ostriker's "Freudianized" reading of Sexton as caught in the rapacious grasp of a Father-God leads her to clump Sexton with Atwood and Wakoski, none of whom, she says, was able to "synthesize opposites or imagine contexts larger than the ancient text of dualism" (Stealing 162). In Sexton's case at least, as I shall show below, I think this conclusion is really not justifiable.

That Sexton did not, and probably could not, dispense with images of masculine sexual influence in her metaphoric store is indisputable. She did not have available the same insights that, post-Mary Daly, post-Elizabeth Fiorenza, post-Linda Gordon, have helped us understand the risks of heterosexuality for women and the phallocentric attachments of the divine. This does not mean, however, that her project to revise the image of a patriarchal God failed. While still incorporating some of the culturally pandemic qualities of masculine power in her image of the divine, Sexton made a serious effort to represent the divine figure as non-dominant, to cut back its aggressive power, to imbue it with the nurturing and sexual qualities of female power (Lauter passim), and to weigh her own woman's poetic power in a more equalized relationship with it. In fact, it is not the inevitable imbalance of power that prescribes an antagonistic relation between the divine and the human. On the contrary, the question is whether Sexton is submissive to, and oppressed by, that power, and she is not. She is, rather, assertive and, as Diane Middlebrook says, "impudent."

As enlightened as feminists may have been by all of the theory that has been worked out since Sexton's time, we still struggle to free ourselves from the orbit of male power. To deny Sexton the successes she undoubtedly achieved in beginning to deconstruct the closed poem and the patriarchal God, because she did not also complete a deconstruction of sexual identity, is to layer our own contexts onto Sexton's and to accede to the interminable power of the patriarchal. I prefer to celebrate the movement along the stages of the journey Sexton began to make toward the remolding of the divine as universal and polymorphous. Her poems in quest of this image are more than simply that. They are also communications in which a relationship with the reader is established by analogy with the poet's relationship with God. In other words, even what we may now view as Sexton's limited renegotiation of the nature of her God nevertheless made it possible for her to embark on a major new poetic venture. As a consequence of this newly defined relationship with a revised God, Sexton now found ways to link what she once saw as opposing and dualistic activities: "Words" (*AW*) represents the creation of poetry and the creation of an omelet as two aspects of the same large process. Earlier thematic oppositions can also be resolved. Processes, connections, and sequences now define the ultimate nature of human experience. Good and evil are essentially interdependent; in order to pursue good, Sexton now suggests that we must recognize and accept evil as an inevitable part of our lives: "one must learn about evil, / . . . . / one must see the night before one can realize the day" ("Evil Seekers," *AW*). In God, the body-soul dichotomy itself can reach a baptismal resolution: "He is all soul / but He would like to house it in a body / and come down / and give it a bath / now and then" ("The Earth," *AW*). And death follows in natural order as part of the process of life. A particularly useful gloss for Sexton's later treatment of death may be found in the presentation of death by another "suicidal" woman who also engaged in the painful effort to carve out a space for her own independent point of view within an unencouraging patriarchal context. The need of Leonard Woolf and Quentin Bell to "explain" Virginia Woolf's suicide as the result of a predictable mental collapse has been revised in a number of feminist readings: by Jane Marcus; by Phyllis Rose—who has challenged not only the "madness" reading of Woolf's death but also the right appropriated by Leonard Woolf and Bell to name her death a suicide; by Rachel Du Plessis—who has shown us that Clarissa Dalloway, perhaps like Woolf herself, interprets suicide "as a symbolic rejection of rapacious power relations" (58); and by Deborah Guth. In a comment on Woolf that is exactly pertinent to Sexton, Guth says that "in no way then is death experienced as disintegration and loss. On the contrary, it is life that has been experienced this way, while death is seen as a triumph of the self, a moment of total being" (225). In other words, death presents a "sense of self-affirmation, defiance and ultimate victory over the hostile, disruptive forces of life" (223). Or, to quote Clarissa Dalloway herself, who satisfactorily sums up the view expressed in Sexton's last poems: "Death was defiance. Death was an attempt to communicate, people feeling the impossibility of reaching the centre which mystically evaded them; . . . there was an embrace in death."

In the same way, Sexton's later poems present death as the savored beginning of a connection, both comically macabre and sexual, for which one prepares as for a wedding; it is no longer a narrow end that opposes and destroys life: "But when it comes to my death / let it be slow, / let it be pantomime, this last peep show, / So that I may squat at the edge trying on / my black necessary trousseau" ("For Mr. Death Who Stands With the Door Open," *DN*). In *The Death Notebooks*, death becomes a freeing experience, a release into spiritual freedom. "The approaches to death are by illumination," said Christopher Smart, and in the psalms modeled on Smart's *Jubilate Agno*, Sexton concludes: "God was as large as a sunlamp and laughed his heat at us and therefore we did not cringe at the death hole" ("O Ye Tongues, Tenth Psalm"). Death is a release of the self into the divine, a speeding up of the rowing toward God, a union which triumphs over life's confining power. In her last books of poetry, Sexton's connection with a Muse-like, inspirational God promotes the changes in theme, tone, and attitude that I have traced above. Most striking, though, is a change of mind that drew Sexton out of the ranks of poets who use the poem as a communication with the self about the self in order to join those who see the poem as potentially enlightening for others. The audience presupposed by her poetry is larger and more eclectic now than before, and the poetic consequences are apparent in the poet's increased awareness of her readers and in her increased sophistication about both overt and covert ways of communication. Overtly, through image, metaphor, and theme, Sexton's poems insistently encourage the reader to participate in or learn from the poet's own experience. The later poems are filled with an assured sense that what has helped the poet reach self-definition and self-affirmation will also help the reader. The poems in *The Awful Rowing Toward God* are neither cries for help nor suicide notes. They are poems of freedom and power that confidently propose an alternative to life and its suffering in the embrace of death and God. These poems teach by example and sometimes by direct insistence on the need for connection: "take off your flesh, unpick the lock of your bones. / In other words / take off the wall / that separates you from God" ("The Wall"). Some of the poetry develops a baroque persuasive fervor:

> If religion were a dream, someone said,
> then it were still a dream worth dreaming.
>
> True! True!
> I whisper to my wood walls.
> . . . .
> For I look up,
> and in a blaze of butter is
> Christ,
> . . . .
> a lamb that has been slain,
> his guts drooping like a seaworm,
> but who lives on, lives on. . . .
>
> ("Is It True?")

The idea inspiring this poetry is expressed at the end of "Welcome Morning": "The Joy that isn't shared, I've heard, / dies young." Another version of the same idea concludes "What The Bird With The Human Head Knew": "Abundance is scooped from abundance, / yet abundance remains." And this abundance is shared by Sexton with the readers of her poetry. Reclaimed from a state of despair herself, she passes on a talismanic flower, given her by a friend, to another in need: "My kindred, my brother, I said / and gave the yellow daisy / to the crazy woman in the next bed" ("The Sickness Unto Death").

IV

By covert means, in the structuring of her last poems, Sexton sought to open lines of communication between herself and her audience. Anne Sexton began as a poet of polished, formalist structures like the variable refrain in "The Starry Night" (*APO*) or the tight narrative in "The Double Image" (*TB*). Her early poems are carefully made and finished: "And we both wrote poems we couldn't write / and cried together the whole long night / and fell in love with a delicate breath / on the eve that great men call for death" ("December 4th," *CP*). Rhythm and line length in the early poems integrate with and affirm the statement: "avenues of fish that never got back, / all their proud spots and solitudes / sucked out of them" ("The Sun," *LD*). And, characteristically, these poems conclude tersely: "As for me, I am a watercolor. / I wash off" ("For My Lover Returning to His Wife," *LP*); "Look, / when it is over he places her, / like a phone, back on the hook" ("You All Know the Story of the Other Woman," *LP*); "O.K. God, / if it's the end of the world, / it must be necessary" ("The Sea Corpse," *CP*).

In the earlier poems, then, the structure is coherent, and the patterns of rhyme, stanza, and syntax are clear and tight. The poem as a finished object expresses a finished experience; in a sense, Sexton's solipsistically closed view of experience predicts a closed, structured control. The already realized statement discourages any possible response. Here, as elsewhere, a strong connection exists between presentations of the self and evidences of the text; as Sexton's point of view altered, so too did the formal nature of her poetry. Together with the thematic and metaphoric invitations of the text, structural clues begin to entice the reader's participation in the experience revealed in the poem. Adrienne Rich has described the movement that occurred in her own poetry as she grew dissatisfied with traditional poetic structures as ways to promote a sense of process and dialogue (Rich 89); this shift from structured form to a sense of process also occurred with Sexton.

As Sexton's poems become less structurally controlled, they begin to incorporate the loose syntax of conversation: "When I was a child / there was an old woman in our neighborhood / whom we called the Witch" ("The Witch's Life," *AW*); "O fallen angel, the companion within me, whisper something holy / before you pinch me / into the grave" ("The Fallen Angels," *AW*). Syntactic structure is not here adjusted to the regular rhythms of traditional poetry but remains spontaneous and apparently arrived at casually. The cataloguing and listing of ideas and images in no ordered, sequential pattern characterizes "Gods" (*DN*), "The Fury of Sunday" (*DN*), "Faustus and I" (*DN*), the psalms of "O Ye Tongues" (*DN*), and "The Death Baby" (*DN*) while the structural elements within these poems also fall into relaxed, episodic relationships. Sexton abandons formal control almost entirely in her later poetry, presumably because such restrictions mirror the life-boundaries she wants to overcome. The adoption of looser forms asserts her sense of personal freedom and encourages the reader to an engagement with the text. As Louise Rosenblatt points out, "When we turn from the broader environment of the reading act to the text itself, we need to recognize that a very important aspect of the text is the clues it provides as to what stance the reader adopts" (81). These casually worded poems with their looser structures retain their power even beyond their conclusions. Sexton achieves this movement of the poem beyond itself into the reader's life by employing open-ended forms. The ways in which the poems in the last volumes conclude are highly significant, with questions asked, potentialities left open, and conditional structures remaining incomplete. Covert tactics of communication, established through the poetic structures, invite the reader to participate in the experience of the poem:

"I had a dream once, / perhaps it was a dream, / that the crab was my ignorance of God. / But who am I to believe in dreams?" "The Poet of Ignorance" (*AW*) asks a question and requires the reader to provide the missing response, as also in "The Play" (*AW*) which concludes:

> The curtain falls.
> The audience rushes out.
> It was a bad performance.
> That's because I'm the only actor
> and there are few humans whose lives
> will make an interesting play.
> Don't you agree?

Similarly, in "The Earth Falls Down" (*AW*) the conditional "if" structure is left incomplete; the following, expected "then" response is to be supplied by the reader. "Is It True?" (*AW*) successfully pushes this cooperative alliance with the reader to its probable limit; the poem, though long, is loosely tied together, forcing the reader to provide the transitions, yet it is certainly one of Sexton's most powerful poetic achievements.

More subtly, poems like "Praying on a 707" (*DN*), "Rowing" (*AW*), "Jesus Walking" (*DN*), "The Witch's Life" (*AW*), and "Riding the Elevator Into the Sky" (*AW*), although their syntactic patterns are complete, evoke experiences the reader is urged to emulate. Especially in *The Awful Rowing Toward God*, Sexton typically chooses not to tie off the ends of her poems, insisting instead on opening options for the reader. At the time when this shifting emphasis was occurring in her poetry, Sexton applauded the kind of poem that could induce its readers to an adequate, active response. Commenting on the way in which Snodgrass's "Heart's Needle" had moved her to reclaim her daughter, she said: "And what could be more beautiful than a poem to move you to action of such a type?" (Heyen Interview 312).

This sense of the reader as a creative respondent reduced Sexton's need to control her poetic statements in an ordered form. She gave up using the formal effects which she dismissed as "tricks," rejecting the "kind of short lyric that remains coin of the realm in American poetry" (Middlebrook, "Poet," 313). The reader was now regularly expected to complete the poem; Sexton absolved herself of the responsibility to do so. As Louise Rosenblatt describes this process, "Instead of functioning as a rigid mold, the text is seen to serve as a pattern which the reader must to some extent create even as he is guided by it" (129). "Listen," says Sexton, "We must all stop dying in the little ways, / in the craters of hate, / in the potholes of indifference— / a murder in the temple" ("The Children," *AW*). Because it accommodates her need to invite the reader to participate in a spiritually illuminating experience like her own, an open-ended form is especially appropriate in Sexton's more emphatically religious verse. Sexton's last poems extend their scope indefinitely into their readers' lives by implying the need to continue beyond the poem's graphemic termination. Finally, her later poems link together the role poetry plays in the writer's life, the consequent forms and functions of the poem, and the role it may play for the reader.

Sexton always acknowledged the difficult and ambiguous relationship of the poet with her art, a relationship specifically complicated when the poet is a woman:

> A woman who writes feels too much,
> Those transports and portents!
> As if cycles and children and islands
> weren't enough; as if mourners and gossips
> and vegetables were never enough.
> She thinks she can warn the stars
> A writer is essentially a spy.
>
> ("The Black Art," *APO*)

Such a poem reveals Sexton's awareness that she is trespassing in alien territory both because of the intrinsically uncooperative nature of language, and because of the limited precedence established by other women poets for a "lady of evil luck" who longs to be what she can only visit ("The Fish That Walked," *AW*). Even though, at their best, the words of poetry are benignant miracles—"doves falling out of the ceiling" ("Words," *AW*)—as it is coming into being, the poem shifts and slips elusively in the poet's grasp: "However, nothing is just what it seems to be. / My objects dream and wear new costumes, / compelled to, it seems, by all the words in my hands" ("The Room of My Life," *AW*). "Words" deals extensively with the fugitive nature of the poem: Words "can be both daisies and bruises," and "often they fail"; "I have so much I want to say, / so many stories, images, proverbs, etc. / But the words aren't good enough / the wrong ones kiss me."

This same sense of frustration in hunting the difficult means of poetic expression is seen in "Said the Poet to the Analyst" (*TB*):

> My business is words. Words are like labels,
> or coins, or better, like swarming bees.
> I confess I am only broken by the sources of things;
> as if words were counted like dead bees in the attic,
> Unbuckled from their yellow eyes and their dry wings.
> I must always forget how one word is able to pick
> out another, to manner another, until I have got
> something I might have said . . .
> but did not.

Sexton sees herself as both "saved and lost," and thus connected with the fallen angels who "come on to my clean / sheet of paper and leave a Rorschach blot," "a sign which they shove . . . around till something comes" ("The Fallen Angels," *AW*). Writing poetry for Sexton is not a neat experience of direct inspiration breathed into the worthy, receptive, and authoritative poet by the gods; it is a messy, human, even gendered process, attractively and acknowledgedly flawed, affirming connections among female poet, open poem, reconstructed God, and participating reader. It is clear that the poetic text was not, for Sexton, an autonomous, organic, unified object—any more than she was herself. Sexton finally does not claim authority over her poem, but passes on to the reader the responsibility of "owning" the text. "Look to your heart," she tells her reader, "that flutters in and out like a moth. / God is not indifferent to your need. / You have a thousand prayers / but God has one" ("Not So. Not So," *AW*). Here, if anywhere, we may relevantly link Sexton's life to her poetic practice. Even without benefit of Carol Gilligan, Nancy Chodorow, or Jean Baker Miller, Sexton was able to construct a sense of herself and her poetry as essentially affiliative and defined by connection rather than by autonomy. She seems to have rejected at the same time both the notion of an autonomous, successful self and the model of a unified, organic, closed text. Even without the later feminist and deconstructionist critiques of phallogocentric aesthetic by critics like Gayatri Spivak, Alice Jardine, and Peggy Kamuf, Sexton wrote poetry whose very form embodies a critique of what has, until recently, been accepted as the dominant Western aesthetic, but which we now recognize as only one among many potential cultural and aesthetic constructs. In addition, Sexton's later poetic style seems to affirm the view that "a poem cannot be understood apart from its results. Its 'effects,' psychological or otherwise, are essential to any accurate description of its meaning, since the meaning has no effective existence outside of its realization in the mind of a reader" (Tompkins ix).

As I have been arguing, Sexton's sense of her own and her poetry's potential came to depend on connections, not drawn in the usual way, detachedly and aesthetically, among elements internal to the poem, but established personally and experientially, among factors which, though external to the poem, nevertheless dictate its theme and form. First, a relationship is established between a polymorphous Muse-God, not detached from the woman poet by conventions of gender, position, or sanctimony, "who owns heaven / but . . . craves the earth, / . . . even its writers digging into their souls" ("The Earth," *AW*), and the writer, who addresses herself in priestly fashion to "the typewriter that is my church / with an altar of keys always waiting" ("Is It True?" *AW*). Ultimately, it seems that Sexton came to view death as a way to embrace this particular connection. Second, a relationship is confirmed between poet and reader, with the poem serving as its connective link. At the end of her career, the writing of poetry was for Sexton an activity akin to the holy, a means of earthly salvation for its creator and a means of communicating the possibility of salvation to the reader. As poet-priestess, Sexton was able to see that "Evil is maybe lying to God. / Or better, lying to love" ("Is It True?") and that good is an authentic realization of the consecrating love that connects us all. An auspicious corroboration of my argument concerning Sexton's commitment to the value of connection is found in the poem Linda Gray Sexton chose to conclude *45 Mercy Street*. Appropriating the two roles most metaphorically exemplary of connection in our culture, Sexton presents herself as mother and priest—agents and beneficiaries of the rich and innumerable connections between divine and human, between individual and individual, between generation and generation, between life and death, between Muse and poet, between poet and reader. In "The Consecrating Mother," Sexton dedicates herself to a womanly consecrating role: "I am that clumsy human / on the shore / loving you, coming, coming, / going, / and wish to put my thumb on you like the Song of Solomon." Such a commitment endorses an experience that seems compatible with many recent feminist formulations; it demands no closure, refuses authority, and exemplifies continuous human process. In a comment that syntactically reflects the opened access to herself and to her poetry, Sexton herself said (Heyen Interview 325), "I have, you know, after all one does grow, change, evolve, and you know, it. . . ."

Notes

[1]There have been recent welcome exceptions to this rule in the work of Estella Lauter and Diane Middlebrook.

[2]Jane McCabe, Suzanne Juhasz, Jeanne Kammer, and Alicia Ostriker approach Sexton sympathetically, but still read in her poetry an eventual loss of control and self-fragmentation. Juhasz suggests that when Sexton abandoned controlled meter, rhyme, and syntax in her poetry, she did so because she had gained control of the poem at another level. It is this level of control I am exploring here.

[3]Joyce Carol Oates, in "The Rise and Fall of a Poet," asserts that "as early as the mid-60's, her poetry had begun to lose its scrupulous dramatic control and to be weakened by a poetic voice that, rarely varying from poem to poem, spoke ceaselessly of emotions and moods and ephemeral states of mind."

[4]For support of this statement, see, for example, Margaret Homans, Suzanne Juhasz, and Gilbert and Gubar's Introduction to *Shakespeare's Sisters.*

[5]Anne Sexton herself commented on this progress in an interview with William Heyen 323-24. Linda Mizejewski and Rise Axelrod document Sexton's themes of regeneration and the role of Eros in *Love Poems, Transformations,* and *The Book of Folly.* Estella Lauter has provided a wonderful reading of Sexton's expansive revision of traditional archetypal patterns.

[6]See Sexton's own description of this development in Marx 30ff.

[7]Sexton's posthumously published poems, as in all such cases, represent some difficulty. Although the poems in *45 Mercy Street, Words for Dr. Y,* and "Last Poems" support my conclusions, I have not concentrated on these works because they were not arranged and edited by Sexton.

[8]There is ample documentation of Sexton's interest in the effect of her poems on her reader. See the material in the "Interviews" section of *Anne Sexton: The Artist and Her Critics.*

[9]The best-known proponents of this view are Carol Gilligan, Jean

Anne Sexton: The Artist and Her Critics.

[9]The best-known proponents of this view are Carol Gilligan, Jean Baker Miller, and Nancy Chodorow.

[10]See Lauter's brilliant reading of Sexton's gradual movement toward a feminized deity.

[11]A Freudian context also heavily conditions Diana George's recent biography of Sexton.

[12]See Walter Michaels' discussion of this connection.

[13]I would like to thank Frances Bixler for this perception.

Works Cited

Axelrod, Rise. "'I Dare to Live': The Transforming Art of Anne Sexton." *Feminist Criticism*. Eds. Cheryl Brown and Karen Olson. Metuchen, N.J.: Scarecrow Press, 1978. 131-41.

Barthes, Roland. *Writing Degree Zero*. Trans. Annette Lauers and Colin Smith. New York: Hill and Wang, 1976.

Chodorow, Nancy. *The Reproduction of Mothering*. Berkeley: U of California P., 1984.

Daly, Mary. *Beyond God the Father*. Boston: Beacon, 1973.

Du Plessis, Rachel. *Writing Beyond the Ending*. Bloomington: Indiana UP, 1985.

Fiorenza, Elizabeth Schussler. *Bread Not Stone*. Boston: Beacon, 1986.

George, Diana Hume. *Oedipus Anne: The Poetry of Anne Sexton*. Urbana: U of Illinois P, 1987.

Gilbert, Sandra, and Susan Gubar. *Shakespeare's Sisters*. Bloomington: Indiana UP, 1979.

Gilligan, Carol. *In a Different Voice: Psychological Theory and Women's Development*. Cambridge, Mass.: Harvard UP, 1982.

Gordon, Linda. *Woman's Body, Woman's Right: A Social History of Birth Control in America*. N. Y.: Grossman, 1976.

Guth, Deborah. "Death as Defiance: A Study of Virgina Woolf." *Southern Humanities Review* 19 (1985): 221-29.

Heyen, William. *American Poets in 1976*. Indianapolis: Bobbs-Merrill, 1976.

Homans, Margaret. *Women Writers and Poetic Identity*. Princeton: Princeton UP, 1980.

Jardine, Alice. "Gynesis." *Diacritics* 12 (Spring 1982): 54-65.

Juhasz, Suzanne. *Naked and Fiery Forms*. New York: Octagon, 1978.

—. "Seeking the Exit or the Home: Poetry and Salvation in the Career of

Anne Sexton." Gilbert and Gubar, 261-68.
Kammer, Jeanne H. "The Witch's Life: Confession and Control in the Early Poetry of Anne Sexton." *Language and Style* 13 (1980): 29-53.
Kamuf, Peggy. "Replacing Feminist Criticism." *Diacritics* 12 (1982): 42-7.
—. "Writing Like a Woman." *Women and Language in Literature and Society*. Eds. Sally McConnell-Ginet, Ruth Borker, and Nelly Furman. New York: Praeger, 1980. 284-99.
Kevles, Barbara. "The Art of Poetry: Anne Sexton." McClatchy, 3-29.
Lauter, Estella. *Women as Mythmakers: Poetry and Visual Art by Twentieth-Century Women*. Bloomington: Indiana UP, 1984.
Marcus, Jane. "Thinking Back Through Our Mothers." *New Feminist Essays on Virginia Woolf*. Ed. Jane Marcus. London: Macmillan, 1981. 1-30.
Marx, Patricia. "Interview with Anne Sexton (1965)." McClatchy, 30-42.
McCabe, Jane. "'A Woman Who Writes': A Feminist Approach to the Poetry of Anne Sexton." McClatchy, 216-43.
McClatchy, J. D. ed. *Anne Sexton: The Artist and Her Critics*. Bloomington: Indiana UP, 1978.
— "Anne Sexton: Somehow to Endure." McClatchy, 244-90.
Michaels, Walter B. "The Interpreter's Self: Pierce on the Cartesian 'Subject.'" *The Georgia Review* 3 (1977): 383-407.
Middlebrook, Diane. "Housewife Into Poet: The Apprenticeship of Anne Sexton." *New England Quarterly* 56 (1983): 438-503.
___. "Poet of Weird Abundance." Rev. of *The Complete Poems: Anne Sexton*. *Parnassus* 12-13 (1985): 293-315.
Miller, Jean Baker. *Toward a New Psychology of Women*. Boston: Beacon, 1976.
Mizejewski, Linda. "Sappho to Sexton: Woman Uncontained." *College English* 35 (1973): 340-45.
Oates, Joyce Carol. "The Awful Rowing Toward God." *New York Times Book Review* 23 Mar. 1975: 3-4.
___. "The Rise and Fall of a Poet." *New York Times Book Review* 18 Oct., 1981: 3 ff.
Ostriker, Alicia. *Stealing the Language*. Boston: Beacon, 1986.
___. *Writing Like A Woman*. Ann Arbor: Michigan UP, 1983.
Rich, Adrienne. "Poetry and Experience." *Adrienne Rich's Poetry*. Eds. Barbara Charlesworth Gelpi and Albert Gelpi. New York: Norton, 1975. 89-98.
Rose, Phyllis. *Woman of Letters: A Life of Virginia Woolf*. New York: OUP, 1978.
Rosenblatt, Louise. *The Reader, The Text, The Poem*. Carbondale: Southern

Illinois UP, 1978.

Sexton, Anne. *The Complete Poems.* Ed. Linda Gray Sexton. Boston: Houghton Mifflin, 1981.

Sexton, Linda Gray and Lois Ames, eds. *Anne Sexton: A Self-Portrait in Letters.* Boston: Houghton-Mifflin, 1977.

Spivak, Gayatri. "Displacement and the Discourse of a Woman." *Displacement: Derrida and After.* Ed. Mark Krupnick. Bloomington: Indiana UP, 1983. 169-95.

— "French Feminism in an International Frame." *Yale French Studies* 62 (1981): 154-84.

Tompkins, Jane, ed. *Reader-Response Criticism*. Baltimore: Johns Hopkins UP, 1980.

IV. Quest

I empty myself from my wooden boat
and onto the flesh of The Island.

"On with it!" He says and thus
we squat on the rocks by the sea
and play--can it be true--
a game of poker.
He calls me.
I win because I hold a royal straight flush.
He wins because He holds five aces.

"The Rowing Endeth"
The Awful Rowing Toward God

ANNE SEXTON'S ISLAND GOD

Diana Hume George

In Anne Sexton's later religious poetry, characterized by a ceaseless search for a God she could believe in, the summer island of her childhood becomes the geographical locus of her spiritual and poetic quest. Her poetry is always preoccupied with legacy and inheritance, in which may be subsumed her religious quest, her sense of herself as a woman, her search of meaning and identity. Squirrel Island is the concentrated core of inheritance and legacy for Anne Sexton—the place where her family came together, where the generations lived side by side, where far-flung people met to confirm their sense of who they were and who they intended to remain, but did not. It was where the fathers of her personal and mythic lives congregated—from Nelson Dingley through Arthur Gray Staples and Ralph Harvey, three generations of her God. What she once called "the lost ingredient" was lost, I think, on Squirrel Island, and found there, in her imagination, at the end of her life.

Linda Gray Sexton and Lois Ames describe the family compound in Maine where Sexton spent her early summers:

> Anne's happy memories centered on Squirrel Island, near Boothbay Harbor, Maine, where the Dingley, Staples, and Harvey clan summered in seven large five-story "cottages." Built atop the shoreline granite with the wind at their back, these summer mansions were anchored into the rock by huge chains. The family lived skin to skin with the sea. From Arthur Gray Staples' study in the "Aerie" the only view that met the eye was one rolling wave after another.
>
> (*Letters* 4)

The sure-thing father-God she finds at the end of *The Awful Rowing Toward God* resides on an island toward which she rows in hopeful need of salvation. He not only resides there; the "island of God" *is* God. This elegiac poet created God in the image of memory. He had been transformed from the loving ragged brother of the early poetry to the authoritarian, arbitrary, alternately loving and rejecting patriarch of the later work. As she became more emotionally isolated, so did her God become more remote from us and from her, until finally he formed the body of a magical and distant island toward which she rowed with deep need, if not quite belief, at the end of her life.

Many readers have been disappointed and perhaps puzzled that the poet who earlier dreamed she could "piss in God's eye," who radically manipulated traditional orthodoxies for happily subversive ends, who dismantled Christian mythology, rewrote the life of Christ and celebrated her own sacraments in new psalms, should have capitulated in the end to a father-god who received her worshipful submission. Sexton never explained the metaphor of God as island. If I am right to track him to Squirrel Island, then the nature of his being, and the terms of her submission to him, are understandable in a new way. I pictured it as a rocky, all but deserted place, studded with few houses on abandoned rock and beach. I looked for it in atlases, but couldn't tell which of the many unnamed islands off Boothbay Harbor it might be. It was too small to be labeled, even on good maps of Maine. A few phone calls and localized atlases later, I found that ferry boats leave Boothbay Harbor for various islands, including Squirrel, regularly throughout the year. I went there on June 2, 1986. It takes about half an hour to get to Squirrel Island by ferry boat. My companion and I were told that sight-seers stay on the boat as it goes around the rest of the harbor area, but that we could stay on the island until the afternoon boat came through to pick us up.

Far from being rocky and deserted, Squirrel Island is a fully developed Maine summer colony. A few summer people were already there, even though this was only early June. Although the island has no stores or food or restaurants, it does have many residents, all of whom arrive with no cars—the island has only a couple of roads—and carry their supplies with them. I approached a formidable older woman as we disembarked because we had only the vaguest idea what to look for. We knew that two of the family houses were called, originally, Dingley Dell and the Aerie, but we didn't know quite where to find them. Our skimpy directions indicated that one was near the boat dock and one was on the other side of the island. I braved the forbidding exterior and asked the woman a few questions.

Yes, she knew Dingley Dell and the Aerie, but she hadn't an idea in the world who Anne Sexton was, and she, Mrs. Hicks, had been coming to the island for, what was it, seventy years. Then I tried using Sexton's parents' names, Mary and Ralph Harvey. Mary she knew—she remembered Mary dancing at the Casino. I thought of "The Double Image" and "The Division of Parts." The Casino? But now she'd clearly had about enough of my questions—I was a nosey off-islander making inquiries that were not welcome. She wasn't rude, just a bit short, and I didn't blame her. Her husband, Mr. Hicks, was more open. He said that Dingley Dell was just next to their house. They were walking up now, and they would show us. On the way up the raised sidewalk, I continued to question Mrs. Hicks as much as I dared. How well had she known Mary Gray? Well enough, but Mary was married, you see. I still don't know what she meant by that, but she repeated it several times.

While walking with her, I looked around at the solid summer houses, all owned by prosperous people on the mainland. None was a typical summer cottage. All were two story and large, some were positively elaborate—normal for this kind of summer colony, but such a colony was not quite what I had expected. The front yards were rocky affairs of granite outcropping such as appear all along the Maine shore. A casino? Yes, but it had burned down. So had the bowling alley. But other structures had replaced them. Yes, Mary Gray liked to dance. I couldn't tell if the reserve and slight disapproval were toward Mary Gray, or toward me for asking about her.

Mr. and Mrs. Hicks gave us a real sense of what the islanders were like: old now, many of them, a bit austere, protective of their privacy, and affectionate toward their island home. We helped Mr. and Mrs. Hicks carry their supplies to the house, and they directed us to Dingley Dell and the Aerie. Mr. Hicks, the chapel historian, said we should be sure to stop in the chapel. The history of the chapel is, in many respects, the history of the island and its inhabitants. After he sold us his booklet for a dollar, we went to Dingley Dell.

Dingley Dell is a planner's and builder's caprice. There is nothing else remotely like it on the island. It gives substance to Sexton's family history in "Funnel" (*TB*):

> The family story tells, and it was told true,
> of my great-grandfather who begat eight
> genius children and bought twelve almost new
> grand pianos.
> . . . .
> Back from the great-grandfather I have come
> to tidy a country graveyard for his sake,
> to chat with the custodian under a yearly sun
> and touch a ghost sound where it lies awake.
> I like best to think of that Bunyan man
> slapping his thighs and trading the yankee sale
> for one dozen grand pianos. It fit his plan
> of culture to dot it big. On this same scale
> he built seven arking houses and they still stand.

The dominant form of the house is indeed an "arc" or arch—

they reappear everywhere, playfully creating a lightness of tone. Dingley Dell would easily have been the most elaborate house on the island when it was built. The family that owns it now was not anywhere in evidence yet, so we looked in the windows at the elegant formal dining room, the gracious living room, the well-stocked kitchen. I recalled a photo in Sexton's *Letters* of her grandfather, Arthur Gray Staples, Anne, and her sister Blanche as children. Clearly, that photo had been taken on the deck of Dingley Dell—I could place it exactly.

Leaving our belongings on the porch, we began the trek through and around the island, toward the Aerie. We stopped at the chapel because a glance at the chapel history revealed that it was a mine of information. Nelson Dingley, Jr., was the first of Sexton's direct forbears to inhabit this island. The island was purchased under his leadership by an association of twelve members in 1870. He and the others raised subscription money for the chapel almost immediately, and it was erected in 1880 with generous funding that allowed for an elaborated structure. From the minutes of the Chapel meetings of 1880, Mr. Hicks records this passage:

> Next Sunday it is hoped to have the chapel formally, and yet heartily, dedicated to a breezy and healthful Christianity—such as the Great Founder of our Faith, who delighted in the lilies of the field, the birds of the air, and the waves of the sea, would have us cherish.

In 1882, Nelson Dingley, Jr. then Governor of Maine, was elected the first President of the Chapel Association. He was Sexton's great-uncle, but Sexton presents him as her great-grandfather in the poetry, for it was he who built the houses in "Funnel" as far as I can determine. It is appropriate that this woman so in search of fathers would call her great-uncle one of her great-fathers.

Mr. Hicks reprints the memorial service eulogy for the Hon. Nelson Dingley, Jr., in 1899. By this time, Dingley had been president of the chapel Association for seventeen years. The island's religious history, and its secular one as well—there was little separation of church and state on the island at this time—bears his indelible mark, and tells us something about the religious past of the highly secular family that, by Sexton's generation, was characterized by the kind of Protestantism Sexton recalls in one of her early poems: Protestants are the people who sing when they're not quite sure. Yet by the end of her life, Sexton was re-seeking the Old Testament God, whose characteristics share much in common with both the god and the mortal fathers of Squirrel Island.

The memorial talk for Governor Dingley was as much about Squirrel Island as about the man. After a hymn of praise to the island and its beauties, the speaker tells of "one whose name is inseparably connected with it," who, on a summer thirty years ago, was sailing past this island. "Under his leadership it was purchased . . . and to that quiet home by the sea he has turned every year since in the season for the rest and recuperation which, as the hard-working and care-worn man that he was, he so much needed." We learn, in the conventional language of eulogy, that "he was a Puritan in principle, but free from the Puritan's repellent austerity of spirit and manner." He never missed a chapel service when he was on the island. Mr. Hicks drew our attention to the fact that Squirrel Island has attracted very distinguished guest preaching throughout the years.

The deserted chapel was well appointed in dark wood tones and lit effectively from the ample windows that the islanders carefully planned. We thought of Philip Larkin's poem, "Church Going," whose speaker tends toward such a cross of ground because such places for a long time held "what since is found / only in separation—marriage, and birth, / And death, and thoughts of these." I walked up to the pulpit and found the nineteenth-century bible presented to the church by the Ladies Association of the island and decided to open it and let may eye rest where it would, and read aloud. My eye fell first on Genesis 28:21-22, which I read:

> So that I come again to my father's house in peace; then shall the Lord be my God: And this stone, which I have set for a pillar, shall be God's house.

Like Larkin's speaker, I intoned "Here endeth." We were quiet for a minute. This island of stone was Sexton's God, to whom she came as to her father's house for the peace she sought at the end of her life. Then my companion recited the end of "Church Going":

> A serious house on serious earth it is,
> In whose blent air all our compulsions meet,
> Are recognized, and robed as destinies.
> And that much never can be obsolete,
> Since someone will forever be surprising
> A hunger in himself to be more serious
> And gravitating with it to this ground,
> Which, he once heard, was proper to grow wise in,
> If only that so many dead lie round.

In fact, no dead lie round the Squirrel Island chapel at all; no one is buried here. But in another sense, they do lie round, particularly Anne Sexton and all her dead, her "straight Maine clan," her pretty ones.

From the chapel, we cut back around to the shore, intending to find the Aerie. Once five stories, now four, it is described in "Funnel":

> One, five stories up, straight up like a square
> box, still dominates its costal edge of land.
> It is rented cheap in the summer musted air

to sneaker-footed families who pad through
its rooms and sometimes finger the yellow keys
of an old piano that wheezes bells of mildew.
Like a shoe factory amid the spruce trees
it squats; flat roof and rows of windows spying
through the mist. Where those eight children danced
their starfished summers, the thirty-six pines sighing,
that bearded man walked giant steps and chanced
his gifts in numbers.

There was no mistaking the Aerie when we came to it. It looks like, well, a shoe factory. It is certainly the largest private structure on the island and is in awful disrepair, unlike the beautifully maintained Dingley Dell. Peering in the windows, we could see that it hadn't been fully inhabited in years. The house sits high on a hill, with an unobstructed view of the sea. Looking at it, one can imagine it in its prime, full of children and their parents—Dingley and Harvey and Sexton and Staples people.

It was here in the Aerie that Sexton's grandfather, Arthur Gray Staples, had his study. Staples is the family figure most intimately connected with the God of the *Awful Rowing*. He was the most literary member of the family, having been for years editor of the *Lewiston Journal* and author of several books of essays, housed in the island library. Among the family members, he could bless her most directly as a writer. She recalls him fondly and frequently in the poetry—he is the grandfather of the bagsful of nickels in *Love Poems*, who belongs to me, she says, like lost baggage.

"Grandfather, Your Wound" (*DN*) takes place in the Aerie, where Sexton stands "in your writing room." The island "you were the man of" is "made of your stuff." She is here, in imagination or in the material world—both her biographer and I think she came to Squirrel Island in the early seventies, not long before her death—mourning his death, his wound, and her own. She is an ocean-going vessel here, as she will be later in the rowboat of *The Awful Rowing*; he is the wooden ceiling of his writing room. She hears him speak "like a horn"—the familiar island foghorn of this sea I am gazing out at?—and the sun goes down, but comes up again in a kind of resurrection. Here is the text:

> The wound is open,
> Grandfather, where you died,
> where you sit inside it
> as shy as a robin.
> I am an ocean-going vessel
> but you are a ceiling made of wood
> and the island you were the man of,
> is shaped like a squirrel and named thereof.
> On this island, Grandfather, made of your stuff,
> a rubber squirrel sits on the kitchen table
> coughing up mica like phlegm.
> I stand in you writing room
> with the Atlantic painting its way toward us
> and ask why am I left with stuffed fish on the wall,
> why am I left with rubber squirrels with mica eyes,
> when you were Mr. Funnyman, Mr. Nativeman,
> when you were Mr. Lectureman, Mr. Editor,
> the small town big shot who, although very short,
> who although with a cigarette-stained mustache,
> who although famous for lobster on the rocks,
> left me here, nubkin, sucking in my vodka
> and emphysema cigarettes, unable to walk
> your walks, unable to write your writes.
> Grandfather,
> you blow your bone like a horn
> and I hear it inside my pink facecloth.
> I hear you, Mr. Iodineman,
> and the sun goes down
> just as it did in your life,
> like a campaign ribbon,
> an ingot from the iron works,
> an eyelash,
> and a dot and a dash.
> Now it comes bright again—

my God, Grandfather,
you are here,
you are laughing,
you hold me and rock me
and we watch the lighthouse come on,
blinking its dry wings over us all,
over my wound
and yours.

The lighthouse is visible from the Aerie where I stood, but is no longer operated by hand as it was when Sexton was a girl on Squirrel Island, when she might in fact have been held by her grandfather in his writing room overlooking the Atlantic. Compare this scene with the final one of "The Rowing Endeth" (*AW*), after she moors her boat at the "island called God":

"On with it!" He says and thus
we squat on the rocks by the sea
and play—can it be true—
a game of poker.
He calls me.
I win because I hold a royal straight flush.
He wins because He holds five aces.
. . . .
He starts to laugh,
the laughter rolling like a hoop out of His mouth
and into mine,
and such laughter that He doubles right over me
laughing a Rejoice-Chorus at our two triumphs.
Then I laugh, the fishy dock laughs
the sea laughs. The Island laughs.
The Absurd laughs.

We may regret that in his transformation from human grandfather to cosmic Grand Father, the figure of Arthur Gray Staples became fraudulent and slightly sinister. It is difficult to applaud this "dearest dealer." But perhaps at the Aerie he was warm and true.

Turning back from the sea toward the derelict house, one may imagine Sexton in her own island room in "Mother and Jack and the Rain" (*LD*). Squirrel Island is clearly the place most identified with Sexton's own version of the primal scene:

> On my damp summer bed I cradled my salty knees
> and heard father kiss me through the wall
> and heard mother's heart pump like the tides.
> The fog horn flattened the sea into leather.
> I made no voyages, I owned no passport.
> I was the daughter. Whiskey fortified
> my father in the next room. He outlasted the weather,
> counted his booty and brought
> his ship into port.

Perhaps no poet, even in this self-consciously post-Freudian era, has so completely eroticized the family as did Anne Sexton. In "Leaves That Talk" (*MS*) Arthur Gray Staples has a love affair with his granddaughter, touching her breast and her neck. Our compulsions meet in the blent air of chapels—and of bedrooms. Anne Sexton blent the air of our collective compulsions when she squarely faced the eros of lineage on Squirrel Island. Collapsing the identities of mother and daughter, this daughter seeks both erotic and spiritual union with the father.

Moving back around the island to make a full circle, we find a beautiful patch of woodland, changing yet again my original notion of what the island looked like. This is the island I had originally imagined, a rocky, wooded rough outcropping. This patch of woodland is the scene of Sexton's "Kind Sir: These Woods" (*TB*):

> Kind Sir: This is an old game
> that we played when we were eight and ten.
> Sometimes on The Island, in down Maine,

in late August, when the cold fog blew in
off the ocean, the forest between Dingley Dell
and grandfather's cottage green white and strange.
It was as if every pine tree were a brown pole
we did not know; as if day had rearranged
into night and bats flew in sun. It was a trick
to turn around once and know you were lost;
knowing the crow's horn was crying in the dark,
knowing that supper would never come, that the coast's
cry of doom from that far away bell buoy's bell
said your nursemaid is gone. O Mademoiselle,
the rowboat rocked over. Then you were dead.
Turn around once, eyes tight, the thought in your head.

These poems form the core of what I call the Squirrel Island group. They show her returning in spirit to Squirrel Island from the beginning to the end of her writing life. The network of references in this group of poems includes some of Sexton's most concentrated themes: fear of madness, sexual anxiety, relationships to the "mother, father, I'm made of," the quest for an ultimate deity.

We find the library, where we hope to uncover more of Anne Sexton's early life, and lifelong compulsions, another time. It is closed this day. Back at Dingley Dell, we sit on the porch, watch the birds, look back into the windows. Dingley Dell and the Aerie are on opposite side of the island. One is merry and waggish in design and faces the mainland; the other looks out to sea, where one might gaze into life's deepest emptiness, its deepest fullness. They reflect a dualism in Sexton's poetry: she seemed sometimes to be two poets, one of delight, the other of despair, one inhabited by the living, the other given over to ghosts. The Aerie looks like the Yorkshire moors. Dingley Dell is like a meadow yellow with flowers. I wonder in which house she spent more time. I will ask her sister Blanche, who cannot imagine how anyone who grew up on Squirrel Island could be unhappy.

Before we leave, we go to buy more copies of the chapel

history from Mr. Hicks. Mr. and Mrs. Hicks come out onto the porch to talk. It is clear that our sincere interest in their island has won them over. From them we find out that there are no mortgages for houses on the island—one must have enough money to buy or build outright. Buy is the wrong word, after all—Nelson Dingley and the original association members stipulated that one could not own any part of Squirrel Island—one leases the property for 999 years. That seems fitting. No one should, no one can, own God.

Waiting back at the dock for the boat to pick us up, I talk to another islander. She seems vaguely to know of Anne Sexton—she thinks two island women gave a short talk on her connection to the island a year or so ago, but it is clear she hasn't read Sexton and knows nothing about her. I regret this. An important poet traces her roots here, and in her work this island becomes God. A modern and at first secular poet, she returns Squirrel Island finally to it religious roots—and whether or not I like that, these people should know of it.

We pull away from the island—I call it the awful outboarding away from God. I imagine Anne Sexton leaving here at the end of her summer childhoods, going back to the mainland to school, to responsibility, to her life to be, and finally to an early death with or without God. With one of her therapists, "Dr. Martin," Sexton used a shorthand for the feeling of loss and loneliness that often overwhelmed her: "like leaving Squirrel," she called it.

At the end of an earlier commentary on Squirrel Island, I wrote this:

> I find it poignant to discover that the "island of God" may have been the island of childhood where she summered. . . . I also confess that I find it beautiful; I contemplate that simplicity, that perfect circle of sought-after comfort, one that brings the middle-aged poet back to the finest moments of a troubled and unhappy past. Perhaps anyone's idea of heaven is some such journey into the past.

Although *The Awful Rowing Toward God* ends with what most readers have regarded as an unfortunate capitulation to paternity, at least two issues regarding that submissive gesture arise. First, only in the final poem of the collection does her God take on his negatively externalized and patriarchal character. Elsewhere he continues to appear in heterodox and polymorphous form: in the chapel of morning eggs, in a whore, an old man or a child, in the private holiness of her hands, in the creation of gender or the act of lovemaking, in the morning laughter. Second, the ocean rower is a woman traveling to land through sea. The island of the father-god rises from the ocean of the mother-goddess. Squirrel Island in its salty sea is not only the father; her journey is through and to both mythic imagos. The God Anne Sexton sought must offer absolution, as perhaps must any god whose qualities serve the needs of a guilt-ridden culture. Absolution is to be had only from the source of that guilt; in Sexton's case, the source is both paternal and maternal, the "mother, father, I'm made of."

Finally, it is important to recall that although *Rowing* was the last collection Sexton prepared for press, it does not represent her last questing words. Those are spoken in poems such as "The Consecrating Mother" (*MS*) and "In Excelsis" (from uncollected last works), which take place in the same liquid medium as *The Awful Rowing*. In "The Consecrating Mother," Sexton's speaker stands before the sea, which says, "Do not give up one god / for I have a handful." She should be entered "skin to skin," says Sexton,

> and in moonlight she comes in *her* nudity
> flashing breasts made of milk-water,
> flashing buttocks made of unkillable lust . . .
> I am that clumsy human
> on the shore
> loving you, coming, coming,
> going . . .

The ocean-god of "In Excelsis" is the same mighty mother:

> I wish to enter her like a dream,
> and walk into ocean,
> letting it explode over me
> and outward, where I would drink the moon
> and my clothes would slip away . . .

She stands on the shore with another woman, "loving its pulse," absorbing "the wild toppling green that enters us today." Only a selective misreading leaves Anne Sexton in the ambiguous embrace of the father-god. She resides in his island arms, but they are both surrounded and enfolded by the mother sea.

Works Cited

Hicks, Marvin D., comp. *Squirrel Island Chapel: 100 Year Diary 1880-1980.*

Sexton, Anne. *The Complete Poems*. Ed. Linda Gray Sexton. Houghton Mifflin, 1981.

Sexton, Linda Gray and Lois Ames, ed. *Anne Sexton: A Self-Portrait in Letters*. Boston: Houghton Mifflin, 1977.

ANNE SEXTON'S "OTHERWORLD JOURNEY"

Margaret Scarborough

In the spring of 1975, about four months after Anne Sexton's death, Mary Daly wrote that the radical journey of women *becoming* "is very much an Otherworld Journey. It is both discovery and creation of a world other than patriarchy" ("Qualitative Leap" 200). Though it is clear that Anne Sexton was never able to arrive in Daly's Otherworld, certainly we see indications in her work of a radical journey toward *becoming*, dramatically registered in clashes between two mythological structures: the dominating patriarchal Christian *mythos* and a deeper archetypal feminine structure that corresponds to the Greek Demeter-Persephone myth, particularly that part of the myth characterized by the quest of Demeter following the rape of Persephone. Like Demeter, Sexton begins in despair, with an "experience of nihilism" that emanates from a profound bifurcation of self and ends at heaven's gate (Zollman 30). However, two related deficiencies sabotage Sexton. Lacking Demeter's rage and her discerning female informant (Hecate, the dark mother), Sexton never learns the whereabouts of her lost self, and her frenzied encounter with the Judaeo-Christian God is a joke, a poker game in which both and neither win.

In the following paper I will discuss Sexton's quest as she descends into herself and backward in time in an attempt to heal her despair, to unite her split self. This will involve discussions of the feminine *mythos* of quest as it differs from and is derailed by the dominant male *mythos* of quest in our culture; the concepts of mother and artist as they inform and direct the quest; the denigration and rejection of the self and all women; and the subsequent sense of an internally divided and isolated self that desires reunion with a lost part. Other pertinent features of Sexton's journey—such as a deepening sense of personal guilt and sin; a descending journey into hell or Hades as she travels backwards in time in attempts to atone for her sin and unite with God; immersion into the life with children and partial self-realization; initiations in the fires of sexual and domestic love; and finally a confrontation with the male deity that reifies Sexton's despair and separation—are matters for another discussion. In any event, the vehicle and impetus for her quest, from beginning to end, is her poetry.

Throughout her quest, Sexton sometimes enacts the trials of Persephone and sometimes those of Demeter. In a woman's quest such a double strategy is unavoidable. To be reunited with herself, a woman must come to terms with the impulses of both the Demeter or mother-creator self (the poet for Sexton) and the Persephone or daughter-wife self. Although Sexton does not succeed, her path is clear. Her system is consistent and may be examined from the point of view of the primordial quest for union "on a higher plane with the spiritual aspect of the Feminine, the Sophia aspect of the Great Mother" (Neumann; Rich 11).

I

The concept of quest in the patriarchal tradition bears no meaning for a woman. Rather than a quester after "authentic being" and "choice-making transcendence," a woman traditionally functions as an "auxiliary to somebody else's development" (Pratt 1-2). Woman exists only as a symbol representing "the totality of what can be known. The [male] hero is the one who comes to know. . . " (Campbell 116). Generally, the result of a woman writer's attempt to turn inward in quest of transcendence and unity is what Annis Pratt calls the "drowning effect": the "encoding or swallowing of patriarchal norms" (6). For Mary Daly, these patriarchal norms find their source in "the myth of feminine evil, expressed in the Fall" and "reinforced by the myth of salvation/redemption by a single human being of the male sex" (198). It is this submergence in the "myth of feminine evil" and the subsequent "drowning" in patriarchal norms that perpetuates Sexton's despair and derails her quest for selfhood. She feels split and male-identified—Persephone underground.

> I see two thin streaks burn down my chin.
> I see myself as one would see another
> I have been cut in two.
>
> ("For the Year of the Insane," *LD*)

"For the Year of the Insane" is a prayer-poem to Sexton's mother and to her image of the Divine Mother to see and save her from this profound internal division. In mythic terms, she laments her enclosure and describes her "Persephone experience" of despair, of being locked away in a kingdom of death and silence. Like Persephone, Sexton imagines that the cause of her split and continued imprisonment is something she ate and pleads with her mother to free her:

> O Mary, open your eyelids.
> I am in the domain of silence,
> the kingdom of the crazy and the sleeper.
> There is blood here
> and I have eaten it.
> O mother of the womb,
> did I come for blood alone?
> O little mother
> I am in my own mind.
> I am locked in the wrong house.

"The Other" (*BF*) and "The Civil War" (*AW*) pick up this

theme of internal schism and the accompanying desire for wholeness with yet more terrible urgency. But, because Sexton (according to the traditions in which she lives) perceives her counterparts for both good and evil to be male, she maintains the split. Consider "The Civil War":

> I am torn in two
> but I will conquer myself
> I will dig up the pride.
> I will take scissors
> and cut out the beggar.
> I will take a crowbar
> and pry out the broken pieces of God in me.
> Just like a jigsaw puzzle,
> I will put him together again.

All this destruction reassembles only a male God; Sexton cannot reconcile this fact with her last stanza, or with her own sex:

> But I will conquer them all
> and build a whole nation of God
> in me—but united,
> build a new soul,
> dress it with skin
> and then put on my shirt
> and sing an anthem,
> a song of myself.

The poet she echoes here is, of course, the utterly male Walt Whitman. Pratt describes this phenomenon, this encoding of male characteristics or myths by female writers, in her study of women's fiction:

> Thus, not only within woman's literature taken as a whole but within the head of the individual woman also, a battle goes on between male myths and a counter-myth . . . , a clash between two contrary *mythoi* which often strikes sparks in our darkness from the very impact of their meeting. (6)

Pratt goes on to explain that this inability of women to identify with female myths funnels them into a veritable sea of male mythology that is either relentlessly narrowing or absolutely contrary to a woman's internal impulses. In consequence, those basic impulses that urge a woman to become a mother, a wise and caring advisor, a creator woman, when filtered through patriarchal patterns and restrictions, deform her into a policing mother, a mother-in-law, or a witch (8). She feels split in two, split between her inner desires toward tenderness and the frustrating restrictions that distort those desires. Fundamental to Sexton's experience of disjunction and to her inability to resolve it is a confused and deformed attitude toward mother, and subsequently, toward that impulse at the heart of her own being that urges her to create. On the one hand, Sexton evidences a deep desire for and an impulse toward the archetypical "good" mother, a Divine Mother. This mother is part of a verdant, green and growing world; she is an image of Demeter:

> Soon it will be summer.
> She is my mother.
> She will tell me a story and keep me asleep
> against her plump and fruity skin.
> ("Three Green Windows," *LD*)

This mother appears to Sexton, as in "Three Green Windows," only at transcendent, half-awake moments, or in memories and fantasies of childhood:

> Oh mother,
> here in your lap,
> as good as a bowlful of clouds
> I your greedy child
> am given your breast,
> the sea wrapped in skin,
> and your arms,
> roots covered with moss . . .

In this fantasy, mother is both of the earth and of heaven, immanent and transcendent; she is the sky, the sea and the earth. She encompasses all that is living, and unity with her is wholeness:

> Oh mother,
> after his lap of childhood
> I will never go forth
> into the big people's world
> as an alien,
> a fabrication,
> or falter
> when someone else
> is as empty as a shoe.

This is the desire, the source and potential satisfaction of Sexton's ever-constant "greed," which she evaluates in traditional Christian terms: as an evil, one of the seven deadly sins. This evaluation (no mere literary convention for Sexton) and her experience with her real mother, Mary Gray, left her, inevitably, bitter and ambivalent. She cannot be reconciled.

"The Double Image" (*TB*) is an early attempt and failure to grapple with ambivalence toward her mother. Addressed to Joyce, her own daughter, the poem moves through seven sections as Sexton attempts to know herself. But ultimately, the resolution she offers is more a desire than a reality. She is blocked in the end by confusion over the identity of the witches in the poem. Sexton, as a mother, links herself with her own mother, her child, and the portraits in hopes of finding a clear view of herself in the interconnections of objects and people. She tells us that at her child's and her mother's illnesses she feels guilt ("The blame, / I heard them say, was mine") and attempts suicide that succeeds only in producing more guilt ("The day life made you whole / I let the witches take away my guilty soul"). Clearly, the witches know the truth, and in the course of the poem we learn that the portraits were initially a device to avoid self-knowledge, to avoid confrontation with what the witches know:

> Too late,
> too late, to live with your mother, the witches said.
> But I didn't leave. I had my portrait
> done instead.

Rather than recognizing that the witches are an expression of her internal but now twisted impulses and values and that she had best contend with them, Sexton explains that she avoided them and tried to petrify herself in time by having a portrait done. She learns only that her guilt-gathering was in itself a means of avoiding the fundamental truths. In spite of what she says, she is unable to tell us why she would rather die than love; *that* truth is possessed by the witches:

> And I had to learn
> why I would rather
> die than love, how your innocence
> would hurt and how I gather
> guilt like a young intern
> his symptoms, his certain evidence.

In poem after poem the witches goad and torment her until, finally, Sexton identifies with them:

> The speaker in this case
> is a middle-aged witch, me—
> tangled on my two great arms
> my face in a book
> and my mouth wide,
> ready to tell you a story or two.
>
> ("The Gold Key," *T*)

Eventually, she recognizes that the witch (like the dwarf and the rat of other poems) is not only construed negatively, as evil; the witch is also recognized as the form her creative impulses take. Such an inversion is contrary to what Campbell describes as the mythic norm of other traditions: the "good" mother is the source of creation and the "bad" mother is the source of destruction. On a higher plane, of course, the two are united. But the current patriarchal demeaning of "bad" mother into bitch, witch, or mother-in-law rather than cosmic force will maintain the divisions. In this secularization the united image is deprived of transformative power. For Sexton, that her creative self appears as evil, as a witch and in conflict with the "good mother" rather than in the form of a goddess or a priestess *and* the "good mother," is a measure of submergence in the patriarchal norms (111). It is the man, not the woman, who is the artist. Woman creates babies.

"The Witch's Life" of *The Awful Rowing Toward God* maintains this view. A woman cannot be both an artist and a mother, and to choose the life of the artist is to abandon good and to take up with evil, to aspire beyond proper limits:

> I am shoveling the children out,
> scoop after scoop.
> Only my books anoint me,
> Yes. It is the witch's life,
> climbing the primordial climb,
> a dream within a dream,
> then sitting here
> holding a basket of fire.

To live a moral life, to win approval from God, it seems, Sexton feels she must abandon her desire to be an artist. In fact, in one of her last poems, "What the Bird with the Human Head Knew," (*AW*) Sexton claims to have transcended her need to create:

> I walked many days

past witches that eat grandmothers knitting booties
as if they were collecting a debt.

Again, the witches are her hungry, creative self that devours her mother or grandmother self who attends to the needs of babies. The dominating *mythos* structuring Sexton's consciousness never enables her to bring together these two aspects of her personality.

II

As a consequence of Sexton's conflict between artist and mother, her image of mother and subsequently of woman is fraught with ambivalence. She is beautiful and all-loving and she is stupid, cruel, and obscene. More often that not, she appears in the latter guise. The Greek corollary to such confusion and self-loathing, we recall, is the "night of flowering," the eve of self-realization and resolution of loss in which women initiates of Eleusis (where the myth of Demeter and Persephone was reenacted) obscenely insult one another. Sexton never achieves the resolution. Without appropriate ritual or direction, she is stalled on this phase of her quest.

A crucial poem for the consideration of this stall, for the consideration of Sexton's attitude toward her own mother and the interconnections between that attitude and her concept of self is "Christmas Eve" (*LD*). The poem opens with imagery of wealth. Sexton's mother is perceived as a priceless but lost diamond, something the daughter longs to possess again. She ponders the old portrait of her mother. Her desire transforms the image from that of the invincible richness of jewels and the sanctifying glow of Christmas lights to fleshy concrete details. The result is a dissolving of Sexton's anticipated joy of imaginative reunion with her mother into disgust and horror:

> I wanted your eyes, like the shadows
> of two small birds, to change.
> Hour after hour I looked at your face.
> Then I watched how the sun hit
> your red sweater, your withered neck,
> your badly painted flesh-pink skin.
> You who led me by the nose,
> I saw you as you were.
> Then I thought of your body
> as one thinks of murder . . .

Shocked by her unexpected loathing, Sexton leaps into a frantic ritual to undo the power of her thoughts:

> Then I said Mary—
> Mary, Mary forgive me
> and then I touched a present for the child,
> the last I bred before your death;
> and then I touched my breast.

It is Christmas eve, and the prayer to her mother, Mary, is also a prayer to the Virgin. The child is both her own and a representation of the Divine Child. To reject her mother, Sexton understands she rejects the universal, divine aspect of Mother and the mother in herself as well:

> and then I touched my breast
> and then I touched the floor
> and then my breast again as if,
> somehow, it were one of yours.

Like Persephone, the rejection of mother is followed by descent: "And then I touched the floor."

"Praying on a 707" (*DN*) picks up and interweaves the strands of conflict about mother, God, and creativity that frayed about the edges of earlier poems. In this poem, the values of the patriarchal deity are clearly those of her mother. She is aligned with laws ("state of letters") and possession ("treasurer's report"). In Greek myth, she is leagued with Zeus and Pluton, who, experiencing only lust, demean and do not connect with the female principles of fertility. Sexual love is not sanctified, and God-mother-daughter breaks the power of it with sarcasm and humor. Sexton wonders that anything happens, that "making love" with such a lack of fullness bears fruit at all:

> If you make love
> you give me the funniest lines.
> Mrs. Sarcasm,
> why are there any children left?

The "encoding" has been complete. The role of mother has been distorted, even on a cosmic level. She has become an exponent of patriarchal morality which, although hated by Sexton, seems to be all-inclusive—the only possibility available.

> Mother,
> each time I talk to God
> you interfere.

Yet, there is another side: The children and the Italian maid who becomes the apotheosis of the "Earth Mother." In spite of the superficial regimentation God-mother imposes on the family, there is a richness, a naturalness and love that also seems to be part of a mother emanating from the lives of the children. As in the positive mother poems, Sexton expresses this vitality in the sensuous, fecund imagery of a pagan fertility goddess, a Demeter. Mother appears as a "great pine of summer," a sea, the moon and gardens. But when Sexton tries to locate this mother in actual events in her life, tries to remember who gave her a doll, she suddenly understands that it must have been the Italian maid, "*She* had a soul" (emphasis Sexton). We recall that Demeter disguised herself as a nursemaid during part of her quest for

Persephone, and as a maid, attempted to effect the growth and transformation of Queen Metaneira's child, Demophoon. Unfortunately for Demophoon, Metaneira interrupted Demeter's work. For Sexton it was the Italian maid who infused the lives of her children and grandchildren with her own earthy, fecund soul, who transformed them from little robots into human beings who "take their children into their arms / like cups of warm cocoa / as you [mother] never could."

But Sexton herself remains caught in the tension between the Italian maid and the rigid, patriarchal morality of her God-mother. Mary Gray, like Queen Metaneira of the Persephone myth, prevented the complete transformation of her last child. In momentary recognition of her dilemma and loss, Sexton is able to make an honest statement of anger and defiance against her God-mother's indictment of her late and continuing quest for transformation, of her desire for self-understanding:

> I talk to God and ask Him
> to speak of my failures, my successes,
> ask him to morally make an assessment.
> He does.
>
> He says,
> you haven't,
> you haven't.

Here there is nothing of the mincing language of "The Double Image" (*TB*). The attack against a dead patriarchal morality is crisp, explosive and to the point:

> Mother,
> you and God
> float with the same belly
> up.

Though at the beginning of the poem Sexton perceived her mother's "interference" as preventing her from getting to God, the spontaneous, nurturing qualities of the maid suggest that it is the adoption of God's values by Sexton's true mother that prevents Sexton from getting to Mother. It is God who "interferes" with mother. Furthermore, the tightness of connection between God and mother at the end of the poem (that her mother and God are of one belly) supports the complexity. The belly "bloats," we remember, not only at death, but also during pregnancy. The rigid, painful and destructive morality and the spontaneous and natural love are merged in and proceed from the same bloated belly. In Sexton, this is a conflict to the end of her poetic quest. She desires the merger, but the nurturing role, commonly in the image of mother, is misplaced by and to the father. The effect is to confuse and nullify the creative power of both of them, to split and grotesquely deform all women, her image of herself, into one-dimensional caricatures.

Such caricatures of women dominate *Transformations.* Not surprisingly, Sexton's views reflect those of the patriarchal fairy tale in which the superficial passivity of the female heroes masks a fundamentally dissatisfied personality. These greedy and desirable females are cruel and heartless, possessed of an evil appetite. The princess of "The White Snake" takes the lives of fifty men. "The Twelve Dancing Princesses" have lost count. Woman is "ever Eve" seeking "the apple of life" ("The White Snake"). Sexton's values are the patriarchal values that maintain distorted images of woman. Integrity violated, woman is just as much a *function* in Sexton's poems as she has been traditionally. "She is the cause and solution to the problem of evil," (Daly; Ricoeur). She is both the torment and the salvation of the male hero (and the source of ironic tension in the poems). Woman is, to repeat Pratt's summation of Campbell's findings, the "auxiliary to somebody else's development" (1-2). Rather than identifying with the male quester, as have many women writers (even to the extreme of adopting male names), or rejecting the female role altogether in a consuming rage, as have many feminist writers, Sexton accepts these roles that lock her into her own damnation, her own Hades. It is from this level, from this sense of involvement and restriction, that Sexton unconsciously participates in the ritual "night of flowering": she denigrates herself as she denigrates other women:

> Snow White, the dumb bunny,
> opened the door
> and she bit into a poison apple . . .

As in the Persephone myth, the virgin is always caught when she ignores the admonitions of her guardians. The consequence is banality, shallowness and dissatisfaction:

> Meanwhile Snow White held court
> rolling her china-blue eyes open and shut
> and sometimes referring to her mirror
> as women do.

The story ends here. The traditional wife, be she Snow White or Persephone, takes her place among all women. Sexton makes no distinctions, but neither can she go beyond the traditions.

The miller's daughter of "Rumpelstilskin" proves to be as stupid and vain as Sexton's Snow White, as sexually motivated as the mythic Persephone:

> Poor grape with no one to pick
> Luscious and round sleek.
> Poor thing.
> To die and never see Brooklyn.

Grapes are the Dionysian symbol for sexual abandon. We recall that in some of the ancient myths, Dionysius rather than Pluton was Persephone's ravisher. The incriminating act, the "picking" of the flower, is constant in all versions.

In "Rumpelstilskin" Sexton reveals to us what she understands to be the cost for women of "marital bliss": the abandonment of her inner creative power, of the mystery, of the poet. By freeing herself from the dwarf, by naming it, the miller's daughter frees herself from her ability to create, from her ability to "spin" golden yarns. She becomes a simple "soft" woman whose singular outstanding feature is her motherhood, who gives her "dumb lactation, / delicate, trembling, hidden, / warm, etc." The narrowing life in this view of woman is, naturally, unacceptable to Sexton. Her sympathy goes out with the dwarf whom she had internalized in earlier poetry:

> Then he tore himself in two.
> Somewhat like a split broiler,
> He laid his two sides on the floor,
> one part soft as a woman,
> one part a barbed hook.

In this book Sexton despairs of salvation. She begins *Transformations* as an energetic witch in quest of answers and ends as the lost, confused little girl, "coming out of prison," pleading with her drunken, sadistic father, to God, to help her in this "life after death" ("Briar Rose").

III

These two parts of her split personality, the "evil" witch and the lost little girl or, from a mythic perspective, the Demeter and Persephone, vie with each other for dominance. But of the two it is clearly the witch who writes the poetry, the witch who is the explorer who, like Demeter, maintains her quest in the face of frequent discouragements and reprimands from both man and gods. As Demeter flew over land and sea in quest of her lost daughter, Sexton imaginatively flies on the wings of her poetry, from subject to subject in quest of her lost self. Now she moves backwards in time, or into the recesses of her mind or of a love affair, then into fairy tales and Christian mysticism—always moving, frenetically, back and forth in hopes of locating the whereabouts of her lost self. Her vehicle, she maintains, is spontaneous, almost automatic, as much the manifestation as the process of inquiry:

> My business is words. Words are like labels,
> or coins, or better, like swarming bees.
> I confess I am only broken by the sources of things;
> as if words were counted like dead bees in the attic,
> unbuckled from their yellow eyes and their dry wings.
> I must always forget how one word is able to pick
> out another, to manner another, until I have got
> something I might have said . . .
> but did not.
>
> ("Said the poet to the Analyst," *TB*)

It is as if the words, guided by an instinct of their own, like bees, would take her to her source, her inner impulses. But, blocked by the patriarchal restrictions encoded in her consciousness, they do not. The block, the resistance, feels like sin to her. "Mother and Jack and the Rain" (*LD*) indicts even her vehicle, poetry. With "let the poem be made" Sexton suggests the opening of Genesis and a God-like creativity that is no business for "good girls." Sexton is cavorting with the devil. Poetry is "The Black Art" (*APO*); it is an attempt to usurp God; it is a statement of dissatisfaction, of wanting more than her lot. Her overseer, the sense of encoded authority within herself, does not approve. Sexton feels damned:

A woman who writes feels too much,
those trances and portents!
As if cycles and children and islands
weren't enough; as if mourners and gossips
and vegetables were never enough.

She thinks she can warn the stars.
A writer is essentially a spy.
Dear love, I am that girl.

And, in fact, what she has as the lost, confused little girl is not enough for the whole creative woman.

Writing, then, is an expression of the dissatisfied, a reification of "need," "greed," and "hunger." It is a statement of desire for a higher fulfillment, for a mending of the elemental split, for a reunion of the writer's dissociated parts. Sexton tells us "Need is not quite belief" in "With Mercy for the Greedy" (*APO*) or "tell them need prevails," in "Doors, Doors, Doors" (*APO*); "I needed you," she admits to Joyce in "The Double Image" (*TB*) and in *The Awful Rowing Toward God* and *Words for Dr. Y.* need is translated to "hunger," Persephone's state: "Scrape off your hunger," she says in "The Wall" (*AW*) or the more subtle "Their mouths are immense" of "The Children" (*AW*); and in "The Bat or To Remember, To Remember" (*DY*) we read the poignant "I swelled with the thought, the deep inner need to life."

But, if it is the symptom of a disease, it is also partly the cure. Poetry, Sexton tells John Holmes ("For John Who Begs Me Not to Enquire Further," *TB*), is more than a means of entering the twisted caverns of her mind. It is as well a way she hopes to fill them, a way of discovering the order at her core by immersing herself in the seeming chaos and emptiness:

Not that it
was beautiful,

> but that,
> in the end, there was
> a certain sense of order there;
> something worth learning.

The method, "introspection leading to release," as Robert Phillips calls it (78), finds its mythological corollary in Demeter's lengthy quest for Persephone and the final descent of Demeter into Hades through the fires of the Telesterion to call forth her lost daughter (Kerenyi 42). Sexton describes her experience similarly:

> there is a big change after you write a poem. It's a marvelous feeling, and there's a big change in the psyche, but I think you really go into great chaos just before you write a poem, and during it, and then to come out of the whole [sic] somehow is a small miracle, which lasts for a couple of days. (Marx 570)

The coming together of her separate parts, of her "witch" or creative and organizing part with her lost child part, in the act of writing a poem, momentarily fulfills her and gives her a passing experience of reunion. But the ambivalence toward these aspects of herself, structured by the finally dominating Christian myth ("[I] have eaten the Cross, have digested its lore. . . ," "The Errand," *DY*) prevents her from sustaining reunion and wholeness for more than a few days. Nevertheless, the satisfaction she obtains from this glimpse of the possibility of wholeness drives her on in poem after poem, to repeat the descending Otherworld journey.

Works Cited

Campbell, Joseph. *The Hero With a Thousand Faces*. Princeton: Princeton UP, 1949.

Daly, Mary. *Beyond God the Father: Toward a Philosophy of Women's Liberation*. Boston: Beacon, 1973.

—. "The Qualitative Leap Beyond Patriarchal Religion." *Quest* 1.4 (Spring 1975): 20-40. Rpt. in *Readings in Recent Feminist Philosophy*. Ed. Marilyn Pearsall. Belmont: Wadsworth, 1986.

Kerényi, Carl. *Eleusis: Archetypal Image of Mother and Daughter*. New York: Pantheon, 1967.

Marx, Patricia. "Interview with Anne Sexton." *Hudson Review* 18.4 (Winter 1965-66): 570.

Neumann, Erick. *The Great Mother*. Trans. Ralph Manheim. Bollingen Series 47. Princeton: Princeton UP, 1972.

Phillips, Robert. *Confessional Poets*. Carbondale: Southern Illinois UP, 1973.

Pratt, Annis. "Archetypal Theory and Women's Fiction: 1688-1975." Women's Caucus, MLA Convention. 27 December 1975.

Rich, Adrienne. "Caryatid." *The American Poetry Review* 2.3 (May/June 1973).

Ricoeur, Paul. *The Symbolism of Evil*. Trans. Emerson Buchanan. Boston: Beacon, 1969.

Zollman, Sol. "Criticism, Self Criticism, No Transformation: The Poetry of Robert Lowell and Anne Sexton." *Literature and Ideology*. Montreal (1974):29-36.

JOURNEY INTO THE SUN: THE RELIGIOUS PILGRIMAGE OF ANNE SEXTON

Frances Bixler

O yellow eye,
let me be sick with your heat,
let me be feverish and frowning.
Now I am utterly given.
I am your daughter, your sweet-meat,
your priest, your mouth and your bird
and I will tell them all stories of you
until I am laid away forever,
a thin gray banner.

"The Sun" (*LD*)

The place I live in
is kind of a maze
and I keep seeking
the exit or the home.

"The Children" (*AW*)

This loneliness is just an exile from God.

April 1, 1963, (*WY*)

Anne Sexton's religious poetry presents different problems to different readers. For those who no longer accept the Christian God as a reality, her search seems dated and inexplicable.[1] Those who empathize with her need to make God a reality may yet feel at a loss to comprehend the twistings, contradictions, and confusions displayed by a large body of her work. Sexton's poetry is also a puzzlement for believers because of her frequent disregard for orthodox theology.

Thus, no reader comes away from her religious poetry feeling fully at ease.

For this reason and because Sexton chose to concentrate so heavily on the theme of religious need, it seems important to attempt a critical analysis of Sexton's religious poems, with an eye to understanding her quest, as much as that is possible, and an ear to hearing variations in tonalities which add to or subtract from the meaning. My aim here is to suggest that by looking at a number of poems ranging over Sexton's entire canon and by taking into account the biographical facts of her life as we now have them, we can arrive at a definition of what Anne Sexton meant when she said she was "both saved and lost"; we can understand more clearly, if not fully, her need for contact with that which is Other—a need more universal than we sometimes admit; and we can also appreciate the struggle of one who was more doubter than believer, more "lost" than "saved."

Such a struggle has a long history in literature. Dante's famous journey, Augustine's *Confessions*, Bunyan's fictive depiction of the Christian life, the search for the Ideal among many of the British Romantics, C. S. Lewis's autobiography, *Surprised by Joy*, and even the fantasy world of J. R. R. Tolkien attempt the recounting of a journey into a world that is different from the natural order. However, Sandra Gilbert identifies the very different experience of the female poet when she attempts a similar journey:

> The female poet . . . writes in the hope of discovering or defining a self, a certainty, a tradition. Striving for self-knowledge, she experiments with different propositions about her own nature, never cool or comfortable enough to be (like her male counterparts) an ironic sociologist; always, instead, a desperate Galileo, a passionate empiricist who sees herself founding a new science rather than extending the techniques and discoveries of an old one. (446)

Gilbert puts her finger on a number of the elements inherent in Sexton's journey. In her quest for God, Sexton was also discovering who she was, defining herself in terms of her relationship with God and especially, Jesus. Her need for establishing—with certainty—the Christian tradition or a new one of her own making is evident. And certainly, Sexton was never "cool or comfortable" about this matter. Her struggle was intense, deeply felt, and constant. In the end, she tried very hard to found a "new science."[2]

To understand the problem Sexton was trying to solve through her religious poetry, the reader must accept Sexton's description of her spiritual condition. She saw her gravest problem as being full of personal, internalized evil. It is this sense of being thoroughly poisoned that she attempts to assuage, to reason with, to kill, and especially to fight with words—those pieces of magic which did sometimes create order out of chaos, did assemble the fragments of the puzzle to make a whole. Sexton's religious poems comprise a great variety of forms and gain complexity with ironic layerings, straight-forward autobiography and confession, despair, prophecy, and celebration, poems that form a mass of imaginative, emotional, and poetic facts which don't always cohere logically, even after several readings. Looked at as a spiritual narrative, however, Sexton's religious poems do begin to speak to each other, and one gains new insights by considering all of her religious work as a unit, or perhaps more explicitly, as the record of a journey which has a specific goal, one fraught with enormous complications—complications the poet attempts to undo in an astounding variety of poetic endeavors.

Several poems shed light on the nature of Sexton's quest. The lightning changes in tone and voice of these selections suggest that Sexton was attempting to get at her subject through many avenues.[3] I have already cited three selections from her work. In "The Sun" Sexton identifies herself with fish who had the bad luck of coming up for sun and getting stuck on earth to rot and with flies that cannot bear the intense heat. They, too, die. My quotation completes the poem. The voice is that of supplication. I take the sun to be a pun on Son, meaning Christ. Thus, I interpret her petition as asking God for a trade-off. In essence, if you will not rot me with your heat or dry me out with your presence, I will do my best to tell what I know about you. Hence, she says, "I am your daughter," a statement affirming her sense of identity with God.[4] The second quotation, in a strikingly different voice, suggests the confusion that is constant on her journey, and the third is a single line published after her death but evidently written much earlier, indicating Sexton's analysis of her problem on one day of her life.

Three other poems provide insight into Sexton's religious quest. The first, "Gods," begins with the sardonic statement, "Mrs. Sexton went out looking for the gods." The searcher looks in books, talks to a poet, prays in "all the churches of the world," goes to the Atlantic and Pacific oceans, goes to the "Buddha, the Brahma, the Pyramids. . . ." She finds no one. Sarcastically, the narrator concludes:

> Then she journeyed back to her own house
> and the gods of the world were shut in the lavatory.
> At last!
> she cried out,
> and locked the door. (*DN*)

Readers of Sexton's poetry are familiar with this voice. It is that of the middle-aged witch in *Transformations* deliberately turning our fairy tales into nightmares, the voice that so often undercuts a serious poem with an ironic ending. This particular mixture of serious subject, deliberate mockery, and shocking images can leave the reader looking for a peg on which to hang meaning. However, I hear in this poem, in particular, a poignance masked by bravado. I also hear the deliberate attempt of the author to scoff at Mrs. Sexton's silly search—an attempt which doesn't quite come off. What does come through finally is the recognition that the search must be an inner one; and, of course, for Sexton this means a solid inquiry into the evil, imaged here by the lavatory, which pervades her life.

Radically different in tone and content is "The Fury of Overshoes" (*DN*). The speaker begins as the adult looking backward to childhood, asking the reader to remember all the indignities of childhood, but she concludes in the naive voice of the child herself:

> Oh thumb,
> I want a drink,
> it is dark,
> where are the big people,
> when will I get there,
> taking giant steps
> all day,
> each day
> and thinking
> nothing of it?

The child, sucking her thumb, speaks, nevertheless, in adult metaphor. The dark is her inability to understand herself and the god she is searching for. Big people are imaged constantly throughout Sexton's work as mothers and fathers, images which become archetypal representations of God. The steps the child is taking go nowhere, and the nothing she is thinking grows out of her ignorance.

A third selection, the short story "Dancing the Jig" (*BF*), supplies yet another aspect of Sexton's search. In this story the main character finds herself dancing wildly to music. She cannot stop, no matter how much she wishes to do so; nor can she control her movements. She is embarrassed and most relieved when the music dies away. Sitting down, she contemplates a chair across the room and thinks how every time her wild desire leaps up in her she attempts to concentrate on something like the chair. Though I think that this story is also about the frenzy of insanity, it lends insight into Sexton's search for a stable, unchanging God. The final lines hint at the underlying meaning: "It [the chair] is fine. . . . It is a relief to dwell on it—a perfect object. So fixed. So always the same" (*BF* 65-71). These several works reveal the central elements in Sexton's spiritual quest: the need for identity, the hunger for security and certainty, the fear of passion, and the recognition that this journey, above all, is interior.

I

Two central religious problems preoccupied Sexton throughout her poetic career—what to do with Jesus Christ and how to assuage her personal sense of evil. In letters dated over a year apart Sexton admitted to her friend, Brian Sweeney, that she was grappling with her questions about faith and God and especially about the divinity of Christ. October 25, 1969, Sexton writes: "Perhaps I should worry about God—he's bigger than any of this. I'm glad you're straight with Him. I have yet to settle the matter. Oh, I really believe in God—it's Christ that boggles the mind" (*Letters* 346). A later letter, dated November 24, 1970, reiterates her thought: "Yes, it is time to think about Christ again. I keep putting it off. If he is the God/man, I would feel a hell of a lot better. If there is a God, Sweeney, how do you explain him swallowing all those people up in Pakistan? Of course there's a God, but what kind is he? Is he our Kind?" (*Letters* 368-69). Both comments reveal that Sexton has no trouble thinking about God as some distant First Cause. She is really not very interested in this kind of God however; her search is for a "husband" (i. e. "the one who carries you through," "The God-Monger," *AW*). Thus, she constantly struggles with the need to believe in Christ, the God/man; yet her doubt just as constantly overrides her faith. Her reference to the terrible episode in Pakistan implies that God doesn't really work miracles. He's a fraud, a fake, someone totally unreliable.

Several poems reflect Sexton's vacillation regarding Christ's divinity. The first appears in one of her best-known poems, "The Division of Parts" (*TB*). In a deadly serious autobiographical voice, Sexton recounts going through her mother's possessions, dividing them with her sisters, remembering her mother's agonizingly slow death from cancer, and the resultant division she feels. The poem is made up of four parts, all happening on Good Friday, the day Christ was crucified. In a sense, this division is a kind of crucifixion for Sexton. She is being separated by death from her mother, but this has only served to bring her face to face with death. "I trip on your death and Jesus, *my stranger,* / floats up over / my Christian home, wearing his straight thorn tree. . . ." Sexton cannot get past the anguish of her mother's death and Christ's death; both seem too impossibly awful to accept as a part of life. She concludes:

> And Christ still waits. I have tried
> to exorcise the memory of each event
> and remain still, a mixed child,
> heavy with cloths of you.
> Sweet witch, you are my worried guide.
> Such dangerous angels walk through Lent.
> Their walls creak *Anne! Convert! Convert!*
> My desk moves. Its cave murmurs Boo
> and I am taken and beguiled.
> Or wrong. For all the way I've come
> I'll have to go again. Instead, I must convert
> to love. . . . (*TB*)

Sadly, Sexton realizes that her faith is really just a part of the "clutter of worship that you taught me, Mary Gray. . . ."

In this poem she discards her religious heritage while acknowledging her human heritage.

A much later poem, "The Falling Dolls," underlines Sexton's conviction that God, if there is a God, should be one who protects, preserves, heals, and feeds (*MS*). She tells of "Dolls, / by the thousands, / falling out of the sky." The implication is that these are people who have no one to help them, to protect them against the cruelties of life. Her rapid-fire questions at the end of the poem catch her anger:

> Why is there no mother?
> Why are all these dolls falling out of the sky?
> Was there a father?
> Or have the planets cut holes in their nets
> and let our childhood out,
> or are we the dolls themselves,
> born but never fed?

Here, as in so many of her poems, the use of mother and father is an archetypal image of God. Sexton, a mother herself, cannot comprehend a caring, loving God who does not feed his children.

Two more poems reflect the intensity of Sexton's sense of being left alone to work out her problems. She says hysterically:

> It makes me laugh
> to see a woman in this condition.
> It makes me laugh for America and New York City
> when your hands are cut off
> and no one answers the phone.
>
> "The Fury of Abandonment" (*DN*)

Typically, Sexton employs synecdoche to intensify her image. For her, "touch is all," yet she here images the woman as having her hands cut off; therefore, she has lost her ability to touch. Equally fatal is the unanswered telephone which Sexton consistently uses to represent the poet's connection to the imagination or to inspiration. With both these faculties out of order, the woman is in dire straits.

Again, using body imagery, Sexton talks about her inner pain:

They hear how
the artery of my soul has been severed
and soul is spurting out upon them,
bleeding on them,
messing up their clothes,
dirtying their shoes.

"The Big Heart" (*AW*)

It is of this pain that she says, "I would sell my life to avoid / the pain that begins in the crib . . . for better or worse / as you marry life. . . ("The Big Boots of Pain," *MS*).

Though Sexton's inability to believe in Christ's divinity caused her much frustration, her sense of being evil was her greatest source of anguish. A number of poems graphically illustrate my point. A short poem dated January 1, 1961, contains the lines, "None of them has / the sense of evil that I have. . . (*DY*). The people Sexton is talking about are her fellow poets, John Holmes, Maxine Kumin, and George Starbuck. Her assessment is probably accurate. Even Maxine Kumin, her sister poet, does not exhibit a similar obsession with evil. Sexton is more precise in "Is It True?":

When I tell the priest I am evil
he asks for a definition of the word.
Do you mean sin? he asks.
Sin, hell! I reply.
I've committed every one.
What I mean is evil,
(not meaning to be, you understand,
just something I ate).
Evil is maybe lying to God.
Or better, lying to love. (*TB*)

I interpret these lines to mean that Sexton's sensitivity to pain and to her own willingness to inflict pain on others leads her to this much more general definition of evil. Sins are acts committed against God or other persons. Evil, however, is a state of being which the poet attempts to capture in the last two lines of the quotation.

"The Evil Seekers" explores the nature of being human, which according to Sexton must of necessity include knowing about evil:

> but one must learn about evil,
> learn what is subhuman,
> learn how the blood pops out like a scream,
> one must see the night
> before one can realize the day. . . . (*AW*)

Nevertheless, the poem ends with an assertion that humans must make a desperate attempt to "bury" evil. The irony embodied in the title thus comes full circle: though we as human beings "seek" evil, we must just as actively try to eliminate it.

Sadly, getting rid of evil is not an easy task for Sexton. The shocking images of "After Auschwitz" reinforce her underlying hatred of humanity's tendency toward mutual self-destruction. The poem begins

> Anger,
> as black as a hook,
> overtakes me.
> Each day,
> each Nazi
> took, at 8:00 A.M., a baby
> and sauteed him for breakfast
> in his frying pan. (*AW*)

Such hyperbole instantly pulls the reader into the horror of WW II and its terrible evil. Probably no Nazi ever fried a baby for breakfast; yet, the image captures the intent of the heart which guided Nazis to serve their country by killing six million Jews. It is the intent of the heart that Sexton cares about. She continues a few lines further to indicate the extent of humanity's degradation:

Man is evil,
I say aloud.
Man is a flower
that should be burnt,
I say aloud.
Man
is a bird full of mud,
I say aloud.

Both flowers and birds figure quite heavily in Sexton's imagery as good, beautiful things. Thus, man, though having the image of the good is nothing but evil in this poem. The voice of the poet here is that of the prophet, crying in the street. It is also one of public and personal confession. She speaks for herself, and she speaks for us all.

If these poems were the only ones concerned with human evil, one could overlook them as samples of the poet having a bad day. Sexton, however, employs numerous images which convey her meaning powerfully. "The Fury of Flowers and Worms" sets up in its title the polar extremes that often appear in Sexton's work. She wishes to be close to the flowers because they help her to be "close to the worms / who struggle blindly / moving deep into their slime, / moving deep into God's abdomen . . . (*DN*). Lest one think that she is talking about real flowers and worms, another poem sets the matter straight:

We are all earthworms,
digging into our wrinkles.
We live beneath the ground

and if Christ should come in the form of a plow
and dig a furrow and push us up into the day
we earthworms would be blinded by the sudden light
and writhe in our distress.
As I write this sentence I too writhe.

"The Wall," (*AW*)

In spite of the obvious pain connected to being an earthworm, Sexton finds good in the fact that the worm is working its way to the light, an example of her "saved and lost" motif which I will explore in depth a bit later.[5]

In addition to the prominent worm imagery, Sexton wrote at least three important poems indicating that inner division provided much of her sense of dis-ease. Her name for this other self was "Old Dwarf Heart" (*APO*). "When I lie down to love / old dwarf heart shakes her head," go the first two lines. This other self is ugly, old, fat, corrupt, full of worldly knowledge, and inseparable. The poem concludes with a parody of the childish prayer:

Oh now I lay me down to love,
how awkwardly her arms undo,
how patiently I untangle her wrists
like knots. Old ornament, old naked fist,
even if I put on seventy coats I could not cover you . . .
mother, father, I'm made of.

Here the implication is that the evil is passed down from generation to generation, with no possibility of escape. "The Other" (*BF*) carries on the same idea of inner division. This time, however, the image is that of "Mr. Doppelgänger. My brother. My spouse. / Mr. Doppel-gänger. My enemy. My lover." Sexton's ambivalence toward this double becomes obvious here. She both loves and hates this part of herself.[6] Finally, Sexton creates a second self in the form of Nana, the great aunt whom Sexton had turned to in her childhood for the nurturing that Mary Gray seemed unable to give. Unfortunately, when Sexton was thirteen Nana suddenly went insane and had to be institutionalized. "The Hex" (*BF*) is in part the recounting of a young girl's terror when her beloved aunt turned strange, but it is is also an interpretation of that event. Nana's accusing voice saying, "You did it, You are the evil" steals the poet's joy of life. Consequently, Sexton names her the "Nana-hex." "Yes! I am still the criminal," Sexton admits. "Yes! Take me to the station house. / But book my double." Her double, though, is too intertwined with her, too much a part of her to be separated. The consequence is "The Civil War" (*AW*) where God is nothing but pieces of a puzzle and the poet is torn in two by her struggle to "build a whole nation of God / in me—but united."

Most invidious of all is Sexton's image of evil as "the rat inside of me." The first poem of *The Awful Rowing Toward God*, "Rowing," includes this image. Indeed, it is the presence of the rat which motivates the rower to keep on rowing "though the oarlocks stick and are rusty / and the sea blinks and rolls / like a worried eyeball. . . ." So urgent is the narrator's need that she makes a prophecy:

> there will be a door
> and I will open it
> and I will get rid of the rat inside of me,
> the gnawing pestilential rat.
> God will take it with his two hands
> and embrace it.

The implication is that God's embrace will somehow make the rat an acceptable animal with which the poet can live. The retelling of the Genesis story in "Rats Live On No Evil Star" (*DN*) creates the myth whereby the rat's existence is explained. Here Adam and Eve appear on the scene and "God looked out through his tunnel / and was pleased." However, the business of the apple becomes the basis for Eve's giving birth to a most vile creature:

with its bellyful of dirt
its hair seven inches long.
It had two eyes full of poison
and routine pointed teeth.
Thus Eve gave birth.
In this unnatural act
she gave birth to a rat.

Thus it is that Anne Sexton, poet, worm, "old dwarf heart," is also rat. One comes to this by being born.

No doubt the most unsettling images of evil are those having to do with excrement.[7] "After Auschwitz" (*AW*) contains the lines, "Man with his small pink toes . . . is not a temple / but an outhouse. . . ." "Is It True?" (*AW*) carries the image further:

When I tell the priest I am full
of bowel movement, right into the fingers,
he shrugs. To him shit is good.
To me, to my mother, it was poison
and the poison was all of me
in the nose, in the ears, in the lungs.

The poet continues employing the same images in "The Sickness Unto Death" (*AW*) when she says she could not "move nor eat bread" because she "was a house full of bowel movement. . . ." Other poems make oblique references to "this country of dirt" ("The Fish That Walked," *AW*), and to the sun which "passes over filth" ("Is It True?" *AW*).

One further note needs to be added in regard to Sexton's spiritual condition. She often conceded that the evil she professed to hate so much was really a good.[8] Typically, nothing is ever simple for Sexton, and her ambivalence toward the dark side of the human self greatly complicated her life. For example, a poem I have already cited, "Rats Live On No Evil Star" (*DN*), is a palindrome. Sexton concludes this poem by saying that "all us cursed ones" end up on the "RAT'S

STAR."[9] She is obviously making use of the reversibility of the words to turn meaning inside out. If one is a rat, one can depend on ending up on a star. The stability of the palindrome guarantees this. Sexton does a similar sleight-of-hand with the name Ms. Dog which she applies to herself in several late poems. Dog is God spelled backwards. I take this reversal to be a bit different in that a transformation is going on. The word is being turned around and so is different, yet related because all the letters are the same. Other indications that Sexton did not hate her evil as much as she said show up in her frequent use of Dalmatians—those black and white dogs. "The Fallen Angels" (*AW*) identifies the poet as "like them—both saved and lost." Furthermore, "they wiggle up life." The epigraph for "Angels of the Love Affair" (*BF*) reads, "Angels of the love affair, do you know that other, the dark one, that other me?" First lines of all six poems in this group begin with similar paradoxical questions:

1. Angel of fire and genitals, do you know slime. . . ?
2. Angel of clean sheets, do you know bedbugs. . . ?
3. Angel of flight and sleigh bells, do you know paralysis. . . ?
4. Angel of hope and calendars, do you know despair?
5. Angel of blizzards and blackouts, do you know raspberries. . . ?
6. Angel of beach houses and picnics, do you know solitaire?

The implication is that knowledge of evil is the source for much of Sexton's poetic energy. Indeed, she admits this quite plainly in a posthumously published poem dated December 4, 1967: "the old sense of evil remains, / evil that wife" (*DY*). Even more to the point is the poem "Baby Picture" (*DN*) in which Anne looks at her baby picture and thinks about who she was:

> I open the dress
> and I see a child bent on a toilet seat.

I crouch there, sitting dumbly
pushing the enemas out like ice cream,
letting the whole brown world
turn to sweets.

Having recognized excrement as one of Sexton's most powerful images for evil, the reader must also come to terms with the paradox of the good/evil which is represented by these lines and images. It is Sexton's double which "cries and cries and cries / until I put on a painted mask / and leer at Jesus in His passion" ("The Other," *BF*). Gilbert's thesis regarding women poets seems to be borne out in Sexton's turning inside out the consequences of evil and her evident disregard for orthodox theology, both as it relates to a definition of evil and as it relates to the nature of Jesus Christ. She does, indeed, seem to be creating "a new science."

II

Gilbert's metaphor built on Galileo and his courageous explorations into the unknown is a useful one to keep in mind when looking at Sexton's religious pilgrimage because she was equally courageous in exploring new foundations for religious faith. One direction she took was to employ the images and concepts of orthodoxy to create a new mythology; another was to renew the old Christian myth, adding dimensions peculiar to her own need.

Several stories and poems link together to form a new mythology—that of woman / poet / human who serves as redeemer. "Making a Living" (*DN*) stands as a clear statement underscoring Sexton's feeling that female sacrifice and death are a necessity. The poem is a retelling of the biblical story of Jonah and the Whale. Jonah finds himself inside the belly of the whale where he clearly understands that he must accept his own death. He diligently works his way toward total acceptance, including the "eating" of his past. Finally, Jonah is vomited up on shore and begins to tell his story to the world. The result is a conflation of the life stories of Jonah and Christ and the poet:

> Then he [Jonah] told the news media
> the strange details of his death
> and they hammered him up in the marketplace
> and sold him and sold him and sold him.
> My death the same.

The suffering of all three persons is meant to be the same, and their mission is also similar. Jonah gave himself to being a prophet, warning people of coming doom. Christ gave himself to death in order to create life in others. The poet gives herself to writing poetry in order to write "books . . . that act upon us like a misfortune, that make us suffer like the death of someone we love more than ourselves. . . " (Epigraph for *APO* vii).

Sexton seems to have been able to explore this idea more fully in stories rather than in poetry, though a number of poems do hint broadly at her re-visioning of Christian orthodoxy. "The Bat" or "To Remember, To Remember" (*DY*) is told by a bat whose "reward" for life has been to be reincarnated the ninth time as a bat who can remember only flashes of scenes from his former eight lives. The scenes make no sense to the narrator, but they do carry meaning for the reader. The motif of crucifixion, which has been present in Sexton's poetry from the very beginning, appears central to this story. Among other scenes, the bat reports seeing himself listening to a man in the street below giving orders to the batman to nail "MISS NO-NAME" against the wall. The bat says, "The girl rises, as he calls up to her to do so and then it's Him, Him, Him *telling, commanding,* and we are the actors in His play" (98-99). The capital H gives away the identity of the director; it is God. As prompted, the bat-man nails the girl, spread-eagled to the wall and kills her with his hunting knife. She takes twenty-four hours to die. In the conclusion of the poem the bat-man calls this a scene of "damnation," but the reader is left to consider the fact that this story holds a strong clue to Sexton's self identity as poet and female.

A second story, "Vampire," (*DY*) contains a black Eucharist in which the woman is the provider of the wine. Again, the narrator is a male who purports to be a normal person, selling life insurance for a living. However, he is captured one day and given a drug which turns him into a human vampire. For his "daily bread," the narrator must go out, taking with him a fresh loaf of French bread, and find a young woman. When he locates his victim, he places his mouth on her navel and sucks blood from her. His description of the act is deeply sensuous, suggesting sexual union. He explains his need for this "transfusion" of life in cold, objective tones, apparently unable to feel guilt over stealing life from someone else so that he can live. The narrator justifies himself this way: "Food! Food! It is perfectly proper and absolutely necessary to have food. . . . I starve. I eat. Plain common sense. Blood and bread, blood and bread, but human blood only, woman blood only. It must be thus. It was ordained" (92). Mr. Ha-ha in "The Ballet of the Buffoon," agrees with this pronouncement. He concludes his oration to the people by saying "Every man kills his wife. It's a matter of history" (*BF* 81). Sexton makes her plainest statement about her new mythology in "The Author of the Jesus Papers Speaks" (*BF*). She tells of having a dream that she was milking a cow and waiting for milk to come forth when, instead, the cow begins to give blood. The poet's reaction is to be ashamed. Following God's instructions, she goes to a well and pulls out a baby, giving birth in a sense as the Virgin Mary did. What follows is the kernel of Sexton's new religion:

Then God spoke to me and said:
Here. Take this gingerbread lady
and put her in your oven.
When the cow gives blood
and the Christ is born
we must all eat sacrifices.
We must all eat beautiful women.

Having given up on believing in the efficacy of Christ's death and resurrection to "save" her, Sexton places herself and other "beautiful women" in the position of bearing the burden of redemption for the human race. Diana Hume George suggests that these lines represent "the other 'sacrifice' of Christianity, corresponding to Christ's sacrifice on behalf of humanity in the person of his male body" (18). Certainly, the Christian church has demanded its pound of flesh from "beautiful women" who have chosen to step out of the boundaries prescribed for them by dogma and tradition. Sexton may also mean to imply in this poem that society asks women, especially female artists, to pay a high price for their calling. She asserts that these chosen ones must dig into into their souls "and ask and ask and ask / until the kingdom, / however queer, / will come" ("Hurry Up Please It's Time" (*DN*).

A discussion of Sexton's new mythology would not be complete without an examination of "The Jesus Papers" (*BF*). Alicia Ostriker sees the "radical vision of 'The Jesus Papers'" as a "systematic and structured . . . reinterpretation of Christian myth". . . ("That Story" 13). Her comment is an apt one. Each of these poems debunks some aspect of Christ's life central to the Christian story. In "Jesus Suckles" the Christ child is at first warmly comfortable at Mary's breast, but the poem ends with the blunt, "No. No. / All Lies. / I am a truck. I run everything. / I own you." Jesus becomes the patriarchal male, determined to dominate and possess everything. Both "Jesus Awake" and "Jesus Asleep" mock Christ's celibacy, but the point of both of these poems is that the loss of touch and sexual union results in terrible pain for humanity. Christ's "celibate life" becomes a medal which is "pinned" on him but at great cost to those he supposedly came to serve. "The Fury of Cocks" (*DN*) serves as counterpoint for these poems where the final lines suggest:

> When they break away they are God.
> When they snore they are God.
> In the morning they butter the toast.
> They don't say much.
> They are still God.
> All the cocks of the world are God,
> blooming, blooming, blooming
> into the sweet blood of woman.

Sexual union, for Sexton, is an image of wholeness. Thus, Christ's refusal to participate in sex makes him small and mean. In "Jesus Asleep" the result of his refusal is that Mary, because she has had no touch from Christ, stays fixed forever on the crucifix with Christ.

An important part of the Gospels are the stories of the miracles Jesus did while on earth. Sexton retells several of these stories in "The Jesus Papers" giving them an ironic twist. "Jesus Raises Up the Harlot" sets the scene where the harlot finds herself in fear for her life because she is being stoned to death. The biblical story places Jesus in the center of the controversy, suggesting to the religious men who were attempting to kill the woman that the one who was without sin should cast the first stone. Of course, none of them can since they probably had all helped to make an adulterous woman out of someone. Sexton's story, however, makes Christ the terrible rescuer. He keeps the harlot from being stoned, but he finds it necessary to "lance her twice on each breast" in order to remove her sickness. The milk flows out and the woman follows Jesus "like a puppy" for the rest of her days. Loss of milk in this context suggests that the woman had lost her god-like qualities and her individuality. She now is "cured," but she has no self. She has traded sickness for a kind of death-in-life.

In both "Jesus Cooks" and "Jesus Summons Forth" Sexton manages to make the miracles of feeding the five thousand and the raising of Lazarus from the dead look like a trick a magician or a con man would use. "Work on the sly / opening boxes of sardine cans," he tells the disciples. The people finally eat well "from invisible dishes." The figure of Lazarus is equally ridiculous. After strenuous efforts to put the body and bones back together, Jesus manages to get his soul dropped down into him only to have the narrator comment that Lazarus was grateful because "in heaven it had been no different. / In heaven there had been no change."

Sexton concludes "The Jesus Papers" with two companion poems—"Jesus Dies" and "Jesus Unborn." In the first poem Jesus is the speaker; his point of view is from the elevation of the cross. Every word he says identifies him as a man dying a cruel death but not a God taking on the sins of the world:

> I want heaven to descend and sit on My dinner plate
> and so do you.
> I want God to put His steaming arms around Me
> and so do you.
> Because we need.
> Because we are sore creatures.

In these lines Jesus is characterized as an empathetic, caring human being, suffering as all humanity suffers, and dying as we all must die. "This is a personal matter," he tells the crowd. Sexton refuses to recognize any global significance in this death.

"Jesus Unborn" is reminiscent of Yeats "The Second Coming." Mary lies in a kind of trance while a "strange being" hovers over her with "executioner's eyes." Mary is obviously one of the beautiful women who must be "eaten" in order for the world to go right. The poem continues in an apocalyptic tone: "All this will be remembered. / Now we will have a Christ." However, the ending of the poem suggests the violence of this act—a rape which ends Mary's own life, "shuts her lifetime up / into this dump-faced day." The birth of Christ costs Mary her life—one life for one life. The sacrifice seems unjustifiable. So ends "The Jesus Papers" with Jesus a patriarchal male, a good person who refuses to touch anyone in need, a helpless human, a con man, a terrifying physician, and a thief of life similar to the vampire in the story I have already mentioned. Sexton's conclusion that under these circumstances "We must all eat beautiful women" seems somehow logical and fitting.

Though Sexton makes a valiant attempt to create a new myth, she appears unsure of herself and unsatisfied with its reality. "The Passion of the Mad Rabbit" (*MS*) suggests that her re-vision turned into a bad dream. In this poem the poet tells of undergoing a "removal" and allowing "a fool" to enter her. His name is Mr. Rabbit. The scene is "bad Friday" and Mr. Rabbit is crucified, taking three days to die. So far these images echo those of the stories and poems I have already cited. Easter comes and the bunny, Mr. Rabbit, is burned while he/she (by now the poet has identified herself with Mr. Rabbit) sings until her blood boils. Nevertheless, the last lines of the poem tell the ironic truth: "In place of the Lord, / I whispered, / a fool has risen." Humble, almost silent, awed by her own blasphemy, the poet admits her failure. It should be noted that most of the poems in which Sexton attempts to construct her new mythology are located in the collection she chose to title *The Book of Folly*. Her next collection takes on entirely new dimensions, employs new voices, and rarely reverts to sardonic irony.

III

The Death Notebooks and *The Awful Rowing Toward God* comprise a new direction for Sexton's religious explorations. In them she returns to Christian myth, but adds her own dimensions to the story. The "O Ye Tongues" sequence (*DN*) is surely one of Sexton's finest achievements. Her appropriation of an apocalyptic voice, her deft handling of a new form, and her weaving together of narrative and lyric elements make these outstanding poems. Included in her achievements in these poems is the creation of a new character whose name is Christopher. I take him to be the sometimes mad religious poet, Christopher Smart, from whom Sexton obviously borrows the form for "O Ye Tongues"; but I also think Sexton is punning on the name and intends Christopher to stand for Christ as well. (Christopher comes from the Greek *Christophoros*—bearing Christ.) These ten psalms compress the story of Sexton's religious pilgrimage while they expand the reader's understanding of her quest.

The psalms begin with the powerful command "Let there be a God as large as a sunlamp to laugh his heat at you." This is the *let* of "Let there be light" spoken by God in Genesis—a statement of great strength and creative power. Immediately, in Genesis, there was light. We can assume that Sexton expects similar results from her commands. She continues creating a new heaven and a new earth in "First Psalm" where things fit together, where a "worm room" makes place for worms, where God does his part to make life good, and life contains laughter and fulfillment.

"Second Psalm" is a petition with the poet making trivial and important requests: "For I pray that John F. Kennedy will forgive me for stealing his free-from-the-Senate Manila envelope. . . . For I pray that God will digest me."

It is in "Third Psalm" that Christopher appears for the first time. Again each line begins with the powerful *let*. "Let

Anne and Christopher kneel with a buzzard whose mouth will bite her toe so that she may offer it up." Together the two come to sacrifice, and this time the sacrificial gift is not a life but a big toe. The psalm continues with all the things that Anne and Christopher will do: "Praise the Lord. . . ." "Humble themselves. . . ." "Serve. . . ." "Bless and rejoice."

"Fourth Psalm" creates the sharpest identity between Sexton and Christopher. It opens with the poignant line, "For I am an orphan with two death masks on the mantel and came from the grave of my mama's belly into the commerce of Boston." The poet's sense of loneliness gives way to joy, therefore, when she says:

> For Anne and Christopher were born in my head as I howled at the grave of the roses. . . .
>
> For Christopher, my imaginary brother, my twin holding his baby cock like a minnow.
>
> For I became a *we* and this imaginary *we* became a kind company when the big balloons did not bend over us.
>
> . . . .
>
> For I shat and Christopher smiled and said let the air be sweet with your soil.
>
> For I listened to Christopher unless the balloon came and changed my bandage.
>
> My crotch itched and hands oiled it.
>
> For I lay as single as death. Christopher lay beside me. He was living.
>
> For I lay as stiff as the paper roses and Christopher took a tin basin and bathed me.
>
> . . . .

> For birth was a disease and Christopher and I invented the cure.

From being an orphan to being a twin who knows touch and love and acceptance, Sexton blossoms forth in new life. She declares jubilantly, "For we swallow magic and we deliver Anne."

"Fifth Psalm" again employs the emphatic *let*.

> Let Christopher and Anne come forth with a pig as bold as an assistant professor. He who comes forth from soil and the subway makes poison sweet.

The psalm continues with all the things that Anne and Christopher will bring as they "come forth"—a mole, a daisy, an orange, a snail, a squid with poison to pour over the Lord, a rose, a daffodil, a spotted dog (Sexton's favorite Dalmatians), a cockroach "large enough to be Franz Kafka," a carp, a leopard, the Mediterranean, and a tree-frog. The succession of items includes many of the natural things we normally abhor as well as some of Sexton's favorite symbolic images such as the mole, the daisy and the orange embodying goodness.

"Sixth Psalm" and "Seventh Psalm" evolve slowly through the now-familiar succession of free-verse lines. "For" is the word introducing the lines in "Sixth Psalm." It is instructive in that the prior psalm employs the grand *let*. One needs to string together the successive elements in this fashion: "Let . . . For . . . ." In this case, the opening lines read, "For America is a lady rocking on a porch in an unpainted house on an unused road but *Anne does not see it*" (my emphasis). This is the first implication that Anne is preparing for death. The psalm contains other hints that death is imminent: "Anne is locked in . . . . She has no one. She has Christopher." However, "Seventh Psalm" turns away from the heavy sound of death to rejoicing. Many lines begin "Rejoice. . . ."

Others begin "Give praise. . . ."

"Eighth Psalm" continues in a celebration of joy. The reasons are given by the poet:

> No. No. The woman is cheerful, she smiles at her stomach. She has swallowed a bagful of oranges and she is well pleased.
>
> For she has come through the voyage fit and her room carries the little people.

Oranges, in Sexton's work, are always images of the sun, of light, and goodness. The poet is, thus, full of God. The voyage, which she explores in much greater depth in *The Awful Rowing*, appears to be over. The psalm continues to tell how dangerous has been the journey, how difficult. Christopher, however, has had a part. He has put her into a "neat package" which will hold together, a line implying that all the troubling inconsistencies of life have been made into a comprehensive whole. The poem continues, suggesting that the poet is "nourished by darkness" and is "a hoarder," putting away "silks and wools and lips and small white eyes." The strange combination speaks of the various riches Sexton has found through her poetic endeavors. Finally, the penultimate moment arrives in stunning birth imagery:

> For she [Anne] is seeing the end of her confinement now and is waiting like a stone for the waters.
>
> For the baby crowns and there is a people-dawn in the world.
>
> For the baby lies in its water and blood and there is a people-cry in the world.
>
> For the baby suckles and there is a people made of milk for her to use. There are milk trees to hiss her on. There are milk

> beds in which to lie and dream of a warm room. There are milk fingers to fold and unfold. There are milk bottoms that are wet and caressed and put into their cotton.

I have no doubt that this baby is the same one of "The Death Baby" sequence. However, these lines indicate a birthing into something new, not just a "final rocking." The abundance of milk images confirm that the baby will find mothering and food enough for any need. The poem concludes:

> For the baby lives. The mother will die and when she does Christopher will go with her. Christopher who stabbed his kisses and cried up to make two out of one.

Sexton personalizes the Christian story to include this intensely personal sharing of an experience by two so closely intertwined that they cannot be separated, even by death.

"Ninth Psalm" is again a psalm of praise for the ordinary, mundane good things in life. "Tenth Psalm" returns, however, to the birth imagery of the "Eighth": "For as the baby springs out like a starfish into her million light years Anne sees that she must climb her own mountain." Here, Sexton adds the dimension she insists upon so strongly in *The Awful Rowing*. She will help herself; she will "do her own wash," and the medium for this will be her words. In this poem the baby grows, becomes a woman, has a child, and walks "up and up" . . . "until she was old as the moon and its naggy voice." Journey's end finds Anne and Christopher working together:

> For Anne sat down with the blood of a hammer and built a tombstone for herself and Christopher sat beside her and was well pleased with their red shadow.
>
> For they hung up a picture of a rat and the rat smiled and held out his hand.

> For the rat was blessed on that mountain. He was given a white bath. (*DN*)

The prophecy of "The Rowing" comes true in these lines. The rat is transformed. Finally, Sexton says

> For God did not forsake them but put the blood angel to look after them until such time as they would enter their star.

The reference to the star, implies that Christopher too is a rat, waiting his time to be translated to this radiant world. Thus, Anne and Christopher share their suffering, their sacrificial living, and their reward. Together, they "hammer" out their salvation.

The Awful Rowing Toward God is largely an expansion of "O Ye Tongues." Written between January 10 and January 30, 1973, just prior to the final settlement of Sexton's divorce, these poems seem flat and prosy after the intense power of the prior sequence. They do, however, add some valuable insight into the particular dimensions Sexton insisted upon in her personal mythology. Enclosed by two poems, "Rowing" and "The Rowing Endeth," the collection carries the reader through the ups and downs of a search for God who is largely missing. Space will not permit me to follow the journey closely, but I would like to discuss briefly several poems which expand the meaning of the "O Ye Tongues" sequence.

"The Sickness Unto Death" appears in the very center of *The Awful Rowing*, suggesting that its placement marks a crucial turning point in Sexton's spiritual journey, which now is definitely a journey toward God. The title of the poem comes from a work by Kierkegaard which Sexton may have read. One of the epigraphs for this collection is also Kierkegaard's: "But above all do not make yourself important by doubting" (vi). In this poem Sexton suggests through images of dry seas and paralysis and an inability to eat or touch that God has left her completely. She cannot hold onto the usual things that comfort people such as Bibles, crucifixes or even her favorite flower, a yellow daisy. In despair she cries, "I who wanted to crawl toward God / could not move nor eat bread." Her solution is to "eat" herself, a phrase which appears many times in her poetry and usually means that she is trying to wash herself clean of the memories and sins of her past life. In doing so, she is eating a "beautiful woman"—herself. The result is that "Jesus stood over me looking down / and He laughed to find me gone, / and put His mouth to mine / and gave me His air." The Anne who is gone is the old, evil Anne; following the biblical and very orthodox paradox, she has lost her life in order to save it. Jesus "inspires" the new Anne; the image is an archetypal one from the Bible where the believer is breathed on by the Holy Spirit and so filled with new life. Evidence of a change comes when Sexton, calling Christ "my kindred, my brother," gives away her yellow daisy—that symbol of life which she cherishes. Several elements in this poem connect with the psalm sequence. There is the death/birth cycle, the brother, the necessary self-renewal of the poet, and the joy of new life.

Following this poem are several of Sexton's most joyous lyrics. "Is It True?" concludes with the poet imagining that all she longs for is, in fact, reality. One should not underestimate the power of the word "imagine" for Sexton; she is, after all, a poet of great image-making power. She has in the "O Ye Tongues" sequence created a new heaven and a new earth. It is not so hard to accept that what she "imagines" here is intensely true. "Welcome Morning" is a paean of praise for the joy she feels. "What the Bird With the Human Head Knew" suggests fulfillment. The poet has walked many days in a dry desert looking for God:

> Then, in the middle of the desert
> I found the well,

> it bubbled up and down like a litter of cats
> and there was water,
> and I drank,
> and there was water,
> and I drank.

The image of thirst has not appeared so often in prior poems; more often it has been of hunger. However, milk has figured very strongly as the ultimate food, so the water image works for both food and drink. Clearly, the poet finds the same satisfaction in this poem that she finds in the "Eighth Psalm" where milk flows everywhere.

Other poems suggest the same deeply felt satisfaction:

> And God is filling me,
> though there are times of doubt
> as hollow as the Grand Canyon,
> still God is filling me.
>
> ("The Big Heart")

"Frenzy," likens the poet's faith to a small wire and suggests that just such a fragile connection can carry faith to a person. "Snow" happily images everything covered with white: "The ground has on its clothes. / The trees poke out of sheets / and each branch wears the sock of God." Purity overlays all the filth and evil of the world. The poet joyfully concludes: "There is hope / There is hope everywhere. Today God gives milk / and I have the pail." Milk and snow, food and cleansing—again the images are reminiscent of "Eighth" and "Tenth Psalm."

"The Rowing Endeth" is a poem which has puzzled many, but a comparison of this poem with "Tenth Psalm" opens new avenues for understanding. Throughout this collection the overriding metaphor has been the image of the poet in her small wooden boat rowing against the waves toward her unknown and perhaps even unknowable destination. In this final poem, however, the suspense is over. "I'm mooring my rowboat / at the dock of the island called God," the poet asserts quietly. As in the psalm, she has "come through the voyage fit. . . ." The poet then empties herself from her wooden rowboat onto "the flesh of The Island." The word flesh is biblical, referring to Christ: "I am the living bread that came down from heaven. If a man eats of this bread, he will live forever. This bread is my flesh, which I will give for the life of the world" (John 6:51). The emptying of herself, like the eating of herself in "The Sickness . . . ," and like the "neat package" Christopher makes of her in "Tenth Psalm," makes it possible for a birthing to occur.

Perhaps most perplexing and certainly amusingly irreverent is the image of God and Sexton playing poker. Some critics have seen this as Sexton's sardonic statement that life is a game of chance which can't be won because God cheats.[10] However, this game of chance is turned into a can't-lose situation by a special set of circumstances. A royal straight flush contains an ace. This is what the poet holds in her hand, and this is what enables her to say she wins. God also wins "because He holds five aces." In a normal deck of cards only four aces appear. It is possible to have two wild cards in a game of Poker which would explain the presence of a total of six aces. Perhaps this is what was in Sexton's mind. What is impossible to overlook are the clear statements that both God and Sexton win, and both share their mutual happiness. Just as Anne and Christopher share their death and together await their removal to their star, so God and Anne share their laughter imaged as union of man and woman, "the laughter rolling like a hoop out of His mouth / and into mine. . . ." Finally, though Anne has had to work very hard herself, she accepts the "win" of another as her "win." If we believe the "Tenth Psalm," Christopher, her brother, has made this possible. He is the "wild card" God throws into the game.

IV

The religious poems of Anne Sexton form an integral part of her work. Equally important is their treatment as religious poems. Though Freudian and archetypal analyses lend valuable insight into the unconscious sources of Sexton's imagery, she deserves to be regarded as a fine religious poet in a long line from John Donne to the present. Such an analysis is always fraught with the danger that the critic sees what she wishes to see, or in Stanley Fish's terms, creates her own text. We all come to a poet's work with our own belief systems interacting with that of the poet. The fact that Sexton was working out her belief system makes her poetry more difficult to synthesize. She emphasized this herself in a letter to Rise and Steven Axelrod concerning *Live or Die*: "The poems stand for the moment they are written and make no promises to the future events and consciousness and raising of the unconscious as happens as one goes forward and does not look backward for an answer in an old poem" (*Letters* 421). In a very good archetypal analysis of *The Awful Rowing*, Kathleen L. Nichols suggests that this is "precisely the problem, for in her [Sexton's] poetry the integrating process must also be attempted over and over again, establishing an exhausting cycle that finally can be stopped only by death" (no. 21). By placing various poems and stories side by side, by juxtaposing images from an entire canon, by attempting to recreate a narrative, by integrating what the poet has not integrated, I am, in some measure, doing violence to Sexton's work. Yet the loss is, in part, replaced by the gain in understanding which a single poem cannot give to the reader. Sexton is most especially a poet who employs clusters of images, recurrent themes, and telling details which only appear important when read in the context of her canon. In gathering up the significance of these details, one tends to simplify or to make systematic that which is anything but a system. Such is not my intent. Sexton was not able to create a "new science," nor was she completely comfortable with the old tradition. What Anne Sexton did was to courageously strike out where no woman poet has gone before, leaving us the record full of pain and joy, full of inconsistencies, of starts and stops, of defeats and victories.

Notes

[1]Middlebrook sees her problem as that of being female (296). George feels Sexton's journey is a "return to the fathers" and a representation of that quest which is native to Western culture, one that she describes as deeply patriarchal ("How We Danced" in *Oedipus Anne,* 24-54).

[2]Ostriker supports Gilbert in suggesting that "knowledge through women's mythmaking is achieved through personal, intuitive, and subjective means. It is never to be derived from prior authority and is always to be tested within the self" (*Stealing the Language* 235).

[3]George's chapter in *Oedipus Anne,* "Sexton's Speakers: Many Kinds of *I,*" is an excellent exploration of the impact of voice upon meaning as well as the recognition of the wide range of voices Sexton is capable of employing. George also makes the point, with which I strongly concur, that though a poet chooses the pronoun *I,* she does not necessarily speak in an autobiographical voice. The very act of creating a poem means that the poet is *creating* a persona or a voice or a situation. Even when the content of a poem is markedly biographical, the tone, the choice of words, the form of the poem put distance between the author and her work. Thus, throughout this paper, though I will speak of Sexton as both author and actor in many of her poems, I readily recognize this important distinction George makes.

[4]Other interpretations can be made of the sun image, but I base my interpretation on Sexton's use of the fish and the fly, two images which she consistently uses to represent good and evil through her work. Also, light or sun appears frequently as an archetypal image of God. See "Hurry Up Please It's Time," (*DN,* 69); "The Fury of Sunrises," (*DN,* 50-51); "Fifth Psalm," images of light, sun, and oranges (*DN,* 87); "Is It True?"—"blaze of butter" (*AW*); "The Room of My Life," "lights keep poking at me," (*AW*); "The Wall," "blinded by the sudden light," (*AW*).

[5]See "The Earthworm," (*MS,* 41).

[6]Gilbert recognizes the tension between the public and the private

woman also. She, in fact, thinks that it is a central problem for many female poets. The female poet, struggling to define herself in a male world, discovers that she has two selves—the one which everyone sees and knows and the other, darker self. "The female poet's second self, however, is associated with her secret name, her rebellious longings, her rage against imposed definitions, her creative passions, her anxiety, and—yes—her art. And it is this *Doppelgänger* of a second self which, generating the woman's uneasiness with male myths of femininity, gives energy as well as complexity to her struggle toward self-definition. For if the first self is public, rational, social, and therefore seems somehow 'natural,' this dark, other, second self is private, irrational, antisocial, and therefore—in the best romantic tradition—associated with the supernatural" (451).

[7]Such imagery is not unique to Sexton, however. Dante (*The Inferno*) and Soltzhenitzen ("A Day in the Life of Ivan Denisovich") are two other writers who employ images of excrement to indicate utter depravity.

[8]Ostriker suggests that "duplicity" in poetry is what gives it its energy, "when, in other words, the poet is driven by something forbidden to express but impossible to repress—is a means of creating high artistic excitement. . ." (*Stealing the Language* 41).

[9]Middlebrook suggests that "star" in Sexton's mythology is the "place—the poetic symbol—where the language of private suffering grows radiant and magically ambiguous" (296).

[10]Middlebrook suggests that Sexton loses because she cannot have an ace in her royal straight flush. However, Sexton says clearly that she wins. Thus, I cannot see how one could say that the "'wild card' signifies the privilege of Him over Her everywhere—the inscrutable possession of dominance" (310). The laughter at the end of the poem, the images of union suggested by the hoops flowing from one to the other, and the double win statements undercut such a reading.

[11]In "Visual Images by Women: A Test Case for the Theory of Archetypes" (64), Lauter discusses the problems with Jungian theory, especially as it relates to the concepts of the anima and the animus. Finally, Lauter suggests that critics cut themselves free from these limiting concepts and look instead for animity—a word coined by Carol Schreier Rupprecht and best understood as "an affirmation of the psychophysical unity of the human person" ("Feminist Archetypal Theory: A Proposal" 227-31). She also disagrees with Neumann's willingness to "subsume all aspects of the feminine under the archetype of the Great Mother" as too confining ("Visual Images" 73). Even Toni Wolff's "medial woman" is an archetype that Lauter rejects in favor of the woman who is herself in-

spired, rather than one who serves the purposes of another person or task ("Visual Images" 74). Sexton as poet / prophet / redeemer seems to fit this latter category very well.

Works Cited

George, Diana Hume. *Oedipus Anne: The Poetry of Anne Sexton.* Urbana: U of Illinois P, 1987.

Gilbert, Sandra M. "'My Name Is Darkness': The Poetry of Self-Definition." *Contemporary Literature.* 18 (1977): 443-57.

Middlebrook, Diane. "Poet of Weird Abundance." Rev. of *The Complete Poems: Anne Sexton. Parnassus: Poetry in Review.* 12-13 (1985): 293-315.

Nichols, Kathleen L. "The Hungry Beast Rowing Toward God: Anne Sexton's Later Religious Poetry." *Notes on Modern American Literature* 3 (Summer 1979), no. 21.

Ostriker, Alicia. *Stealing the Language: The Emergence of Women's Poetry in America.* Boston: Beacon Press, 1986.

___. "That Story: Anne Sexton and Her Transformations." *The American Poetry Review.* July-Aug. 1982: 11-16.

Sexton, Anne. *The Complete Poems.* Boston: Houghton Mifflin, 1981.

Sexton, Linda Gray and Lois Ames, eds. *Anne Sexton: A Self-Portrait in Letters.* Boston: Houghton Mifflin, 1977.

Epilogue

Every time I get happy
The Nana-hex comes through.
Birds turn into plumber's tools,
a sonnet turns into a dirty joke,
a wind turns into a tracheotomy,
a boat turns into a corpse,
a ribbon turns into a noose . . . .

"The Hex"
The Book of Folly

ITINERARY OF AN OBSESSION: MAXINE KUMIN'S POEMS TO ANNE SEXTON

Diana Hume George

Max

Max and I
two immoderate sisters,
two immoderate writers,
two burdeners,
made a pact.
To beat death down with a stick.
To take over.
To build our death like carpenters.
When she had a broken back,
each night we built her sleep.
Talking on the hot line
until her eyes pulled down like shades.
And we agreed in those long hushed phone calls
that when the moment comes
we'll talk turkey,
we'll shoot words straight from the hip,
we'll play it as it lays.
Yes,
when death comes with its hood
we won't be polite.

Anne Sexton ("The Death Baby," *DN*)

Years pass, as they say in storybooks.
It is true that I dream of you less.
Still, when the phone rings in my sleep
and I answer, a dream-cigarette in my hand,
it is always the same. We are back at our posts,
hanging around like boxers in
our old flannel bathrobes. You haven't changed.
I, on the other hand, am forced to grow older.

—Maxine Kumin, "Itinerary of an Obsession"

Soon I will be sixty.
How it was with you now hardly more vivid than how
it is without you, I carry
the sheer weight of the telling
like a large infant, on one hip.
I who am remaindered in the conspiracy,
doom, doom on my lips.

—Maxine Kumin, "Apostrophe to a Dead Friend"

MK: She had all my regard and sympathy and affection, and I guess I had all of hers. A day never passed that we didn't speak, on the phone if we didn't see each other, usually several times a day. It was that kind of relationship.

DHG: Does a day ever go by now that you don't think of her?

MK: Hardly. And I think up until a year ago I would have said never, but now I think it's almost ten years. I think occasionally a day passes when she's not in the front of my mind. But rarely. It isn't a conscious thing at all, it's just that . . . she's just there.

—Interview, Maxine Kumin and Diana Hume George, October 1983, Erie, PA.

"As the world knows, we were intimate friends and professional allies," wrote Maxine Kumin in "A Friendship Remembered" (83). Stable and strong, I think the poetry world would call Kumin, in direct contrast to Sexton's famous instability and fragility. While Sexton wrote about suicide, Kumin wrote about chopping wood. If Maxine Kumin has cut a rather sedate and restrained figure in contrast to her baroque "sister," she has also secured more respect. She does not stand accused of Sexton's many sins—although, happily from my point of view, she has certainly committed them.

I begin with this paradox: a famous friendship between two women poets of the same time and place, an enduring sisterhood that the public perceives as a unity of opposites, poetic as well as personal. Even Maxine Kumin has shared this assumption about their poetry, one she specified in a 1975 interview for the *Massachusetts Review*: "Anne Sexton was a very close personal friend. I know that sounds odd because we're so different; our voices are so different" (Meek Interview 29). As late as 1983, Kumin continued to see theirs as a collaboration if not of opposite sensibilities, then at least of vastly different ones. In response to my question about similarities in their poetry—one I asked to counter exactly this assumption of fundamental difference—Maxine Kumin replied: "There are probably more differences than there are similarities, although we empathized enormously with what each other was doing. My focus was always more on the natural world. Anne's focus was always more on human relationships" (George Interview). Maxine Kumin acknowledges that in recent years, she has become "able to deal with human relationships to a degree that perhaps I wasn't able to early on":

> I've become . . . much more apocalyptic than I ever dreamed I would be. So that in a way I've overtaken a lot of her themes. . . . Anne encouraged me and drew me out in ways that I was just barely ready for then. So that my directness, my openness, my ability to confront feelings, I think is a natural outcome of our relationship. (George Interview)

Among Kumin's many public tributes to Anne Sexton, this is one of the most telling for anyone who reads Maxine Kumin; for hers has become one of the most courageous and powerful voices in contemporary poetry. Indeed, she has "overtaken" many of Sexton's themes, in more than one sense: she has overtaken in the sense that she has caught up to those themes, and she has also taken them over, by which I mean that since Sexton's death, Kumin has become Sexton's successor, her inheritor, the voice that speaks both of and for Sexton now that Sexton is silent. In *House, Bridge, Fountain, Gate, The Retrieval System* and *Our Ground Time Here Will be Brief*, American poetry inherited an intricate amalgam of the styles, themes, and voices we once separated, and associated with Sexton or Kumin, seldom both.[1]

Kumin has "respectfully declined" to be "the protector of Sexton's reputation" in the critical sense; that is not, as she perceives it, her role. Nor do I think that she has deliberately set out to write like Anne Sexton, or even to keep Anne Sexton's themes alive. But that is exactly what her poetry accomplishes, not by crude imitation or sentimental affectedness, but through the deeply felt perspectives she has developed in the process of living and writing in the wake of her dearest friend's death. Theirs was always a relationship in which mutual influence was more profound than perhaps either poet suspected. The development of Kumin's poetry was already, well before Sexton's death, pursuing this mutual direction in which their voices, always distinguishable, had become choral. Years of workshopping each other's poetry on an almost daily basis had already resulted in a poetic collusion far deeper than what they called the "tricks of technique."

Had Anne Sexton lived, we cannot know whether or not this coming together would have deepened and continued. Anne Sexton did not live, and Maxine Kumin has been left, as she says in "Apostrophe to a Dead Friend," with a tremendous burden to carry, "like a large infant, on one hip:"

> I who am remaindered in the conspiracy,
> doom, doom on my lips.

Kumin's poems to Sexton after Sexton's death make their continued collaboration from beyond the grave seem an inevitability. "I will be years," she writes, "gathering up our words." In her recent poetry, Kumin does "gather up our words," and makes of them something new. How could it be otherwise, for the poet sister left alive, "remaindered in the conspiracy" of eighteen years, who wears the dead poet's clothes, her shoes, who must "put my hands in your death / as into the carcass of a stripped turkey?"

If I seem to be agreeing that Kumin and Sexton were once near-opposites in their poetic styles and voices, and that Kumin developed a Sexton-like voice after Sexton's death and only thereafter became similar to Sexton, I must qualify myself. The differences between them are genuine and have always been clear, reflected even in the titles of each poet's collections during those years of friendship. While Sexton was publishing titles such as *To Bedlam and Part Way Back* and *Live or Die,* Kumin was publishing the far more restrained *Halfway* and *The Privilege.* Sexton never wrote about horses or woodchucks or mushrooms or splitting wood, and Kumin seldom wrote about suicide or madness or God in her poetry. But Kumin was never as afraid of dealing with human relationships as even she might now think. "The Pawnbroker," a poem to her father that appears in her second collection, *The Nightmare Factory,* published in 1970 and written well before Sexton's death—perhaps at the first peak of their collaborative influence on each other's work—might as easily be a Sexton as a Kumin title. Its content is as personal, as "confessional," as anything one might find in Sexton's work of the same period. Sexton and Kumin were both dealing with family relationships, loss, dreams, mourning, and death from a perspective we might now term "feminist" long before Sexton died. Kumin grants Sexton credit for being the first of the two to deal with such subjects. In response to an interviewer's question about the extent to which she and Sexton had "changed the face of poetry," Kumin is nearly self-effacing:

> I think she has much more than I. She is a very original voice in American poetry. She certainly was responsible in large measure for the outpouring now of what I would call feminist verse. . . . She made it possible for women to write about the quality of womanhood in a way that just could not have been taken seriously twenty years ago. I don't put myself in that category; I don't know to what degree I may or may not have been an inno-

vator. (Meek Interview 32)

While it is true that Sexton preceded Kumin chronologically in her exploration of what migh be called feminist themes, Kumin was not far behind her. By 1970 she was doing her share of innovating on such subjects in *The Nightmare Factory*; and in *Up Country* and *House, Bridge, Fountain, Gate,* both in print by 1975, she was doing her own *kind* of innovating with the Hermit poems and the Amanda sequence.

I will concentrate on Kumin's "Itinerary of an Obsession" because of its concrete statement of both poetic and personal relationship and the ways in which it demonstrates that Maxine Kumin's is now a poetic voice that combines the strengths of her own earlier voice and Anne Sexton's. Perhaps the genuine differences in Sexton's and Kumin's styles reflect essential differences in their deeply entwined souls: one of them was, is, a survivor. Survival was one of Anne Sexton's most consistent, unroutable poetic themes, even if she lost the struggle. In the wake of her death it has become Kumin's, for only she is remaindered in that old and dear conspiracy. But Anne Sexton remains a living part of Kumin's own struggle "somehow to endure":

> Dear friend, last night I dreamed
> you held a sensitive position,
> you were Life's Counselor
> coming to the phone in Vaud or Bern,
> some terse one-syllable place,
> to tell me how to carry on
> and I woke into the summer solstice
> swearing I will break
> your absence into crumbs
> like the stump of a punky tree
> working its way down in the world's evening
> down to the forest floor.
>
> —Maxine Kumin, "Progress Report" (*RS*)

Mother's Lap: Itinerary of an Obsession

Maxine Kumin has published five poems to or about Anne Sexton. "How It Is" (*RS*) takes as its moment a day one month after Sexton's death in 1974, while "Apostrophe to a Dead Friend" (*GT*) and "Itinerary of an Obsession" (*GT*) take place years later. Two earlier poems that appear in *The Retrieval System* ("Progress Report" and "Splitting Wood at Six Above") are fixed at different intervals after Sexton's death: four months, and two years. In the hiatus between the early poems and the later "Apostrophe" and "Itinerary" we hear little of Sexton from Kumin, but the later poems make it clear that the absence has been only public—or perhaps only poetic, since during the intervening years, Kumin has continued to "carry the sheer weight of the telling" in interviews and essays. If the poems did not give us clues of composition dates, any reader might think them the product of one period of sustained mourning and writing, for they are largely of a piece in tone, subject, style, and quality of intimacy. The conversation between poets has gone on for nearly a decade; we are privileged to overhear on occasion. Sexton is with Kumin in every possible activity of daily life: while she is walking in the woods, cutting and splitting logs, flying over Paris, listening to the Pope in St. Peter's Square, dreaming dreams old and new. Kumin picks up each conversation *in medias res*; any of these poems might have begun with "furthermore . . . ." While the tone is consistently intimate, it is never simple, for in all of these poems Kumin entangles her complicated passions toward this dearest friend: she is living, compassionate, bereaved, betrayed, sometimes ironic to the point of bitterness. Her project is to tell the truth, and when that truth is tough, even acid, Kumin will not back down. Here, as in their lives together, the words are "living meat."

In "Itinerary of an Obsession," Kumin speaks to Sexton in a voice as newly raw as it is familiar. The isolated notes of bitter irony in other poems Kumin wrote to Sexton gather here into a chiding chorus of resentment, both good-humored and earnest. As "Peeling Fence Posts" is the sub-text for "Splitting Wood at Six Above" (*RS*), the title poem of Kumin's 1978 collection is the sub-text for "Itinerary." "Our Ground Time Here Will Be Brief" takes place aboard an airplane, where the speaker contemplates the situation of all the passengers, herself included:

> Wherever we're going
> is Monday morning.
> Wherever we're coming from
> is Mother's lap.

Above the plane, on the "cloud-pack," lie "the souls of the unborn." The poem never mentions its title, nor does it elaborate on that theme, taken, as all plane travelers would know, from the loudspeaker of a plane landing temporarily to take on cargo or passengers. The implication is that we whose bodies house our unique souls must make room for the souls of the unborn, "my children's children's / children and their father." Mortality and the rhythmic cycles of human existence underscore the images; wherever we are going is some sort of beginning, and wherever we have come from, no matter our age or our mission aboard an airplane flight or in this life, is "Mother's lap," that home-place of security and belonging that is at once both false (Mother can't save us), and the only truth we know.

The epigraph for "Itinerary" establishes the poem's elaborate relationship to time. "Just remember that everything east of you has already happened," quotes Kumin from a time-zone chart. The poem situates itself in past and future as well as present, re-doing what has been done, imagining what the future might be when it has already come to pass. The "obsession" of the title is the speaker's concern with

Sexton's death, and by implication, with her own. She is telling Sexton the story of her trip to the Holy Land with a "planeload of pilgrims, / none under seventy"—she is, we assume, the exception in that respect as well as in others, for the never stated object of her pilgrimage is probably different from those of her fellow passengers, among whom are two nuns. At the moment when one of the nuns says to her, *"pas loin,"* pointing up, signalling that it is not far to their destination—either the Holy Land or, by grimly comic inference, the ultimate one—Kumin is visited by a vision of Anne Sexton:

> lulled by motion or distance here you come
> leaping out of the coffin again,
> flapping around the funeral home
> crying Surprise! I was only fooling!
> while your lovesick dog chases a car
> the twin of yours and lies dead
> years back in a clump of goldenrod.

The detail of Sexton's dog's death deepens the poem's time frame. We know that the vision of Sexton leaping out of the coffin has happened before—she is doing it "again"—and that it alludes to her actual death and Kumin's wishful resurrection of her; but we don't know if the dog died before or after Sexton's death. Everything here has indeed "already happened," and happens again and again in the poet's mind. The dog's death is either a foreshadowing or an echo; perhaps it is both in the speaker's memory. The comic tone makes one envision Sexton, perhaps in flamboyant reading attire, running about the funeral home like a cross between a chicken and a corpse. But why should this vision have come to Kumin at this moment? *"Pas loin"* may be the immediate stimulus; Kumin, like all of us, has "not far" to go to her own death, and to the reunion with her friend with which this poem will end. Thinking as she is about time, the poet catches herself in her usual wish to undo what has been done. As she wrote in "How It Is," she would "unwind" that last day of Sexton's life, running the home movie backward "to a space / we could be easy in." If everything east of you has already happened, then everything west of you has not; and Paris can be construed to be either east or west of Boston.

Next the poet is in St. Peter's Square in Rome, listening to the Pope bless the crowd in "the static shower of Latin," when once again Sexton shows up, this time "coolly as Pascal,"

> arranging to receive
> extreme unction from an obliging priest
> with a bad cold. You swivel your head
> to keep from inhaling his germs. Pigeons
> swoop past, altering the light.
> I put my hand into your death
> as into the carcass of a stripped turkey.

The reference here is to an actual event in Sexton's life. A bit more than a year before her death, when she was searching desperately for something to save her and leaning more and more toward an authoritarian and male God, she found a priest whom Kumin describes elsewhere as "elderly and sympathetic." She "accosted" this priest, according to Kumin, in an effort to be made a Catholic and to receive the last rites. The priest refused, but he helped her more than any last rites could have; he told her "God is in your typewriter," thus keeping her alive, thinks Kumin, "at least a year beyond her time" (Kumin, "How It Was," Foreward, xxiii). In the fantasy scenario of "Itinerary," Sexton's wish for the last rites is granted, ironically, after her death, inspired perhaps by the presence of the Holy Father. The vision is comically and grotesquely detailed by Sexton's swerve to avoid the priest's germs—surely unnecessary if she is either about to die or already dead. Aware that she is still, after all these years, as deeply involved as ever in Sexton's life and death, Kumin finishes this section with what may be the most powerful, and is surely the most grotesque, of her images to explain the depths of her involvement in this death. If "the body is dumb, the body is meat," as Sexton had said, then her death is meat eaten from a body now stripped and skeletal. Kumin can claim herself finished neither with the need for nourishment from their long meal together—their best moments occur in a "kitchen place"—nor with the leftovers she tears from the carcass of her friend's body.

Continuing her travel "itinerary," Kumin finds herself next at the Red Sea, where she meets up with a fellow tourist who has been searched for contraband by the authorities. "Do I look like a terrorist?" he asks. Walking to Solomon's mines, Kumin "stumbles through mirages," seeing the ghosts of slaves dying of thirst on the desert. "My feet weep blisters, sand enters the sore, / I bite on sand." Even this reminds her of Sexton, and brings back the theme of clothing familiar from other poems:

> On the floor of your closet
> smolder a jumble of shoes, stiletto heels,
> fleece-lined slippers, your favorite sneakers
> gritty from Cape Cod, all my size.

In her vision, the shoes on Sexton's closet floor are hot—they "smolder"—like the desert through which Kumin walks without her; yet they are also, in direct contrast to Kumin's circumstances on the desert, images of style or comfort or happy leisure. Sexton's "desert" was not this merciless stretch of Holy Land, but rather the sands of Cape Cod. Although she does not say so, the appearance of a vision of Sexton's closet of shoes while she wanders on the desert suggests a wish that she could wear those shoes, be home with Sexton, safe with her, before or beyond her death.

All through this trip to the Holy Land, then, during

which we might infer that Kumin, in however secular a fashion, is searching out some spiritual truth, she is haunted by visions of Anne Sexton dead, Anne Sexton alive, Anne Sexton resurrected and restored to her. Sexton's own search was for transcendent sacredness, a patriarchal God of unquestionable authority and comfort. Kumin's search seems to be for connection of the human sort, transcendent over death and time. While Sexton searched for God, Kumin searched for whatever it was she had, and lost, with Anne Sexton: a friendship stronger than death, a solidarity of souls that must continue. "Words are the only 'holy' for me. The only sanctity really, for me, is the sanctity of language" (Meek Interview 25). That language is the words between friends who are poets—"our words like living meat"—words turned by Sexton's death into a "carcass," which the living poet must try to reconstruct. She can do so only by bringing Sexton back from the grave. And she does so one final time in the last section of "Itinerary," where she finds that even if she "dreams of you less," she is still obsessed:

> Still, when the phone rings in my sleep
> and I answer, a dream-cigarette in my hand,
> it is always the same. We are back at our posts,
> hanging around like boxers in
> our old flannel bathrobes. You haven't changed.
> I, on the other hand, am forced to grow older.
> Now I am almost your mother's age.
> Imagine it! Did you think you could escape?
> Eventually I'll arrive in her
> abhorrent marabou negligee
> trailing her scarves like broken promises
> crying yoo-hoo! Anybody home?

"Itinerary" conflates all of the thematic strands of Kumin's five poems to Sexton: the wish to reverse time, the identification of the poet with her friend, the poet's own preoccupation with mortality as it is expressed through this special death, the equation of the holy with language, the salvation of "soul" and its relationship to "body," the poet's progression through "the middle age you wouldn't wait for," the double haunting of the poet's language. The living poet is not only haunted by her dead friend; Kumin's determination is not only to live her own nightmare to the end, but to resurrect Sexton to live through it with her. Maxine Kumin is the living ghost who tries to haunt Anne Sexton's spirit, as she herself is haunted. Unable—or unwilling—to let Sexton's spirit rest, she haunts her unremittingly; and although there are some elements of a friendly, intimate aggression in this haunting, the object of these poems is not to torture Anne Sexton, but to make her remain among the living, to bring her back to finish her work—the work of the partnership, the conspiracy of poets, of friends, of women.

Sexton and Kumin are among American poetry's most powerful interrogators of the relationship between mothers and daughters, and in this poem's ending that mutual theme is illuminated, and darkened. The multiple ironies of this final section depend on an understanding of both poets' previous work on the issues of mothering. Sexton and Kumin both knew that maternal light, and its sister darkness. In "The Double Image" Sexton called her mother, with whom she had a troubled and painful relationship throughout her life, "my mocking mirror, my overthrown / love, my first image" (*TB*). In her own role as mother to daughters, she wrote poems such as "The Fortress" (*APO*), "Little Girl, My Stringbean, My Lovely Woman" (*LD*), and "A Little Uncomplicated Hymn" (*LD*), in which she looks for uncomplicated hymns from mother to daughter and finds that "love has none." She can promise, as she does in "The Fortress," to give her daughter "the images I know"; she can promise the moments in which "we laugh and we touch." But she also knows that she "cannot promise very much":

Darling, life is not in my hands;
life with its terrible changes
will take you, bombs or glands,
your own child at
your breast, your own house on your own land.
Outside the bittersweet turns orange.
Before she died, my mother and I picked those fat
branches, finding orange nipples
on the gray wire strands.
We weeded the forest, curing trees like cripples.

Sexton is good at this kind of love, the kind that sends a child into the world with the assurance of love, but without false securities the mother could promise but never perform. Her advice to her daughter Linda at her puberty is characteristic of this strong, self-assured, genuinely nurturing affection:

Darling,
stand still at your door,
sure of yourself, a white stone, a good stone—
as exceptional as laughter
you will strike fire,
that new thing!

Any daughter might wish to be sent into the world with this maternal blessing. Yet this was the same mother whose mental breakdowns were first occasioned by post-partum depression, who tortured herself with guilt over having, she thought, abandoned her children during her illness. And this was the same daughter who, at least in her poetry, endured her own mother's accusation of something far worse than desertion:

On the first of September she looked at me
and said I gave her cancer.
They carved her sweet hills out
and still I couldn't answer.

("The Operation," *TB*)

This is, too, the daughter who knows that at her mother's death, she becomes "one third thief of you," exposing the underbelly of inheritance. This is the daughter who cannot let go of her dead mother after her death, who returns to her ghost throughout her life, trying to please and appease her, knowing that especially in the wake of her death, she can never succeed. This is the mother and the daughter who knows that "death too is in the egg."

The passage below, from Kumin's poem about her daughter, "Sunbathing on a Rooftop in Berkeley" (*RS*), might have come from a Sexton poem, as so many of Sexton's lines might have come from Kumin's pen:

> O summers without end, the truth is
> no matter how I love her, Death
> blew up my dress that day
> while she was in the egg unconsidered.

Kumin's passionate love for her daughters shares all the fundamental assumptions of Sexton's, and is sometimes so similar in tone and in imagery that one infers a collaboration of spirits deeper by far than technique. "Leaving My Daughter's House" (*GT*) was written long after Sexton's death, and it speaks of a stage of the mother-daughter relationship that Sexton did not live to see; yet if Sexton had lived, if her daughters had left her as permanently as Kumin feels this European daughter has left, no one would be surprised to read the same kind of statement from Sexton. Kumin is beside her daughter, a day before she will have "crossed the ocean, gone beyond time,"

> where we stand in a mannerly pose at the window
> watching the ancient iron strike flint from stones,
> balancing on the bit that links us and keeps us
> from weeping o God! into each other's arms.

So internally possessive is her love that in "Seeing the Bones" (*RS*), she remembers her daughter's junior high biology class in which the class boiled a chicken down to its bones, "four days at a simmer in my pot." The class project was to recreate the hen by wiring its bones back together. The poet's life is filled with reminders of her daughter's life with her and away from her:

> Working backward I reconstruct
> you. Send me your baby teeth, some new
> nail parings and a hank of hair
> and let me do the rest. I'll
> set the pot to boil.

She knows that "at the hour / of my death my daughters will absorb me," knows that they will "carry me about forever / inside them, an arrested fetus"; and that this is a fate devoutly to be wished by every mother, every daughter, for it lets us carry on:

> May we, borne onward by our daughters, ride
> in the Envelope of Almost-Infinity,
> that chain letter good for the next twenty-five
> thousand days of their lives.
>
> ("The Envelope," *RS*)

But in "The Fairest One of all" (*NF*), Kumin announces the dark side of this guarantee of what she elsewhere calls "the celestial arrangement." Like Sexton's "Little Girl . . . ," the poem begins as a celebration of newly acquired womanhood, with a nursery rhyme and fairy tale motif as background for the bodily drama. "Pirouettes of you are in order." There ought to be, says the mother, appropriately celebratory rituals to make your passage, and accouterments to match: "slithers of satin," "diamonds buckled to your ears," and "gold ropes cunningly knotted / under your breasts."

Sexton's daughter Linda, younger than Kumin's Jane at the time of the writing of each poem should also step into her rituals:

> Let high noon enter . . .
> and someday they will come to you,
> someday, men bare to the waist, young Romans
> at noon where they belong,
> with ladders and hammers
> while no one sleeps.

But here the similarity between the two poems ends, for in Sexton's, daughter and mother remain together, the mother very "here," even if "an old tree in the background." In Kumin's poem, what "ought to befall" does not. The future she predicts, even promises, is different:

> But let there be
> no mistaking how the dark scheme runs.
> Too soon the huntsman will come.
> He will bring me the heart of a wild boar
> and I in error will have it salted and cooked
> and I in malice will eat it bit by bit
> thinking it yours.
> And as we both know, at the appropriate moment
> I will be consumed by an inexorable fire
> as you look on.

The end of Kumin's "The Fairest One of All" is duplicated in Sexton's canon in "Snow White and the Seven Dwarfs" (*T*), written at about the same time as Kumin's poem. Here Sexton retells the story of Snow White, and ends with the scene Kumin has transferred to her own life:

> First your toes will smoke
> and then your heels will turn black
> and you will fry upward like a frog,
> she was told.

And so she danced until she was dead,
a subterranean figure,
her tongue flicking in and out
like a gas jet.
Meanwhile Snow White held court,
rolling her china-blue doll eyes open and shut
and sometimes referring to her mirror as women do.

The close collaboration of Kumin and Sexton—Kumin contributed, among other things, the title of the *Transformations* collection—is here as concretely interpenetrative as might be possible. Each woman told the same story of mothers and daughters, with Kumin, surprisingly, being the one who personalized it most. Sexton echoed, or foreshadowed, Kumin's images of mother-daughter power struggles and identifications in many other poems as well. In "Those Times . . ." (*LD*) the speaker did not know that her life, in the end, "would run over my mother's like a truck." And in "Housewife," (*APO*) Kumin's "Envelope" is duplicated in another metaphor—women marrying their houses:

Men enter by force, drawn back like Jonah
into their fleshy mothers.
A woman *is* her mother.
That's the main thing.

Addendum to that truth from the conclusion of "Itinerary": a sister who outlives her sister becomes that sister's mother. The time theme that travels through Kumin's poems to Anne Sexton foreshadows this conclusion in "the middle age you wouldn't wait for" of "Progress Report." The ambiguity of "Now I am almost your mother's age" can be cleared up by a few biographical details. Sexton's mother, Mary Gray Harvey, was in her late fifties when she died; and Maxine Kumin was about the same age when she wrote "Itinerary." Without that intimate detail, a reader might wonder about the meaning of such a line. Almost your mother's age *when*?

The answer is, when your mother died; not when Sexton died, ironically, for Sexton's mother had been dead for about fifteen years when Sexton died. So it is the poet's own death she contemplates here, identified with the death-age of her friend's mother. "Imagine it!" Recalling their old friendship, one of sisters and equals, the poet asks her dead friend to imagine that impossibility, that she has been left to become the age of that monumental parental presence whom they cared about and were contemptuous of in that special way that people can be about family—and this regardless of how well Kumin knew Mary Gray, for she "knows" her in this poem as yet another alter ego, a generation removed by the time that has elapsed and made her not Sexton's contemporary, but Mary Gray's.

In the final lines of "Itinerary," Kumin transforms herself into Mary Gray, and follows Sexton to the grave, arriving as a gaudy, inappropriately dressed ghost who promises to continue disturbing Sexton's sleep. Because she is now Mary Gray's age, she can take on her identity by the same act throughout her poems to Sexton: she is wearing the dead woman's clothes. Just as the poem begins with Sexton "leaping out of the coffin again, / flapping around the funeral home," it ends with Kumin pulling the same trick on Sexton, this time leaping, in effect, into the coffin, where she herself now flaps, announcing her arrival on the scene of the afterlife in the same exasperating tones of Sexton's mother at the earthly door: "yoo-hoo! Anybody home?" Thus, she threatens, will she take her own helpless and undeliberate revenge upon the friend who deserted her in this life. "Did you think you could escape?" The question is a challenge, for Sexton died in part to escape her ghosts, who would not leave her alone in life, the "mother, father, I'm made of" who pursued her from their own graves.

In this poem, Kumin clearly resents having been cast by time into the role of the mother to this ghost who began as her sister, and who remains a sister in her consciousness. In a 1983 interview, Kumin was explicit about this familial bond:

> I never had a sister and although Anne had sisters, she was never close to them. So that I think in each other's life we fulfilled a desire for sisterhood that had gone long unfulfilled. That was the kind of bonding that we had, we really were each other's sister—closer than sisters. (George Interview)

A sister is a member of one's own generation, to whom one is bound by mutual concerns, loves, and struggles. A sister is one with whom one suffers and celebrates, for the challenges of a sister's life are the challenges of one's own. The relationship, as archetype, is never untroubled, marked as it must be by competition as well as by mutuality. But at least it does not necessarily imply the kind of dark complexities inherent, "by celestial arrangement," in the parent-child bond. It is not, in particular, marked by the dark design of death, by which the daughter must survive her mother. And that is the final irony of this other, bitter "transformation" effected by Sexton's relinquishment of life; for having survived Sexton after her death, Kumin was compelled to play out, first, the role of daughter-survivor; and finally, the role of mother. And she had meant, from the start, to keep the sister she had found.

The revenge imagined in the end of "Itinerary" is in this respect a just one; Maxine Kumin, having no sense of the sacred beyond the poetry of the human spirit which she shared above all else with Anne Sexton, valued that living person beyond all price; and at least in the person of her poetic persona, she needed to be able to count on her lasting presence throughout life. Sexton took that away from her by dying. Sexton didn't do this to hurt Kumin, of course; but that doom on the lips of the live and lone conspirator was the inevitable result of her death. And Kumin's arrival beyond the grave in the guise of Sexton's mother will be similarly inevitable. The revenge is not purposeful, for Kumin would do nothing deliberately hurtful to this ghost; it's simply part of the dark plan, by which both conspirators get what they have feared most deeply: the loneliness of living for Kumin, the return of the mother for Sexton. There is no hint here that Kumin's ghost will be that of the mother who offers succor and nourishment. Rather, she is the mother who trails her scarves in Mary Gray's high and haughty style, like "broken promises."

One other pattern characterized by opposition recurs in Kumin's poems to Sexton. Kumin thinks of Anne Sexton at many moments of her life; she lets Sexton know that Sexton is with her in the wood as well as in the air, throughout all elements and activities. Sexton's spirit accompanies Kumin down to the forest floor in the world's evening, and to the Holy Land she reaches by means of flight. In "Address to the Angels" (*RS*), she is once again flying, once again "up here grieving, tallying / my losses," and once again thinking of Anne Sexton:

> Angels, where were you when
> my best friend did herself in?
> Were you lunching beside us
> that final noon, did you catch
> some nuance that went past my ear?

The angels are no consolation, for we are, "each one of us, our own / prisoner. We are / locked up in our own story," which is the same as our own nightmare. Kumin thinks of Sexton while she is flying and while she is splitting wood, and I think it is no accident that Sexton recurs more than once in each of these opposing situations, one earth-bound, one aspiring.

While I do not wish to oversimplify what is clearly a

complexity beyond simple summaries or neatly bifurcated oppositions, I think these physical, geographical extremes echo the polar oppositions of Kumin's poetry, especially the poems to and about all her pretty ones: the locales correspond, however incompletely, to body and soul. These attributes or elements are never divorced from each other in Kumin, for splitting wood is as clearly spiritual an activity as is a trip to the Holy Land—probably it is more so for Kumin. It is the physically grounded activity of splitting wood that releases the souls of trees; and even on the cloud-pack, Kumin never forgets the body. She would like, as she says in many poems and in interviews, to get them together, as she tries to do in "Body and Soul: A Meditation" (*RS*). Yet they do not cooperate with her or each other, in spite of the best efforts of all three. As she wanders up the mountain with her body, "Old Paint, Old Partner," in this "sedate roundup" in the "meander of our middle age," looking for the "same old cracked tablets," her "airmail half-ounce soul" touches tongues with her and "Old Paint"; but

> somehow it seems less sure;
> somehow it seems we've come
> too far to get us there.

It is in part by working with and through Anne Sexton's death, with and through the relationship between Sexton's body, so like Kumin's, and Sexton's soul, that small round entity like a "sun-yellow daisy heart," that Kumin tries to unite her own uneasy partners. Sexton gave up the search, in a sense, even before she died, by turning away from complex uncertainties of the kind they had both tried to work with together back when, for Sexton as for Kumin, "need was not quite belief"; her need was finally too strong, so that it became its own version of belief in a patriarchal God. Kumin cannot join her friend in this kind of search, which she knows to be a dead end, in the literal as well as figurative sense. Instead, she puzzles her way through, aware that her ground time here will be brief, that she has only a limited time to come to terms with body and soul. And that, for her, means coming to terms with the forest floor and the infinite sky, in both of which Anne Sexton lives on.

Notes

[1]Maxine Kumin's poetry from the following collections is documented by these abbreviations:

The Nightmare Factory	*NF*
The Retrieval System	*RS*
Our Ground Time Here Will Be Brief	*GT*

Ground Time includes selections from all of Kumin's earlier collections including *The Privilege* (*P*) and *Halfway* (*H*). *House, Bridge, Fountain, Gate* was published in 1975, dedicated "In Memoriam, Anne Sexton, 1928-1974." The poems in *HBFG* were written before Sexton's death; I include the volume in this list because of its publication date.

Works Cited

George, Diana Hume. Interview. "Kumin on Kumin and Sexton." *Poesis: A Journal of Criticism* 6:2 (1985), 1-18.

Kumin, Maxine. "A Friendship Remembered." in Kumin *To Make a Prairie: Essays on Poets, Poetry, and Country Living*. Ann Arbor: U of Michigan P, 1979. (Rpt. in *Anne Sexton: The Artist and Her Critics*. Ed. J. D. McClatchy. Bloomington: Indiana U P, 1978.)

___. "How It Was," Foreward to *Anne Sexton: The Complete Poems*. Boston: Houghton Mifflin, 1981.

___. *The Nightmare Factory*. New York: Harper & Row, 1970.

___. *Our Ground Time Here Will Be Brief.* New York: Viking Press/Penguin Books, 1982.

___. *The Retrieval System.* New York: Viking Press/Penguin Books, 1978.

Meek, Martha George. Interview. In Kumin, *To Make a Prairie*, 19-34.
Sexton, Anne. *Anne Sexton: The Complete Poems*. Boston: Houghton Mifflin, 1981.

NOTES ON CONTRIBUTORS

BRENDA AMETER, a professor of English at Indiana State University in Terre Haute, received her Ph.D. from Indiana University. Her interests range from Samuel Richardson's *Clarissa* to Anne Sexton's poetry. Currently she has been exploring Jungian archetypal theory and its application to literature written by or about women. She is a contributor to MLA teaching guides dealing with eighteenth- and early nineteenth-century writers and to MHRA.

ANNE MARIE SEWARD BARRY is an assistant professor at Boston College. She writes and teaches in the areas of literature, film, and advertising. An active communications consultant and court mediator, she holds Master's degrees in American Literature and Marketing Communications and a Ph.D. in Perceptual Psychology, Literature, and Film from Boston University, where she was a University Scholar.

FRANCES BIXLER is a faculty member at Southwest Missouri State University. She received her Ph.D. from the University of Arkansas at Fayetteville. Her critical studies include articles on Chaucer, Robert Penn Warren, Richard Wilbur, and Anne Sexton. She has published articles in *Publications of the Arkansas Philological Association* and *"Time's Glory": Original Essays on Robert Penn Warren*, edited by James Grimshaw. Recently she has received a grant to continue research on Richard Wilbur's poetry. She is married and the mother of two children.

MICHAEL BURNS is a poet and faculty member at Southwest Missouri State University. He holds an MFA from the University of Arkansas at Fayetteville, where he studied under Miller Williams and James Whitehead. His poetry has been published in two collections titled *When All Else Failed* and *And As For Darkness.* He has published in the *New Orleans Review, Quarterly West, The Chariton Review* and *Poetry Magazine.* New work is scheduled to appear in *The Southern Review.*

KAY ELLEN MERRIMAN CAPO is on the Literature faculty at the State University of New York College at Purchase. She received her Ph.D. in Performance Studies at Northwestern University in 1978. Professor Capo is on the editorial board of *Literature in Performance* and the forthcoming *Text and Performance Quarterly.* Several essays and reviews have appeared in the *Journal of Literature in Performance.* Her essays also have appeared in *Soundings* (1987) and *Performance of Literature in Historical Perspectives* (1983). An essay entitled "Redeeming Words" will be published in *Anne Sexton: Telling the Tale,* edited by Steven Colburn (1988). She is working on a book-length study of Sexton's poetry.

DIANA HUME GEORGE is a professor of English at The Pennsylvania State University/Behrend College, where she teaches poetry, creative writing, and women's studies. Her critical studies include *Blake and Freud* (nominated for the Pulitzer Prize in 1980), *Epitaph and Icon* (with M. A. Nelson), and *Oedipus Anne: The Poetry of Anne Sexton;* her poetry chapbook is titled *The Evolution of Love.* She is the editor of *Sexton: Selected Criticism,* and co-editor with Diane Wood Middlebrook of *Selected Poems of Anne Sexton.* She has published many articles on poetry, psychoanalysis, feminist theory, and American attitudes toward death, in journals including *College English, Hartford Studies in Literature, The Centennial Review, Poesis, Enclitic, The Journal of American Culture,* and *Women's Studies.* Grants and fellowships from the National Endowment for the Humanities and The American Council of Learned Societies have supported her work. George is currently working on two manuscripts: *Words Like Living Meat: Anne Sexton and Maxine Kumin,* and *Eating Beautiful Women,* a study of Marilyn Monroe and Anne Sexton.

JENNY GOODMAN is a poet and graduate student in the Creative Writing Program at Syracuse University, where she is also a teaching assistant. She received her undergraduate degree in Creative Writing and Comparative Literature at Brown University. At Brown, she studied with C. D. Wright and Philip Levine; at Syracuse, she is presently studying with Tess Gallagher and Hayden Carruth.

CAROLINE KING BARNARD HALL received her Ph.D. in English and American literature in 1973 from Brown University. She is the author of *Anne Sexton,* to be published by G. K. Hall (Twayne Publishers) in 1988, and of *Sylvia Plath,* published by Twayne in 1978. Her academic career has included two senior Fulbright lectureships in modern American literature and women's studies, at the University of Klagenfurt in Austria in 1980-81 and at the University of Copenhagen in Denmark in 1986. She currently lives in New Orleans and teaches at Xavier University.

LYNETTE MCGRATH is a native of Australia who has lived in the United States for twenty-five years. She holds a Bachelor's degree from the University of Sydney and

Master's and Doctoral degrees from the University of Illinois in Urbana. She is on the faculty of West Chester University, West Chester, Pennsylvania where she is Professor of English and Women's Studies, having also held the position of Coordinator of the Women's Studies Program there. She teaches undergraduate and graduate courses in seventeenth-century non-dramatic literature and in women's literature, especially a course in Feminist Poetry. The author of numerous articles on 17th-century and contemporary poetic theory and practice, she has recently published translations of contemporary Catalan women poets. Her political commitments are feminist and pacifist; she is the mother of three daughters.

DIANE WOOD MIDDLEBROOK is the Howard H. & Jessie T. Watkins University Professor in English and Feminist Studies at Stanford University. Her books include *Walt Whitman and Wallace Stevens* (1974) and *Coming to Light: American Women Poets of the Twentieth Century*, edited with Marilyn Yalom (1985). With Diana Hume George she edited *Selected Poems of Anne Sexton* (1988), and is writing a critical biography of Anne Sexton, to be published by Houghton Mifflin Company in 1990.

MARGARET SCARBOROUGH received her Ph.D. in English literature from the University of Washington. She has published criticism and poetry in *Modern Drama, Encounter, Oregon English, Crosscurrents*, the *Washington English Journal*, and elsewhere, and written the English introduction to *Bird Cries*, a collection of poetry by the Chinese poet, Gno Gno Cheung. She is also the author of two full-length medieval Christmas masques and a one-act production about Anne Sexton, both of which were produced in Seattle. Presently, she is completing a book on Sylvia Plath, Anne Sexton, and Adrienne Rich. She edits two academic publications: *Crosscurrents* and *The Washington English Journal.* She lives in Seattle with her husband, three cats, four chickens, and a boa constrictor, Imhotep.